Useful Assessment and Evaluation in Language Education

Useful Assessment and Evaluation in Language Education

Editors

John McE. Davis, Yorktown Systems Group
John M. Norris, Educational Testing Service
Margaret E. Malone, Georgetown University
Todd H. McKay, Georgetown University
Young-A Son, Georgetown University

GEORGETOWN UNIVERSITY PRESS
Washington, DC

The publisher is not responsible for third-party websites or their content. URL links were active at time of publication.

Library of Congress Cataloging-in-Publication Data

Names: Georgetown University Round Table on Languages and Linguistics (2016 : Washington, D.C.), author. Davis, John McE., 1970- editor.
Title: Useful Assessment and Evaluation in Language Education / editors, John McE. Davis, John M. Norris, Margaret E. Malone, Todd H. McKay, Young-A Son.
Description: Washington, D.C. : Georgetown University Press, 2018. Series: The Georgetown University Round Table on Languages and Linguistics series | Includes bibliographical references and index.
Identifiers: LCCN 2017019313 (print) | LCCN 2017032351 (ebook) | ISBN 9781626165410 (ebook) | ISBN 9781626165397 q(hc : qalk. paper) | ISBN 9781626165403 q(pb : qalk. paper)
Subjects: LCSH: Language and languages--Study and teaching--Evaluation--Congresses.
Classification: LCC P53.63 (ebook) | LCC P53.63 .G46 2016 (print) | DDC 418.0071--dc23
LC record available at https://lccn.loc.gov/2017019313

∞ This book is printed on acid-free paper meeting the requirements of the American National Standard for Permanence in Paper for Printed Library Materials.

19 18   9 8 7 6 5 4 3 2 First printing

Printed in the United States of America

Contents

PART 3. VALIDITY EVALUATION

◆ Preface

JOHN McE. DAVIS

THIS VOLUME COLLECTS A selection of presentations from the 2016 Georgetown University Round Table (GURT) conference, a springtime tradition sponsored every year by the Georgetown University Department of Linguistics. GURT differed somewhat in 2016 in that it was primarily organized by the Assessment and Evaluation Language Resource Center (AELRC), a federally funded research entity, newly hosted (at the time) at Georgetown, and created to conduct research, outreach, training, and professional development in support of language assessment and language program evaluation across the broad domain of US foreign and world language education.[1]

The involvement of AELRC in GURT 2016 was notable in that the center's focus on language assessment and evaluation guided the conference theme in important ways. The unique focus of the AELRC—and GURT 2016—is captured in the title of the conference and this volume: *Useful Assessment and Evaluation in Language Education*. The emphasis on assessment and evaluation 'usefulness' issues directly out of the AELRC mission and connects with an explicit proposition put forward by the AELRC that assessment and evaluation are "key elements in a comprehensive approach to education that is accountable to the needs of learners, the values of scholarly disciplines, and the well-being of society."[2] Put another way—and going beyond traditional conceptions of assessment and evaluation as employed to capture achievement or proficiency, or make decisions about placement, admission, or accountability—the AELRC views assessment and evaluation as tools of educational transformation, "essential mechanisms for understanding, improving, and demonstrating the worth of foreign language education."[3]

At the heart of the AELRC mission is the foundational idea that assessment and evaluation are critical processes of educational inquiry that can and should play a transforming role in language programs. Accordingly, the specific (and varied) ways in which language assessment and evaluation are able to impact learning and teaching have become an important research concern, particularly as educators are increasingly called upon to implement these processes for improvement, accountability, or curricular development. In the United States, particularly, mandates for assessment and evaluation embedded in federal government legislation or arising out of reforms in higher education accreditation have expanded the range of educational assessment and evaluation uses toward such activities as monitoring institutional performance, innovating instruction, and improving and demonstrating educational effectiveness. Certainly, particular veins of contemporary assessment research and practice have emerged in response to these currents, or have otherwise tried to innovate assessment and evaluation approaches along a number of novel lines. As an example, a diverse set of approaches has aimed to push assessment beyond the conventional bounds of estimating or capturing student abilities and toward directly engendering language learning processes themselves. Terms such as "learning-oriented assessment," "assessment-for-learning," and "dynamic assessment" (among others) denote assessment methods or processes designed to be integral and intrinsic to the learning occurring in language classrooms and across educational systems. The large English-language assessment companies (e.g., ETS, Pearson, Cambridge) have each innovated their suites of assessment instruments in this direction (focusing, for example, on the use of automated feedback) in an effort to supply educational organizations with tools that not only capture achievement and proficiency, but also support and drive learning. Accordingly, as assessment is used to intentionally and concretely influence educational processes, new learning-oriented constructs and development-oriented methods have emerged that call for innovative approaches to assessment design, piloting, and validity evaluation. Moreover, an abiding concern with assessment use and consequences connects with key developments in language program evaluation. An established emphasis on evaluation usefulness implies that practitioners must attend carefully to the ways in which assessment and evaluation (and educational programs) actually function and, thereby, the mechanisms or factors that lead to intended assessment or evaluation uses and desired program outcomes.

Enhancing language education via impactful, useful assessment and evaluation practice has thus become a focal concern within different domains of applied linguistics research, not to mention for the many teachers and administrators called upon by outside authorities (or otherwise motivated) to use assessment and evaluation for informing and reforming their educational practices. The GURT 2016 conference explicitly sought to explore these (and other) themes, collecting a wide-ranging and novel set of research projects on assessment and program evaluation in contemporary language education. Along diverse lines of inquiry, then, the GURT 2016 conference explored a variety of queries. How, for example, can assessment and evaluation be designed to most usefully and productively impact language learning and related educational processes? What are the conceptual and epistemological dimensions of focusing on utility, learning, or educational transformation via assessment and evaluation practices? What are the methodological and contextual considerations that condition the impact and efficacy of learning or otherwise educationally oriented assessments? Given a more diverse array of possible educational assessment uses, what are the implications for thinking about and demonstrating validity? What are the implications for design, measurement, and validity evaluation when undertaking assessment for learning-oriented and related educational purposes? And how can program evaluation contribute usefully to educational innovation and improvement in language programs?

In a similar spirit, this volume endeavors to capture a selection of the research and examples of praxis showcased at GURT 2016. To this end, the book is divided into three sections. The first section—Connecting Assessment, Learners, and Learning—explores theoretical considerations and practical implementations of assessment conducted specifically for the purpose of enhancing and developing language learning. The second section—Innovating, Framing, and Exploring Assessment in Language Education—collects a diverse set of projects addressing novel assessment implementations such as the formative use of task-based assessment specification frameworks in primary schools, the implementation of technology-mediated speaking performance assessment, validation of educational placement decisions for immigrant learners, and the use of assessment to help identify neurolinguistic correlates at different levels of established proficiency benchmarks (e.g., ILR, ACTFL, CEFR). Finally, chapters in section three—Validity Evaluation—address different instances and examples of assessment validation, many reporting on the use of argument-based approaches to demonstrating validity of assessment score interpretation and use, as well as for conducting language program evaluation. The volume ends with an innovative proposal from Michael Kane on the role of evaluation in validating assessment when put to educational or formatively oriented uses.

To conclude on a personal note, I feel especially fortunate to have been involved in GURT 2016 via my role (at the time) as codirector of the AELRC and also to have had the opportunity to bring this volume to fruition. For these fortuities, I am indebted to a number of individuals. First, I am deeply grateful to my esteemed colleagues and coeditors, John Norris and Margaret Malone, for their mentorship and support during my time at the AELRC and also for their editorial contributions during the creation of this work. Both have made indelible impacts on my professional development and have been valued partners during GURT 2016 through to the final realization of the conference vision in this volume. I also want to express my gratitude to our two invaluable PhD student coeditors, Todd McKay and Young-A Son. The volume would not have been possible without their tireless labor and shrewd editorial judgment (and general cheerfulness during some taxing editing tasks). I am also grateful to Clara Totten and Hope LeGro at Georgetown University Press for their especially helpful support and assistance. Special thanks also to AELRC assistant and Georgetown PhD student Amy Kim for accomplishing a number of key support tasks during the final stretch. Finally, a debt of gratitude is owed to the volume's chapter authors for their high-quality contributions and for enduring and accommodating multiple rounds of revision (with substantial reductions in some cases) in good humor. Via the realization of this volume, each of the above individuals and entities has helped further the AELRC mission and advance important conceptualizations of assessment and evaluation as means of educational transformation, innovation, and betterment.

Notes

1. AELRC is sponsored by a grant from the US Department of Education (P229A140012).
2. "Assessment and Evaluation Language Resource Center," Georgetown University, http://aelrc.georgetown.edu/.
3. Ibid.

Part One

Connecting Assessment, Learners, and Learning

Chapter 1

◆ Developing Students' Self-Assessment Skills

The Role of the Teacher

RICHARD KIELY
University of Southampton, United Kingdom

THIS PAPER EXPLORES THE role and implementation of student self-assessment in language teaching. The first section describes the relationship between teaching and assessment in language education and identifies three rationales for including self-assessment in curricula. These rationales draw on second language acquisition (SLA) in instructed settings; educational considerations focusing on student participation, investment, and agency in the curriculum; and assessment theory, where the rationale supports active development of assessment awareness within language learning. The second part describes an integrated research and teacher professional development initiative to enhance student self-assessment in a language program. This initiative has two principal activities: (a) exploring teacher beliefs and cognitions about assessment and the positioning of assessment practices in their pedagogy, and (b) developing classroom activity models that teachers can adapt and integrate. The data from this process captured the teachers' beliefs about and attitudes toward assessment and how their practice positioned assessment in their pedagogy. The analysis shows the complexities of the teacher's role in enhancing self-assessment and the need to engage with these complexities to support transformation of programs and language-learning experiences.

Assessment in Language Education

The relationship between language teaching and testing is both close and complex. Teacher education provides an important perspective for examining this relationship; the principles and norms that shape teacher training reflect perceptions of effective teaching. Three characterizations of this relationship, which correspond to three phases of development in recent decades, can be identified: *keep it out*, *bring it in*, and *hand it over*.

Keep It Out

Wallace (1991) points out that teachers should focus on activities that promote learning and not concentrate on test preparation strategies. As Gitlin and Smyth (1989) point out, teachers and students have traditionally been evaluated by test results; thus, teachers are predisposed to teach to the test. In the 1960s and 1970s, when current teacher-training schemes for language teachers were developed, the dominant strategy for assessment was discrete-point items, such as multiple choice (MC) questions (Lado 1964; Oller 1979). Language-teacher education curricula (Richards and Nunan 1989; Wallace 1991) focused on the teacher's role in facilitating learning and supporting learners rather than judging their progress or preparing them for tests. In the 1980s and 1990s, new constructs of language proficiency (Canale and Swain 1980; Swain 1985) and new frameworks for assessing proficiency (Bachman and Palmer 1996) resulted in limitations to MC formats and introduced communicative tasks as integral to language proficiency assessment (Fulcher 2000). These developments contributed to aligning language teaching and assessment; both were shaped by constructs of language use rather than focus on language form. For example, the four skills—listening, speaking, reading, and writing—have become critical for both teaching methodology and materials development and language tests (Hall 2011).

Bring It In

Recently, assessment has been an important influence on language teaching. First, in general education, the focus on teacher talk as interaction rather than instruction meant a focus on how teachers respond to student contributions. Such interactions enable the teacher to personalize instruction to support student growth (Black et al. 2003; Tunstall and Gipps 1996). Second, in applied linguistics and language-teaching methodology, SLA-informed recommendations provide salience for classroom interaction. From error analysis to corrective feedback, styles assessment and feedback was identified as a consistently important success factor in instructed SLA (Norris and Ortega, 2000, 2001). Assessment routines thus are not merely test preparation but are integral to the kind of pedagogy that best supports language-learning processes. Ellis's (2001) account of focus-on-forms (FonFs) teaching and Rea-Dickins's (2006) classroom-based assessment both integrate assessment into teacher education degree programs (Andrews 2007; Johnson 2009). Once teachers understand the learning potential of assessment and its related pedagogic practices, teachers can next work with students to involve them as active and informed participants in these routines. This involved handover in the classroom, a teachers' commitment to raise awareness about and develop capacity in monitoring and developing language-use skills.

Hand It Over

According to FonFs pedagogy, teachers take the lead in assessment; their contributions are seen as crucial to learning. However, according to assessment for learning (AfL), student involvement in assessment enhances levels of engagement, motivation, and the metacognitive and reflective skills that underpin effective learning

(Black and Wiliam 1998). In language learning, research on language-learning strategies (Griffiths 2013; Oxford 2011), learner autonomy (Benson 2003, 2011), and learner investment and agency (Norton 2000), the evidence is clear: when students reflect, identify the needed change, and marshal the resources to effect this change, the likelihood of learning increases. In practice, taking control of language learning is challenging for many students. Such an approach may be inconsistent with their institutional cultures and may push the students' comfort levels. The next sections examine in greater detail the nature of self-assessment and the challenge for teachers and students to focus on classroom learning and developing these skills.

Self-Assessment

The rationale for including the development of self-assessment skills and practices in the language curriculum is based on arguments from language learning, education, and language assessment theories.

The Language-Learning Rationale

Research supports two ways that self-assessment can drive language learning. First, in language instruction, a set of techniques informed by SLA research (Ellis, Basturkmen, and Loewen 2002; Ellis 2003) allows the teacher to respond to particular issues in student contributions to classroom talk: "In focus-on-form instruction the primary focus of attention is on meaning. The attention to form arises out of meaning-centered activity derived from the performance of a communicative task. For example, students might be asked to perform an information-gap task and in the course of doing so have their attention drawn to one or more linguistic forms which are needed to perform the activity or that are causing the students problems" (Ellis, Basturkmen, and Loewen 2002, 420).

Focus-on-form techniques are designed for students "to engage in meaning-focused language use" (Ellis, Basturkmen, and Loewen 2002, 422). These opportunities typically emerge in assessments in classroom interaction, usually guided by the teacher, but also by peers and by students in self-assessment. Further support for this assessment role comes from sociocultural SLA; through scaffolding in classroom interaction, teachers help students develop control of new language and enhance opportunities for language learning (Lantolf and Poehner 2008; van Lier 2007). These techniques for managing assessment within classroom interaction require effective teacher listening and response. The opportunities for learning are largely in the students; performance or attempted performance and the teacher's response can transform student understanding. Thus, assessment is central in classroom talk, and this role requires students to actively self-assess.

A second perspective in language-learning theory emphasizes student agency in learning management (Benson 2003; Norton 2000). Capacity for taking responsibility for learning, and acting autonomously to progress it, can transform formative assessment into self-assessment, depending on student participation and investment, resulting in students taking control and developing expertise in their own learning. A similar rationale for self-assessment has also emerged in general education.

The Educational Rationale

In general education, research by Black and Wiliam (1998), Boud (1995), Gibbs (2006), and Boud and Falchikov (2007) suggests that student self-assessment progresses learning. The AfL principles set out by the Assessment Reform Group (ARG) specifically focus on self-assessment: "Assessment for learning develops learners' capacity for self-assessment so that they can become reflective and self-managing. Independent learners have the ability to seek out and gain new skills, new knowledge and new understandings. They are able to engage in self-reflection and identify the next steps in their learning. Teachers should equip learners with the desire and the capacity to take charge of their learning through developing the skills of self-assessment" (ARG 2002, 2).

The "handover" implicit in achieving this principle involves transforming both the teacher role and the student mindset. Teachers must hand over responsibility for assessment to students and actively guide them in reflection and self-management; the complexity of this transformation has not been fully understood (Opfer and Pedder 2011). The present study explores the complexity of teachers helping students learn autonomy in developing their own "desire and the capacity to take charge of their learning through developing the skills of self-assessment" (ARG 2002, 2).

The Assessment Rationale

Self-assessment has been viewed positively as a dimension of the language curriculum for some decades (Blanche 1990; Heilenman 1990; Legutke and Thomas 1991; Oscarson 1989). Drawing on the experience of a range of assessment initiatives in the 1970s and 1980s, Oscarson (1989) defines benefits for learning and classroom practice through increased awareness and goal orientation. Diversifying assessment type can reduce teachers' assessment burden and establish capacity for autonomous learning as a program outcome. Empirical work has been in two areas. First, research has focused on self-assessment as valid, reliable, and useful and on how it can realistically reduce teachers' assessment burden. Blue (1988, 1994), Matsuno (2000), and Huang (2010) demonstrate in statistical studies that self-assessment of writing is unreliable and idiosyncratic as well as inappropriate for formal grading contexts. In contrast, Butler and Lee (2010), Kato (2009), and Chen (2008) show that, with progress in learning and practice in self-assessment, students' capacity to self-assess increases. Kato (2009), in a project with university students of Japanese as a foreign language, focused on goal setting and monitoring as well as consequent self-assessment. The study found high levels of student engagement with the self-assessment study, suggesting that students have a greater capacity for and perception of usefulness of responding to the texts they produce than to planning for learning. Chen (2008) found that, with increased familiarity, students' self-assessment measures of oral skills aligned more closely with teacher assessments. More recently, Butler and Lee (2010) reiterate: "The learning aspect of assessment relates to its potential role in advancing students' learning. By providing students with opportunities to evaluate their performance as well as giving them feedback based on the results of their assessment, students can become more aware of their own learning process and performance, and in turn they can become more proficient in learning" (2010, 6).

To appropriately guide students, teachers also need training. Rea-Dickins and Leung and colleagues have explored teachers' work with assessment activities within school curricula and define two challenges. First, assessment schemes are complex, particularly when moving beyond correct and incorrect language use, or interpreting performance based on a scale and potential for learning (Davison and Leung 2009; Leung 2005, 2010; Rea-Dickins 2007). Second, when implementing assessment for learning, practices tend to focus on enhancing teacher contributions over student inclusion (Rea-Dickins 2006; Teasdale and Leung 2000). Thus, while the introduction of self-assessment practices requires active teacher participation, this approach could also emphasize the teacher and lesson handover to students.

Teacher Literacy

Teacher knowledge of, attitudes toward, and confidence in the role of assessment activities in learning influence the success of classroom assessment initiatives (Carless 2005; Rea-Dickins 2006; Towler and Broadfoot 1992). Fulcher (2000) and Scarino (2014), arguing for greater attention to teacher assessment literacy, illustrate the challenges of including students in the development and uses of such literacy. The demanding nature of assessment literacy, incorporating awareness of its historical and policy aspects (Shohamy 2006), as well as understanding of testing principles and practices, means that there is always a risk that increasing teacher responsibilities in testing and self-assessment leaves students as passive and unengaged participants.

Thus, this study gives teachers the central role in student self-assessment development by exploring how teachers integrate assessment into their work, how student capacity for self-assessment can be enhanced, and how to change the focus from "Does self-assessment work?" (Blue 1994) to "How can it be made to work?" The next section outlines a continuing professional development project designed to support teachers' participation in the project.

Enhancing Self-Assessment Skills

Enhancing Self-Assessment Skills (ESAS) is an ongoing project for UK teachers of adult ESOL (English for speakers of other languages) students. The foci of the project are to develop activities that enhance students' self-assessment skills and document the processes. The first stage of the project involved understanding the issues and affordances for the teachers. The ESAS design was informed by four dimensions of curriculum development: (1) the teacher's role, (2) the innovation strategy, (3) how teachers change their practices, and (4) the design of self-assessment activities.

The Role of the Teacher

Recent accounts from TESOL indicate that teacher alignment with developmental initiatives is essential for successful change. Much evidence shows that teachers' practices do not easily change in response to curriculum reforms and policy changes (Kiely 2012; Wedell 2009). Changes in practice follow changes in thinking;

proposed innovations in practice must be integrated into teachers' thinking and have a "sense of plausibility" (Prabhu 1990, 172) for teachers, to become routine and automated in classroom life. In this paper, I use "teacher thinking" as a broad, inclusive term covering teachers' pedagogical knowledge (Shulman 1986); beliefs, assumptions, and knowledge (Woods 1996); and situated teacher cognitions (Borg 2003; Tsui 2003), which guide decisions in classroom interactions. Research suggests both teacher thinking and practice evolve with experience (Barkhuizen 2014; Kiely and Davis 2010). However, such changes are less amenable to direct manipulation than policymakers and program leaders often assume. Teachers are mediators of curriculum rather than deliverers; few simply implement an existing curriculum. Arguably, such creativity is at the heart of the philosophy of education, according to Dewey (1933) and Stenhouse (1975). In recent decades, the shift to teaching as mediation provides insights into how curriculum change can be effectively managed. It is important to recognize both how complex teaching is and how teachers themselves drive change, and to build on these factors when introducing innovation.

The Innovation Strategy

The innovation strategy was informed by action research principles (Burns 1999; McNiff 1988) and the post-method approach of Kumaravadivelu, where teachers engage with the ways their classrooms work in terms of *what is required (particularity)*, *what seems to work (practicality)*, and *what is possible (possibility)*; (Ellis 2010; Kumaravadivelu 2004). Thus, teachers "own" what is implemented as an innovative practice in the classrooms and feel committed to its success. This study's approach to innovation was shaped by Leadbeater's (2014) frugal innovation theory. Leadbeater (2014) posits that, for innovations to be successful, they must be *lean*, *simple*, *clean*, and *social* (2014, 57). Lean means the innovation should not be demanding or wasteful of resources; simple connotes implementation in a range of contexts without much disruption to routine; clean affords opportunities for recycling and restoring; and social suggests agreeable collaboration. A second influence was nudge theory (Sunstein 2014; Thaler and Sunstein 2008), which promotes change and innovation through suggesting potentially beneficial, useful, and possible behaviors that might not occur without nudging. In ESAS, this approach to innovation involves developing innovative activities *with* rather than *for* teachers and builds on teacher agency in ways that previous models of change (Rogers 1983) do not. This approach accepts that experienced teacher practice has social and emotional as well as pedagogical dimensions, and that change is gradual and messy (Freeman 2002; Kiely and Davis 2010) as teachers fit new ideas to their classrooms and curricula.

The Ways Teachers Change Their Practices

Recent work in pedagogic change builds on the notion that transforming thinking is necessary for innovation (Borg 2003; Woods 1996). Ellis (2010) and Hunter and Kiely (forthcoming) use the word "idea" as a starting point for development of practice. Ellis, discussing the role of SLA input on teacher development programs, suggests that "topics covered in an SLA course should consist of *ideas* rather than *models* … teachers' theoretical positions should emerge out of the *ideas* discussed in the course" (2010, 196, emphasis added). Hunter and Kiely (forthcoming) further this notion in a research study that explores how ideas transformed practices of teachers following teacher development courses. The study found that the ideas with transformative impact had three features:

- Identified as valuable by a participant and stored for potential future use
- Personally appropriated by the teacher to form part of their own knowledge
- A resource for the transformation of practice

Recent studies of teachers in Japan (Hiver 2013; Hiver and Dörnyei, forthcoming) show that teachers must engage at a deep level with the ideas that underpin innovation and change. Using a narrative approach, these studies approach the notion of "teacher immunity" to change that impedes many top-down curriculum innovations. A key part of the strategy they suggest involves exploring ways that novel activities can be tried out and, with adaptations, become part of the teacher's regular practices.

The Design of Self-Assessment Activities

Boud (1995) identifies two core self-assessment activities: identifying and understanding criteria for judging one's work, and making judgments on the extent to which these criteria are reached. As broad processes of engagement with the processes of self-assessment, these informed the design of three specific activities that teachers could introduce in the study reported here. The first activity, a rating exercise, involved the teacher in selecting samples of work and giving students the task of rank ordering them as well as identifying strengths and weaknesses. After the group-work phase, the teacher could discuss the students' rank ordering and the strengths and weaknesses and share perspectives. The second activity involved explicit discussion of formal assessment criteria, teacher demonstration of ways to identify these criteria against work samples, and opportunities for students to "apply" the criteria to their work before submitting it. The third activity involved asking students to reflect and consider questions such as:

- How am I doing?
- What factors influence my performance?
- What can I change to improve?

This activity could be undertaken as a written, learning-journal activity or a classroom-discussion activity.

Enhancing Teacher Self-Assessment Literacy: The Research Process

Phase one of ESAS involved talking to teachers to identify (1) the place of assessment in their work, (2) how to include self-assessment in teaching, and (3) the impact of introducing self-assessment activities. Four teachers participated in the project. Their motivation was to think critically and creatively about their practice and "stimulate a bit of intellectual curiosity about the work" (Teacher B). The teachers had more than fifteen years of teaching experience, master's degrees in applied linguistics and language education, and leadership responsibilities in their professional settings. Both the teachers' expertise and their programs' curriculum design centered on language use and developing communicative language skills. Many of the programs also focused on academic preparation; the students enrolled wanted to join university programs taught in English and had to achieve a recognized proficiency level on a recognized assessment. When arranging the interviews, I shared the research questions for ESAS:

RQ1. How can a focus on enhancing self-assessment skills be achieved in a complex English language curriculum (general and academic) in terms of instructional materials and learning activities?

RQ2. What factors shape teacher engagement with a focus on enhancing self-assessment?

RQ3. What factors shape student engagement with self-assessment as a learning strategy?

RQ4. What are the impacts of the ESAS initiative in terms of learning achievement and student satisfaction with the whole program?

This paper focuses on RQ2 and analyzes the teacher perspective in enhancing self-assessment skills within the language curriculum.

Data Collection

The interviews had two purposes. First, the interviews involved teachers describing and explaining how assessment and assessment practices shaped their work and how their assessment practices evolved. Second, we discussed the nature and potential of self-assessment in the language curriculum and specific activities that might help develop students' self-assessment capacity. The goal was to nudge the teachers to try these activities in ways consistent with their style and students' needs. We conducted nine forty-five- to sixty-minute interviews over ten months, as table 1.1 shows.

Although Teachers C and D were enthusiastic, they did not continue with the project after month 4. Teachers A and B worked together on different programs, and most interviews were conducted during lunch breaks. The first interview with each teacher explored four thematic areas, which were sent to the teachers before the interview:

Table 1.1. Sequence of data collection

Teacher	Month 1	Months 2–4	Months 6–8	Months 8–10
A	Individual interview	Joint Interview (A and B)	Joint Interview (A and B)	Joint Interview (A and B)
B	Individual interview			
C	Individual interview	Individual interview	...	...
D	Individual interview	Individual interview	...	...

1. Assessment and teaching
   a. Teaching philosophy
   b. Set curriculum
   c. Training
2. Assessment in classroom interaction
   a. Strategies for feedback
   b. Language items
   c. Social factors
3. Assessment for learning
   a. Role in learning
   b. Student view
4. Self-assessment
   a. Teacher input
   b. Skills development
   c. Student autonomy

At the end of Interview 1, I introduced the three self-assessment activities to develop a focus on self-assessment and discussed ways to use them. These activities first concretized how self-assessment skills might develop in classroom practice. For example, a task on the collaborative ranking of student writing samples showed how to discuss criteria. Second, the activities provided a nudge via activities teachers could adapt and implement. Subsequent interviews allowed teachers to discuss their experience in using these activities.

The interviews were transcribed and analyzed in two ways. First, an initial thematic analysis was carried out in the week after the interview and sent with the transcript to each teacher, with an invitation to clarify, comment, or provide more information. All four teachers provided additional information by email after the first interview, and Teachers A and B continued to collaborate. Second, I coded the interviews using a grounded, content analysis approach which resulted in lists of excerpts describing teachers' experiences, beliefs, and thinking relative to specific students. Three thematic areas emerged:

- Teachers' beliefs about and experiences with assessment
- Self-assessment and student factors
- Self-assessment and curriculum factors

The interview and email follow-up data included episodes and narratives from lessons, and are analyzed as situated cognitions as well as stated beliefs. The theme "teachers' beliefs and experiences" captures the complexity and fluidity of teachers' thinking about assessment. The theme "student factors" draws together ways teachers see the student in how they conduct their teaching. "Curriculum factors" captures accounts and explanations that relate to the program and institutional setting.

Findings
Teachers' Beliefs and Experiences about Assessment
A key theme in the teachers' beliefs suggests teachers view assessment and teaching separately, but shows that teacher feedback is viewed as a way to progress student

learning. All the teachers linked assessment to end-of-course tests and believed it was important in designing tests. Institutions, not teachers, determined the tests, and sometimes the design was based on formats developed for the International English Language Testing System (IELTS). Teacher C, describing a year-long program preparing students for university study in English, observed that there was

> quite a bit of testing related to IELTS, to see how far off they are, what areas they need to improve on. But it's not specifically my philosophy.

Teacher B, discussing a similar program, said that she used the IELTS criteria to assess students in later stages of the program:

> I certainly don't use the specific measurement . . . until after Christmas. I don't use them for the first term, but in the comment that I write, it would be usually along the lines of good effort . . ., well done, whatever it is, with some comments on perhaps, what they need to do to improve.

The teachers were all hesitant to align teaching too closely to tests and test formats, differentiating between preparation for academic study in English and preparation for a specific high-stakes test. The former involves working toward stated program goals, while the latter represents the specific instrument that determines achievement of these goals. For the teachers, test preparation is necessary although not always viewed as positive for language learning, as described in the next section.

A feature in the data is a distinction between measurement and feedback. The teachers were hesitant about grading students but enthusiastic about providing feedback and described many approaches. They were aware of the importance of teacher feedback both for promoting learning and for maintaining a supportive social learning environment. Teacher B described her teaching as characterized by responding to students in class and individually. She listed her classroom strategies:

- Comments and questions in homework
- Peer feedback forms and activities
- One-to-one meetings outside of class
- Small group talk within class
- Classroom talk: "get them to tell me"
- Collaborative analysis and discussion of students' sentences on the board
- Silence to enable students to work it out for themselves
- Goal-setting talk: the bridge to next year and coping with subject study

She notes that the purpose of guiding and nudging students is to allow them to become "more active, mature, and responsible learners." Teacher B describes how she often worked with sample sentences from students' work on the board. This activity was useful for improving sentence-level accuracy, which was one criteria in that program's writing test. She felt that activities where students discussed complete texts would provide similar opportunities to engage with task completion, another test criterion, and agreed to try this approach. In a later interview, she said that the text rating was useful in helping students to understand task completion. It did not replace the board work but allowed her to follow up on writing tasks. Teacher C similarly describes a rating exercise that became a discussion of the writing criteria on which the students' work is assessed in formal tests. The students' ratings focused on grammatical accuracy and spelling. After guidance from the teacher on other criteria, she noted that students showed understanding of task completion and they became proficient at self-assessing it.

The data illustrate the range of teachers' beliefs, cognitions, and classroom practices regarding assessment. The data also represent feedback and domains of classroom talk that extend student awareness and self-assessment skills, benefitting learning and, indirectly, possibly improving test performance. In the interviews, the teachers described two transformative impacts of reflecting on their practices. First, the interviews required reflection and sense-making, such that the beliefs and cognitions shaping practice were clarified as they were articulated. Second, the prototype tasks explored in the interviews served as nudges, and often represented practical ways to achieve teachers' existing goals.

Self-Assessment and Student Factors

Two dimensions emerged relative to self-assessment. First, teachers did not see self-assessment, either as practice or as a skill, as important for classroom teaching. Second, the self-assessment practices described in the AfL framework—developing learners' capacity for self-assessment to become reflective and self-managing—are important for all the teachers. Thus, the technical aspect of assessing fairly and consistently was perceived as less important than developing informed and thoughtful students. Teachers all showed concern with broadening students' horizons, from understanding effective speaking as not just "sounding like a native speaker" (Teacher D) or what IELTS band a piece of work was consistent with (Teacher A). While this aspect of the teachers' work aligned closely with developing students' understanding of the assessment criteria used in high-stakes tests, the teachers saw it more generally, developing, as Teacher B puts it, "a more mature attitude to working collaboratively...with people from a different language because [they wanted] to be more active and gain more confidence." Teacher B then notes that

> the assessment part … I haven't thought that through yet … I don't know how … at least they have some feedback.

Although they acknowledge and work with the reality of high-stakes assessments and their implications for students, they also seek to protect their students' from the harsh judgements that such assessments might entail if they had more impact on classroom outcomes. The complexity of the teachers' positioning can be understood relative to three aspects of the AfL self-assessment framework: engagement in self-reflection, identifying the next steps in their learning, and equipping learners with the desire and the capacity to take charge of their learning.

Engagement in Student Self-Reflection

Much feedback that teachers provide is aimed at promoting reflection. Teacher A notes the satisfaction experienced when students ask "why" questions:

> Questions that I like them to ask me: "Why" … you know … why have you underlined these words? We always encourage our students to ask "Why" … you know … critical thinking … critical analysis … why.

Teacher D describes a specific strategy to encourage self-reflection:

> This reflective task that I give them. … I don't write on that either. I read it and I generally will give them some general feedbacks. And some indications that I've read it.

This account illustrates the complexity of the teacher's work; she does not write on the students' texts to avoid any impression of an evaluative stance toward it. However, she does make sure that students know she has read the text.

Identifying the Next Steps in Their Learning

This point in the AfL approach suggests individualization, and its occurrence in teacher practices is evident in two ways in the interview data. First, the scaffolding work that teachers undertake to extend students' understanding and capacity in interaction is evident. Teacher B describes this:

> I rarely assess, in the sense, correct students' language in the whole class discussions. More likely, I would do it when they are working in pairs or groups. Then I would … when I walk in the class and listen to … you know … specifically what they say and I would try to think how they might say it. I try to get them … basically to tell me what is wrong.

This approach is particularly strong on individualized attention to a particular problem and aligns with Tunstall and Gipps's (1996) "constructing the way forward" (400). Teacher B shows understanding of where students are in their learning and clarifies how to progress. The second aspect of identifying next steps for student learning is increasing students' confidence. This emphasis on student confidence is evident in the care Teacher B takes when providing feedback; this strand emerges in all the interviews. By helping students increase their confidence in their progress toward goals, students move to the next phase independently. Thus, teachers can equip learners with the desire and the capacity to take charge of their learning.

Equipping Learners with the Desire and the Capacity to Take Charge of Their Learning

All the teachers mentioned confidence as a focus; teachers reference it as a learning need, condition for learning, learning outcome, and factor to be negotiated when assessing and providing feedback. Attention to confidence means focusing on students as individuals rather than as a group, as Teacher B states above. When discussing confidence, the teachers all mention individual students with specific confidence issues. For example, Teacher C talked about Student X's awareness that her speaking skills needed work, and Teacher C needed to avoid overtly confirming that both privately and in the classroom. These narratives of individual students illustrate the centrality and complexity of the confidence aspect of learning for teachers, because it has an influence on how they assess students and provide feedback. They focus less on the technical aspects of language development than on maintaining student optimism and engagement to thus equip learners with the desire and capacity to become autonomous.

Self-Assessment and Curriculum Factors

The teachers described two particular features of their curriculum contexts that influenced student self-assessment. First, teachers have a high level of autonomy in syllabus design and teaching methods. Institutions determine learning outcomes, while teachers determine how to accomplish these goals. Some decisions are collective, involving small groups of collaborating teachers, but many are individual. Rather than using prescribed materials, these teachers draw on material banks and their own resources. Teacher B described an email writing project over several lessons that developed from a classroom discussion. The individual ways the teachers construct the curriculum may obscure the affordances for the development of self-assessment skills in classrooms. However, all teachers noted the importance of formal assessments on curriculum design. The formal assessments included both external examinations and institutional tests. The formats of both are fixed, so teachers must integrate preparation within their teaching, regardless of their views of the assessment. Teacher D describes how the criteria for speaking assessments included characterizations of pronunciation and fluency based on native-speaker models that were inconsistent with her own beliefs and values.

A key factor in integrating the development of self-assessment skills is what Teacher B calls "connectability." In planning and implementing lessons, the teacher makes connections and helps students see their relevance. The connections that occur in classroom interaction, especially teacher talk, link particular instances of language use to general rules of accuracy and appropriateness. Thus, student performances are linked to assessment criteria that demonstrate how assessment criteria work, how such insights can construct further learning, and how students can transform these insights into self-assessment tools that enhance language learning. In analyzing one interview with Teacher B, we identified six ways that connections shape the curriculum:

1. Connecting communicative classroom activities with real-word communication to promote learning
2. Connecting assessment and self-assessment training with the activities appropriate for a specific classroom
3. Helping students see the links between what they are supposed to be doing and what they are actually doing
4. Using task-specific criteria to better connect student thinking to assessments
5. Using increasingly precise codes to align student perceptions with what the teacher considers important
6. Using assessment to connect activities, such as iterations of drafts of emails or other texts

This notion of connectability illuminates the ways teachers position assessment and self-assessment in the curriculum and shows how innovations, including this projects' self-assessment activities, can become part of routine practice.

Discussion

The accounts above illuminate three dimensions of the complexity of enhancing students' roles in classroom self-assessment. First, assessment seems to suggest a teacher-centered classroom, and teachers must mitigate the effects of this. To achieve this, they separate feedback from assessment, the former characterized by a learning focus and the latter characterized by a measurement focus. Although high-stakes assessments at the end of the programs have salience for teachers, they filter the impact to ensure that their classes are not merely test preparation. Teachers see feedback as focused on the learning needs and potential of each student and manage to build student confidence. Feedback is regarded by teachers as distinct from assessment, the latter being more focused on providing a mark or grade independent of social context and emotional need. Another teacher strategy appears to be a delay in the assessment focus until the end of the program. Thus, the use of marks does not feature until later in the program, and specific work unpacking criteria and enhancing student understanding of how these work is also delayed.

Second, this low profile for assessment makes the handover implicit in self-assessment difficult. All the teachers all felt that their students were dependent on them to guide their language learning. Where teachers perceive students as not yet ready for managing their own learning, they had to educate and persuade so that the development of informed language learners was part of a maturation process, and progressed from school-based learning to university- or workplace-based adult learning. Teacher practices demonstrated serious attention to formative assessment and engagement. The practices of experienced teachers are shaped by processes of situated learning and reflection; they are the outcome of a range of experiences and alignments, of tacit analyses and positions. Processes of teacher learning and curriculum change are sustained by a reflective disposition.

Third, these teachers were innovators, aware of the need to change as student profiles and expectations change. The focus of this project increased reflection on existing practices, and sometimes resulted in unexpected developments. Teacher C, for example, found the rating exercises on pieces of writing difficult, but she made the technique work in the context of speaking skills development.

Conclusion

This chapter has set out the rationale for enhancing student self-assessment skills as part of a dynamic, student-centered curriculum that equips students for a lifelong process of language learning. It demonstrates that, to be integrated into practice, teachers must both understand and own policy initiatives such as AfL so that they are integrated into classroom practice and become part of the learning development of students. This chapter illustrates the complexity of this for teachers, particularly in the ways they manage the social and emotional dimensions of classroom life.

References

Andrews, Stephen. 2007. *Teacher Language Awareness*. Cambridge: Cambridge University Press.
ARG. 2002. "Assessment for Learning: 10 Principles." Accessed June 2016. http://cdn.aaia.org.uk/content/uploads/2010/06/Assessment-for-Learning-10-principles.pdf.
Bachman, Lyle F., and Adrian S. Palmer. 1996. *Language Testing in Practice: Designing and Developing Useful Language Tests*. Oxford: Oxford University Press.

Barkhuizen, Gary. 2014. "Narrative Research in Language Teaching and Learning." *Language Teaching* 47:450–66. http://dx.doi.org/10.1017/S0261444814000172.

Benson, Philip. 2003. *Autonomy in Language Learning*. Basingstoke, Eng.: Palgrave Macmillan.

———. 2011. *Teaching and Researching: Autonomy in Language Learning*. London: Pearson.

Black, Paul, Christine Harrison, Clare Lee, Bethan Marshall, and Dylan Wiliam. 2003. *Assessment for Learning: Putting It into Practice*. Berkshire, Eng.: Open University Press.

Black, Paul, and Dylan Wiliam. 1998. "Assessment and Classroom Learning." *Assessment in Education: Principles, Policy & Practice* 5:7–74. doi:10.1080/0969595980050102.

Blanche, Patrick. 1990. "Using Standardised Achievement and Oral Proficiency Tests for Self-Assessment Purposes: The DLIFLC Study." *Language Testing* 7:202–29. doi:10.1177/026553229000700205.

Blue, George M. 1988. "Self-Assessment: The Limit of Learner Independence." In *Individualisation and Autonomy in Language Learning*, edited by Arthur Brookes and Peter Grundy, 100–18. ELT Documents 131. London: The British Council/Macmillan.

———. 1994. "Self-Assessment of Foreign Language Skills: Does It Work?" *CLE Working Papers* 3:18–35. http://files.eric.ed.gov/fulltext/ED396569.pdf.

Borg, Simon. 2003. "Teacher Cognition in Language Teaching: A Review of Research on What Language Teachers Think, Know, Believe, and Do." *Language Teaching* 36:81–109. http://dx.doi.org/10.1017/S0261444803001903.

Boud, David. 1995. *Enhancing Learning through Self-Assessment*. London: RoutledgeFalmer.

Boud, David, and Nancy Falchikov. 2007. *Rethinking Assessment in Higher Education: Learning for the Longer Term*. London: Routledge.

Burns, Anne. 1999. *Collaborative Action Research for English Language Teachers*. Cambridge: Cambridge University Press.

Butler, Yuko Goto, and Jiyoon Lee. 2010. "The Effects of Self-Assessment among Young Learners of English." *Language Testing* 27:5–31. doi:10.1177/0265532209346370.

Canale, Michael, and Merrill Swain. 1980. "Theoretical Bases of Communicative Approaches to Second Language Teaching and Testing." *Applied Linguistics* 1:1–47. http://ibatefl.com/wp-content/uploads/2012/08/CLT-Canale-Swain.pdf.

Carless, David. 2005. "Prospects for the Implementation of Assessment for Learning." *Assessment in Education: Principles, Policy & Practice* 12:39–54. doi:10.1080/0969594042000333904.

Chen, Yuh-Mei. 2008. "Learning to Self-Assess Oral Performance in English: A Longitudinal Case Study." *Language Teaching Research* 12:235–62. doi:10.1177/1362168807086293.

Dewey, John. 1933. *How We Think*. Boston: D. C. Heath & Co.

Davison, Chris, and Constant Leung. 2009. "Current Issues in English Language Teacher-Based Assessment." *TESOL Quarterly* 43:393–415.

Ellis, Rod, ed. 2001. *Form-Focussed Instruction and Second Language Learning*. Special issue of *Language Learning*. Oxford: Blackwell.

———. 2003. *Task-Based Language Learning and Teaching*. Oxford: Oxford University Press.

———. 2010. "Second Language Acquisition, Teacher Education and Language Pedagogy." *Language Teaching* 43:182–201. http://dx.doi.org/10.1017/S0261444809990139.

Ellis, Rod, Helen Basturkmen, and Shawn Loewen. 2002. "Learner Uptake in Communicative ESL Lessons." *Language Learning* 51:281–318. doi:10.1111/1467-9922.00156.

Freeman, Donald. 2002. "The Hidden Side of the Work: Teacher Knowledge and Learning to Teach. A Perspective from North American Educational Research on Teacher Education in English Language Teaching." *Language Teaching* 35:1–13. http://dx.doi.org/10.1017/S0261444801001720.

Fulcher, Glenn. 2000. "The 'Communicative' Legacy in Language Testing." *System* 28:483–97. doi:10.1016/S0346-251X(00)00033-6.

Gibbs, Graham. 2006. "How Assessment Frames Student Learning." In *Innovative Assessment in Higher Education*, edited by Cordelia Bryan and Karen Clegg, 23–36. London: Routledge.

Gitlin, Andrew David, and John Smyth. 1989. *Teacher Evaluation: Educative Alternatives*. Lewes, Eng.: Falmer Press.

Griffiths, Carol. 2013. *The Strategy Factor in Successful Language Learning*. Clevedon, Eng.: Multilingual Matters.

Hall, Graham. 2011. *Exploring English Language Teaching: Language in Action*. London: Routledge.

Heilenman, L. Kathy. 1990. "Self-Assessment of Second Language Ability: The Role of Response Effects." *Language Testing* 7:174–201. doi:10.1177/026553229000700204.

Hiver, Philip. 2013. "The Interplay of Possible Language Teacher Selves in Professional Development Choices." *Language Teaching Research* 17:210–27. doi:10.1177/1362168813475944.

Hiver, Philip, and Zoltán Dörnyei. Forthcoming. "Language Teacher Immunity: A Double-Edged Sword." *Applied Linguistics*. doi:10.1093/applin/amv034.

Huang, Li-Shih. 2010. "Do Different Modalities of Reflection Matter? An Exploration of Adult Second-Language Learners' Reported Strategy Use and Oral Language Production." *System* 38:245–61. doi:10.1016/j.system.2010.03.005.

Hunter, Duncan, and Richard Kiely. Forthcoming. "The Idea as a Mechanism in Language Teacher Development." *Journal of Second Language Teaching and Research*.

Johnson, Karen, E. 2009. *Second Language Teacher Education: A Sociocultural Perspective*. New York: Routledge.

Kato, Fumie. 2009. "Student Preferences: Goal-setting and Self-assessment Activities in a Tertiary Education Environment." *Language Teaching Research* 13:177–99. doi:10.1177/1362168809103447.

Kiely, Richard. 2012. "Designing Evaluation into Change Management Processes." In *Managing Change in Language Education*, edited by Christopher Tribble, 75–91. London: The British Council.

Kiely, Richard, and Matt Davis. 2010. "From Transmission to Transformation: Teacher Learning in English for Speakers of Other Languages." *Language Teaching Research* 14:277–96. doi:10.1177/1362168810365241.

Kumaravadivelu, B. 2004. *Understanding Language Teaching: From Method to Postmethod*. Mahwah, NJ: Routledge.

Lado, Robert. 1964. *Language Testing: The Construction and Use of Foreign Language Tests; A Teacher's Book*. New York: McGraw-Hill.

Lantolf, James P., and Matthew E. Poehner. 2008. *Sociocultural Theory and the Teaching of Second Languages*. London: Equinox Pub.

Leadbeater, Charles. 2014. *The Frugal Innovator: Creating Change on a Shoestring Budget*. Basingstoke, Eng.: Palgrave Macmillan.

Legutke, Michael, and Howard Thomas. 1991. *Process and Experience in the Language Classroom*. Harlow, Eng.: Longman.

Leung, Constant. 2005. "Classroom Teacher Assessment of Second Language Development: Construct as Practice." In *Handbook of Research in Second Language Teaching and Learning*, edited by Eli Hinkel, 869–88. Mahwah, NJ: Lawrence Erlbaum.

———. 2010. "Language Teaching and Language Assessment." In *The Sage Handbook of Sociolinguistics*, edited by Ruth Wodak, Barbara Johnstone, and Paul Kerswill, 545–64. London: Sage.

Matsuno, Sumie. 2000. "Self-, Peer-, and Teacher-Assessments in Japanese University EFL Writing Classrooms." *Language Testing* 26:75–100. doi:10.1177/0265532208097337.

McNiff, Jean. 1988. *Action Research: Principles and Practice*. London: Macmillan.

Norris, John M., and Lourdes Ortega. 2000. "Effectiveness of L2 Instruction: A Research Synthesis and Quantitative Meta-analysis." *Language Learning* 50:417–528. doi:10.1111/0023-8333.00136.

———. 2001. "Does Type of Instruction Make a Difference? Substantive Findings from a Meta-analytic Review." In *Form-Focused Instruction and Second Language Learning*, edited by Rod Ellis, 157–213. Oxford: Blackwell.

Norton, Bonnie. 2000. *Identity and Language Learning: Gender, Ethnicity and Educational Change*. Harlow, Eng.: Longman.

Oller, John. 1979. *Language Tests at School: A Pragmatic Approach*. London: Longman.

Opfer, V. Darleen, and David Pedder. 2011. "Conceptualizing Teacher Professional Learning." *Review of Educational Research* 81:376–407. doi:10.3102/0034654311413609.

Oscarson, Mats. 1989. "Self-Assessment of Language Proficiency: Rationale and Applications." *Language Testing* 6:1–13. doi:10.1177/026553228900600103.

Oxford, Rebecca L. 2011. *Teaching and Researching Language Learning Strategies*. London: Longman.

Prabhu, N. S. 1990. "There Is No Best Method—Why?" *TESOL Quarterly* 24:161–76. http://www.jstor.org/stable/3586897.

Rea-Dickins, Pauline. 2006. "Currents and Eddies in the Discourse of Assessment: A Learning-Focused Interpretation." *International Journal of Applied Linguistics* 16:163–88. doi:10.1111/j.1473-4192.2006.00112.x.

———. 2007. "Classroom-Based Assessment: Possibilities and Pitfalls." In *The International Handbook of English Language Teaching*, edited by Chris Davison and Jim Cummins, 505–20. New York: Springer.

Richards, Jack C., and David Nunan, eds. 1989. *Second Language Teacher Education*. Cambridge: Cambridge University Press

Rogers, E. M. 1983. *Diffusion of Innovations*. New York: The Free Press.

Scarino, Angela. 2014. "Learning as Reciprocal, Interpretive Meaning-Making: A View from Collaborative Research into the Professional Learning of Teachers of Languages." *Modern Language Journal* 98:386–401.

Shohamy, Elana. 2006. *Language Policy: Hidden Agendas and New Approaches*. Routledge: London.

Shulman, Lee S. 1986. "Those Who Understand: Knowledge Growth in Teaching." *Educational Researcher* 15:4–14. http://www.jstor.org/stable/1175860.

Stenhouse, Lawrence. 1975. *An Introduction to Curriculum Research and Development*. London: Heinemann.

Sunstein, Cass R. 2014. *Why Nudge?: The Politics of Libertarian Paternalism*. New Haven, CT: Yale University Press.

Swain, Merrill. 1985. "Communicative Competence: Some Roles of Comprehensible Input and Comprehensible Output in Its Development." In *Input in Second Language Acquisition*, edited by Susan M. Gass and Carolyn G. Madden, 235–56. New York: Newbury House.

Teasdale, Alex, and Constant Leung. 2000. "Teacher Assessment and Psychometric Theory: A Case of Paradigm Crossing?" *Language Testing* 17:163–84. doi:10.1177/026553220001700204.

Thaler, Richard H., and Cass R. Sunstein. 2008. *Nudge: Improving Decisions about Health, Wealth, and Happiness*. New Haven, CT: Yale University Press.

Towler, Lee, and Patricia Broadfoot. 1992. "Self-Assessment in the Primary School." *Educational Review* 44:137–51. doi:10.1080/0013191920440203.

Tsui, Amy B. M. 2003. *Understanding Expertise in Teaching: Case Studies of Second Language Teachers*. New York: Cambridge University Press.

Tunstall, Pat, and Caroline Gipps. 1996. "Teacher Feedback to Young Children in Formative Assessment: A Typology." *British Educational Research Journal* 22:389–404. doi:10.1080/0141192960220402.

van Lier, Leo. 2007. "Action-Based Teaching, Autonomy and Identity." *Innovation in Language Learning and Teaching* 1:46–65. doi:10.2167/illt42.0.

Wallace, Michael J. 1991. *Training Foreign Language Teachers: A Reflective Approach*. Cambridge: Cambridge University Press.

Wedell, Martin. 2009. *Planning Educational Change: Putting People and Their Contexts First*. London: Continuum.

Woods, Devon. 1996. *Teacher Cognition in Language Teaching: Beliefs, Decision-Making and Classroom Practice*. Cambridge: Cambridge University Press.

Chapter 2

◆ Young Learners' Processes and Rationales for Responding to Self-Assessment Items

Cases of Generic Can-Do and Five-Point, Likert-Type Formats

YUKO GOTO BUTLER
University of Pennsylvania

SELF-ASSESSMENT (SA) HAS GAINED substantial attention in recent years among educators of young foreign language learners (conventionally defined as children from six to twelve years old [Nikolov 2016]). Researchers have developed various types of SAs for young learners, including the speaking can-do statements in the European Language Portfolio (CILT 2006) and Lingua Folio Junior (National Council of State Supervisors for Languages 2014) based on the American Council on the Teaching of Foreign Languages proficiency guidelines. These readily available SAs tend to be generic (i.e., somewhat decontextualized) because they are meant for use across various contexts. Textbooks and other materials for young learners often include SAs in different formats, such as can-do (i.e., a dichotomous format), Likert-type, and open-ended response formats. In some cases, including Japan where the present study was conducted, SA has been implemented as part of language education policy; the teachers may be required or strongly recommended to implement SA for summative or formative purposes or both.

Despite the popularity of SA among educators of young language learners, we have limited information about many aspects of SA for such learners, including the relationship between children's age and the ability to self-assess their performance in a foreign language; how the context of SA implementation (e.g., wording, scaling, examples, and timing) influences children's judgment; and how children make evaluative judgments (e.g., comparisons with other children, comparisons with previous performance, etc.). For example, in responding to the item "I can say simple greetings in English," we do not know what a child considers to be a "simple greeting," what counts as evidence of a "simple greeting," and how children evaluate their performance. Therefore, as part of a larger project investigating young learners' processes and rationales underlying SAs, this study focuses on generic SA items with two different response formats: (a) a typical dichotomous format (can-do descriptors) and a five-point, Likert-type format (using the same items from the dichotomous format but with a graded scale).

Background
Learners' Ability for Self-Evaluation

SA involves "internal or self-directed" activities (Oscarson 1989, 1), and thus it differs from other types of assessments, which are based on judgments by external agents, such as teachers and test administrators. Because of the subjective nature of SA, primarily from a traditional perspective of assessment (i.e., assessment of learning) where the primary objective of assessment is to make accurate inferences of learners' abilities, concerns have emerged with respect to SA's validity and reliability. Despite such concerns, previous studies on SA, at least those conducted among adult learners, indicate that SA results generally show reasonably high correlations with other external criteria such as objective tests, teachers' judgments, and course grades (e.g., Bachman and Palmer 1989; Blanche 1990; Leach 2012; Oscarson 1997). However, researchers have also identified a number of factors that could influence the accuracy of learners' SA results; such factors included skill domains being assessed (receptive skills vs. productive skills; Ross 1998); item wordings and constructions (e.g., Heilenman 1990); and various factors specific to individual learners, such as proficiency level and experience with SA (e.g., Blanche and Merino 1989; Heilenman 1990; Stefani 1994; Sullivan and Hall 1997; Suzuki 2015).

Information on SA among young language learners remains limited. However, researchers examining children's development of achievement-related cognitions and motivations observed that children maintain high self-appraisal irrespective of their actual performance until they reach early primary-school grades. Sometime after around the age of eight, children begin to self-assess their performance more accurately; this coincides with the time when they start using social-comparative information to judge their own performance against others. Importantly, however, while social-comparative information starts influencing children's self-appraisal of *performance* at around age seven to eight, it won't influence their self-appraisal of *abilities* until they are around eleven to thirteen years old (R. Butler 2005).

Researchers' interpretation of children's judgment of their own performance and abilities has changed over the years. In the past, strongly influenced by Piaget's (1929) cognitive development theory, children's failure to accurately self-assess their performance and abilities was attributed to the immaturity of their internal mental structures. However, researchers began to realize that children's self-evaluative abilities vary depending on kinds of tasks they engage in (i.e., children can more accurately self-evaluate their performance in familiar tasks or cognitively less demanding tasks), learning contexts (i.e., children with greater social interaction with others are better at assessing themselves using social-comparative information than children with less social interaction), experience with SA, the ways that assessment items were constructed and delivered, and the availability of scaffolding (Y. Butler 2016). In other words, the observed increase in accuracy of self-evaluation by age appears to be largely due to "age-related changes in children's typical experiences and contexts, rather than their internal cognitive structures" (R. Butler 2005, 208). Thus, when implementing SA with young learners, we need to pay careful attention to learning and assessment contexts and their age-related experiences in addition to their chronological age.

SA's Potential Benefit for Enhancing Learning

One of the major reasons for the recent popularity of SA is its potential benefit for enhancing students' learning (Y. Butler 2016). By self-reflecting on learning and performance through SA, it is thought that learners can develop self-regulation—defined as "self-regulated thoughts, feelings, and behaviors that are oriented to attaining goals" (Zimmerman 2002, 65)—which in turn leads to further learning. According to social cognitive theory, developing a greater degree of self-regulation requires learners to have goals and motivation, and learners' self-efficacy—"the judgments that individuals hold about their capabilities to learn or perform courses of actions at designated levels" (Pajares and Usher 2008, 395–6)—plays a critical role in sustaining their goals and motivation for regulatory behaviors and, ultimately, in facilitating learning. Self-evaluation gives learners an opportunity to self-monitor their learning processes and outcomes, and positive evaluation brings learners feelings of efficacy about their goals and motivation for further learning. Social cognitive theory also holds that individuals' personal factors, such as self-evaluation, self-efficacy, and motivation, have reciprocal relationships not only with their behaviors (e.g., high self-efficacy may lead to self-regulatory behaviors, and achieving high performance may lead to higher self-efficacy) but also with environmental factors (e.g., receiving positive feedback from teachers may increase self-efficacy, and high self-efficacy may influence the way the teacher provides the feedback to the learner). Finally, social cognitive theory also predicts that environmental factors mutually interact with behavioral factors (Bandura 1986).

Judgment Processes When Responding to SA

According to social cognitive theory, learners' SA should be influenced by both behavioral factors (e.g., mastery experiences) and environmental factors (e.g., feedback from teachers, peer-group comparisons, etc.) and vice versa. However, we have very limited information on how language learners self-assess their performance and attainment in the target language. In psychology, Higgins, Strauman, and Klein (1986) proposed a model of the self-evaluation process composed of four stages: (1) stimulus representation, (2) identification, (3) interpretation, and (4) general appraisal. If we apply their model to a situation in which a child responds to an item in SA related to a second or foreign language, such as "I can understand questions about myself," we can hypothesize the process as follows:

1. The child comprehends what the item refers to (e.g., getting the meaning of "understand questions about myself").
2. The child retrieves relevant instances in which they engage in the performance or action in question (e.g., thinking about instances in which the child was asked about themself in English).
3. The child sets the reference point(s) for evaluation (e.g., setting reference points such as other classmates' performances, one's own past performance, etc.).
4. The child determines each scale level and makes an evaluative judgment (e.g., evaluating performance in the retrieved instances against the reference points that the child set).

However, according to Higgins, Strauman, and Klein (1986), not all learners necessarily proceed through each step. If learners are asked to self-evaluate something outside of their experience, for example, they may not retrieve any instances of previous performance or may even go directly to the final stage.

In a rare example of a study that examined language learners' processes of responding to SA, Moritz (1996) conducted semistructured, retrospective interviews with twenty-eight French-learning college students, with the aim of understanding reference points that the students used. She coded the data based on Higgins, Strauman, and Klein's classification scheme for standards of self-evaluation and found that her college students mostly relied on the following three types of reference points (1986, 26–27, cited in Maritz 1996, 7):

1. *Social category*: The "'average' performance or attributes among the members of some social category or group" (e.g., compared with average students' performances in my class)
2. *Meaningful other*: "The performance or attributes of another individual who is meaningful to the evaluator" (e.g., compared with my study mate)
3. *Autobiographical*: "The evaluator's own past performance or attributes," which can be either "a single instance or distribution of instances" and "recent or remote" instances (e.g., compared with my performance in the last semester)

Regarding young learners, however, their processes of responding to items in SA (referred to as SA items hereafter) remain largely unclear. To understand such processes would be informative for educators of young learners when they implement SA and interpret the results of SA.

Research Questions

As previously discussed, this study is part of a larger project that aimed to understand young foreign language learners' processes and rationales for responding to various types of SAs. The original project compared young learners' responses and rationales to SA items depending on (a) different response formats (i.e., dichotomous versus Likert-type formats); (b) different "concreteness" in item descriptions (whether items contain concrete examples or not); and (c) different "contextualization" in administration (i.e., SA is administrated generically or immediately after particular tasks). The present study focuses on the two different SA response formats when administered generically, and it is exploratory by nature. More specifically, this study addresses the following research questions:

1. How do young learners respond to two different SA formats (namely, can-do [dichotomous] and five-point, Likert-type formats)?
2. What are young learners' processes and rationales when they respond to SA items?
3. How do young learners' processes and rationales differ according to their age?

Methods

Participants

Thirty-one English-learning, primary-school students in Japan participated in this study. They were divided into two age groups: a younger group (ages eight through nine, $n = 17$) and an older group (ages ten through twelve, $n = 14$). They were recruited from among children who passed the silver level of the Eiken Junior test within the three months prior to recruitment. The Eiken Junior test is designed to examine young learners' general English proficiency (receptive skill domains only), and the silver level roughly corresponds to the A1 level in the Common European Framework of Reference (CEFR). The recruitment announcement was posted online, and the participants came from both private and public schools in the Tokyo metropolitan area.

In 2015, when this study was conducted, Japanese policy required fifth- and sixth-grade students (ages ten through twelve) to engage in "English language activities" once a week, focusing on oral English activities, and SA is recommended to teachers of these grade levels. The age grouping in this study (the younger and older groups mentioned above) was partially motivated by this policy. It was also motivated by the previous research suggesting that children's self-appraisal of performance and abilities seems to change sometime around nine and ten years of age (see the literature review section). Because primary schools in Japan may have extended English instructional hours, the amount of English instruction that children received at school varied. In addition, according to a warm-up interview with the children and a questionnaire distributed to their parents, all of the participants in this study had at least some additional English lessons outside of school. Such different levels of accessibility to English instruction both in school and outside of school allowed us to recruit students of different ages while roughly controlling for their general proficiency level (measured by the Eiken Junior test). Perhaps partially due to the current policy's emphasis on SAs in English education in Japan, all the participants indicated that they had some experience with SAs, but this experience varied both in degree and in format.

Self-Assessment Instrument

The SA instrument used in this study was composed of nine items. Eight items were selected from the can-do speech bubbles in the European Language Portfolio

(CILT 2006). The items selected from can-do speech bubbles resembled the kinds of SA items that have often been used in Japanese primary classrooms. We used the can-do speech bubbles in this study because they also have been used in a large-scale research project conducted by a group of primary-school teachers in Japan (Kuno, Aida, and Irie 2014). In addition to the items from can-do speech bubbles, one more item was included (item #7 Speak 3 with an asterisk below). Item #7 is a locally popular SA item that was designed to deal with a learning issue specific to Japanese learners of English. Thus, as shown below, there were four listening items, four speaking items, and one reading item altogether, reflecting the current curriculum emphasis on the three skill domains at Japanese primary schools (i.e., listening and speaking are the main focus with some reading instruction, while writing is not taught).[1]

1. Listen 1: I can understand questions about myself.
2. Listen 2: I can understand the teachers' instructions.
3. Listen 3: I can follow short stories.
4. Listen 4: I can follow someone else's conversation.
5. Speak 1: I can name some foods.
6. Speak 2: I can say simple greetings in English.
7. *Speak 3: When speaking in English, I can express myself naturally and "English-like."
8. Speak 4: I can introduce myself to others in English.
9. Read 1: I can read a short story.

The items were delivered in both a can-do format and a five-point, Likert-type format and written in the children's first language (Japanese). An example of the SA sheet given to the children is shown in appendix A. As suggested by Dörnyei and Taguchi (2010), smilegrams were used instead of numerical anchors. The happiest face, the neutral face, and the unhappy face indicate "do it well," "so-so," and "still difficult," respectively. The children were asked to circle one of the faces.

Procedure

The assessment procedures involved a warm-up chat with an interviewer, after which participating children were asked to respond to the can-do items first, and then the five-point, Likert-type items for which they were asked to circle the most appropriate smilegram. Immediately after the children completed the items, they participated in a semistructured, retrospective interview. Based on the hypothesized four stages of SA processes described above, the interviewer asked the children questions to explore how they comprehended the items (e.g., "What do you think 'questions about myself' are?" "What does 'understand' mean here?"). Then, pointing to an item, she asked the children to explain to her how they decided to evaluate themselves on that item in order to understand the rest of their processes but without assuming that the children would articulate the process in the order suggested above. When necessary, scaffolding was provided to help the children better articulate their SA-response process. The children were also allowed to ask questions at any time during the entire process. The session took approximately twenty to thirty minutes per child. All the interactions between the children and the interviewer were recorded and transcribed.

Analysis

For research question 1, the children's evaluation to the SA in the two different response formats was compared. In order to answer the second and third research questions, the verbal information elicited through the interviews was analyzed according to the four stages of SA processing described above: (1) comprehend the items, (2) retrieve relevant instances, (3) set the reference point(s) for evaluation, and (4) make an evaluative judgment. In order to enhance coding reliability, two researchers (one of them the author of this chapter) randomly selected five students' verbal data, which we then coded independently. Any discrepancies were discussed and resolved, and then the researchers coded another five students' data to ensure reliability. After we reached one hundred percent agreement in coding, the author coded the rest of the data. Additional details for the analyses are described in the results section.

Results

Young Learners' Responses to Can-Do and Five-Point, Likert-Type Formats

The children's responses on the can-do and the five-point, Likert-type formats are shown in table 2.1. Although the number of items was quite small, the children generally responded positively to speaking items (except for Speak 3, an added item). By contrast, their responses to the receptive-skill items were more split. This variability in responses to the receptive items is interesting given that the children's general English proficiency in the receptive-skill domains was assumed to be relatively similar (as far as the Eiken test results were concerned). This is also curious considering that adult learners more accurately self-assess their performance in the receptive domain than in the productive (i.e., speaking and writing) domain (Ross 1998) although the present analysis could not test the accuracy of the children's responses.

The patterns of the children's responses between the two formats varied across items; unexpected responses were observed in some items (e.g., checking "not yet" in the can-do format and "do it well" in the five-point, Likert-type format for the same item such as Listen 2 and Listen 4). Some SA items also had relatively high frequencies of choosing the neutral face (the middle answer) in the five-point, Likert-type format (e.g., 10 children in Listen 1 and 8 children in Speak 3). On average (across the 9 items), 6.4 children out of 31 children (approximately twenty percent of the participating children) chose the neutral face, whereas they were forced to choose a dichotomous answer in the can-do format.

Young Learners' Processes and Rationales When Responding to the SA

Results shedding light on young learners' self-evaluation were analyzed in terms of the extent to which the four cognitive processes were evidenced in children's interview responses. The discussion to follow presents results in each of the four

◆ **Table 2.1.** Children's responses to can-do and five-point, Likert-type SA items

Listen 1	😀	🙂	😐	🙁	⊗	Total
Can	3	15	4	1	0	23
Not yet	0	2	6	0	0	8
Total	3	17	10	1	0	31

Listen 2	😀	🙂	😐	🙁	⊗	Total
Can	7	11	2	1	0	21
Not yet	1	1	5	3	0	10
Total	8	12	7	4	0	31

Listen 3	😀	🙂	😐	🙁	⊗	Total
Can	5	5	6	2	0	18
Not yet	0	0	1	8	4	13
Total	5	5	7	10	4	31

Listen 4	😀	🙂	😐	🙁	⊗	Total
Can	4	3	5	1	0	13
Not yet	2	0	2	13	1	18
Total	6	3	7	14	1	31

Speak 1	😀	🙂	😐	🙁	⊗	Total
Can	17	10	3	1	0	30
Not yet	0	0	0	1	0	1
Total	17	10	3	1	0	31

Speak 2	😀	🙂	😐	🙁	⊗	Total
Can	19	5	6	0	0	30
Not yet	0	0	1	0	0	1
Total	19	5	7	0	0	31

Speak 3	😀	🙂	😐	🙁	⊗	Total
Can	4	3	1	0	0	8
Not yet	0	1	7	11	4	23
Total	4	4	8	11	4	31

Speak 4	😀	🙂	😐	🙁	⊗	Total
Can	12	11	4	2	0	29
Not yet	0	0	1	1	0	2
Total	12	11	5	3	0	31

Read	😀	🙂	😐	🙁	⊗	Total
Can	9	2	0	0	0	11
Not yet	0	1	4	8	7	20
Total	9	3	4	8	7	31

Note: 😀 = can do it very well; 😐 = so-so; and ⊗ = still difficult

processing categories (comprehension, retrieval, reference-point setting, appraisal), exploring themes arising from respondents' interviews with each domain.

1. Comprehending Item Descriptions

Regardless of age, the children reported that they had no problem understanding the items in general. However, the interview data revealed that their interpretations of some commonly used words in the SA, such as "follow" and "understand," varied across individuals. In the case of Listen 3 ("I can follow short stories"), for example, most children indicated that they usually could guess the meaning of words and some sentences when they listened to short stories. But some children did not think guessing was sufficient because "guessing and understanding are two different things" (ID#19, age ten). More precisely, for some children, "following stories" meant being able to understand not just select words or sentences but most or all of the words or sentences used in the stories. According to the participating children, teachers usually tell the same story multiple times in class. Thus, for some children, "following stories" meant that one should grasp a storyline when listening to the story for the first time—before teachers give the students any hints and explanations. For others, "following stories" meant that one should be able to retell the story to others in Japanese, reflecting their classroom routine (teachers usually ask the students questions in Japanese to check their comprehension).

Such variability in the interpretation of SA items may result in a deviation from what teachers or item writers intended. The item, Speak 3, is a good example. This item is not from the can-do speech bubbles but was added because of its popularity in Japanese classrooms for addressing a specific English-learning issue among Japanese-speaking students. (This item was also included in the previously mentioned large-scale study conducted by primary-school teachers in Japan [Kuno, Aida, and Irie 2014.]) Translating the original item (英語らしく自然に話せる) into English is difficult, but it would be something like, "I can speak English naturally and [sound] 'English-like.'" This item is meant to convey that the respondent can speak English without having a "Japanized" pronunciation. Japanese has many loan words from English, but when English words are used in Japanese, the original pronunciation and accent pattern adjust to the Japanese phonetic and phonological system. "Japanized" pronunciation has been a prevailing concern among English teachers in Japan, and students sometimes intentionally keep such pronunciation in English classes due to peer pressure (Otsuka and Ueda 2011).

While some children in this study referred to a pronunciation issue (e.g., "pronunciation produced by foreigners or native speakers") as expected, many children had more extended interpretations of how they sounded while speaking. Some children interpreted this item as fluency and reflecting a smooth transition from one word to another. Other children interpreted it as an issue of automaticity, making unconscious effort, or having no hesitation in speech: "[Speaking naturally and 'English-like'] means speaking without thinking. Words should come out from my mouth without thinking. What I do now is to look for words that are stored in my closet in the brain and take it out slowly" (ID#22, age eight). Somewhat similarly, some children interpreted the item as referring to having control over the language—in other words, to being able to say anything without worrying about how to say it, as if they were speaking their own language (i.e., Japanese).

2. Retrieving Instances

According to the original self-evaluation process model by Higgins, Strauman, and Klein (1986), the retrieving stage is more likely to evoke emotion, which may lead to positive or negative self-evaluation. Although our participating children usually did not overtly express their emotional experiences associated with retrieved instances, they did mention successful instances and unsuccessful instances for some items. We also noticed that the children sometimes talked about situations that went beyond their immediate learning experiences and even talked about hypothetical or imagined scenarios. Given these findings, we coded the children's retrieved instances based on the following types: (a) the child did not have much relevant experience or demonstrated difficulty in retrieving instances, (b) the child mentioned only successful instances, (c) the child mentioned unsuccessful instances (as well as successful instances), and (d) the child mentioned instances that went beyond their own immediate learning experiences. (Note that these categories are not necessarily mutually exclusive.)

As indicated in table 2.2, the children retrieved different types of incidences depending on the item. Interestingly, the children, older children in particular, often thought about instances that went beyond their own immediate learning experiences. This tendency was particularly evident in the listening items. For example, for Listen 1 ("I can understand questions about myself"), young children tended to mention their own experiences (e.g., instances that they could not handle well in class or other places, such as after-school programs), whereas many older children indicated hypothetical or imagined instances that they would not yet to be able to handle well. One child (ID#6, age eleven) who likes math said, "If somebody asked me what school subject I like, I would understand it. But, if the person started asking me about what kind of math I like or details about math in English, I would not be able to understand." Similarly, in responding to Listen 2 ("I can understand the teacher's instructions"), a number of children indicated that their teachers controlled the level of English in their instructions: "I could understand my teachers' instructions because my teachers only use English that we should be able to understand—things that we have learned already. But, I know that there are many instructions that I would not be able to understand" (ID#9, age ten).

The inherent "openness" of generic descriptors, such as "someone else's conversation" in Listen 4 ("I can understand someone else's conversation"), seemed to be confusing for the children and invited a variety of responses among them. In response to this item, the children thought about different situations, including (a) foreigners or teachers, who have high proficiency, talking together (in class or outside of class); (b) teachers talking to other students in class; and (c) students talking to other students in class. Depending on what situation the item evoked for the children, they arrived at different self-evaluations.

3. Setting Reference Point(s)

According to Higgins, Strauman, and Klein (1986), one's self-evaluation typically relies on *factual points of reference*—a type of standard that is set based on the evaluator's beliefs about one or more individuals' actual performance or attributes, such as social categories, meaningful others, and autobiographical references (reference points mentioned in Moritz's study as well). Higgins, Strauman, and Klein (1986) propose that evaluators may also use *acquired guides*—"what they hoped for, wanted, or believed ought to happen" (36)—or *imagined possibilities*—"the level of performance they imagine a significant other would have achieved on the same task or they themselves

◆ Table 2.2. Retrieved instances (percentages and frequencies)

Item	Not much experience/ hard time retrieving		Successful instances only		Unsuccessful and successful instances		Go beyond own learning experience	
	Younger	Older	Younger	Older	Younger	Older	Younger	Older
Listen 1	5.9%(1)	…	11.8%(2)	7.1%(1)	64.7%(11)	28.6%(4)	17.6%(3)	64.3%(9)
Listen 2	11.8%(2)	…	29.4%(5)	14.3%(2)	58.8%(10)	7.1%(1)	…	78.6%(11)
Listen 3	35.3%(6)	21.4%(3)	17.6%(3)	7.1%(1)	35.3%(6)	28.6%(4)	11.8%(2)	42.9%(6)
Listen 4	17.6%(3)	…	11.8%(2)	14.3%(2)	52.9%(9)	21.4%(3)	17.6%(3)	64.3%(9)
Speak 1	…	…	58.8%(10)	57.1%(8)	5.9%(1)	7.1%(1)	35.3%(6)	35.7%(5)
Speak 2	5.9%(1)	…	58.8%(10)	57.1%(8)	11.8%(2)	28.6%(4)	23.5%(4)	14.3%(3)
Speak 3	5.9%(1)	…	11.8%(2)	14.3%(2)	17.6%(3)	…	64.7%(11)	85.7%(12)
Speak 4	5.9%(1)	…	41.2%(7)	42.9%(6)	17.6%(3)	…	35.3%(6)	57.1%(8)
Read 1	41.2%(7)	28.6%(4)	29.4%(5)	42.9%(6)	11.8%(2)	7.1%(1)	17.6%(3)	21.4%(3)

Note: Zero frequency is indicated as "…".

would have achieved if they had tried harder" (36–37). For the present study, an extended coding scheme was developed based on Moritz's (1996) framework. We added *feedback and approval* (e.g., teachers' and parents' explicit acknowledgement of the child's performance as a reference point) to two of Moritz's social or environmental factual reference points (social category and meaningful other). The autobiographical category was further divided into *past performance* (using relatively remote past performance, such as performance in the past semester or year), *average multiple instances* (using the average performance of multiple recent instances), and *recent specific instance* (using a specific instance that occurred recently). The above-mentioned *acquired guides* and *imagined possibilities* in Higgins, Strauman, and Klein (1986) were also included, but we combined these two categories (labeled "goal/imagined instances") because they were not always clearly distinguishable in the data. Finally, *intuition and unclear cases* (including no reference point mentioned) and *others* were added.

As we can see in table 2.3, there were variations across items. However, in most cases, the children used *recent multiple instances* and *goal/imagined instances* as a reference point, followed by *recent specific instance*. Curiously, the social or environmental factual reference points (social category, meaningful other, and feedback/approval) were used much less frequently among the participating children, which was different from Moritz (1996).

A close examination of the data reveals some tendencies by age group. While no notable age difference was observed in the frequencies of using *recent multiple instances*, the reference points of having *goals/imagined instances* were observed more frequently among older children (see figure 2.1). An example of an imagined instance comes from one child's (ID#14, age twelve) response to Listen 4 ("I can follow someone else's conversation"): "I understand conversations at my word level. But, I wouldn't

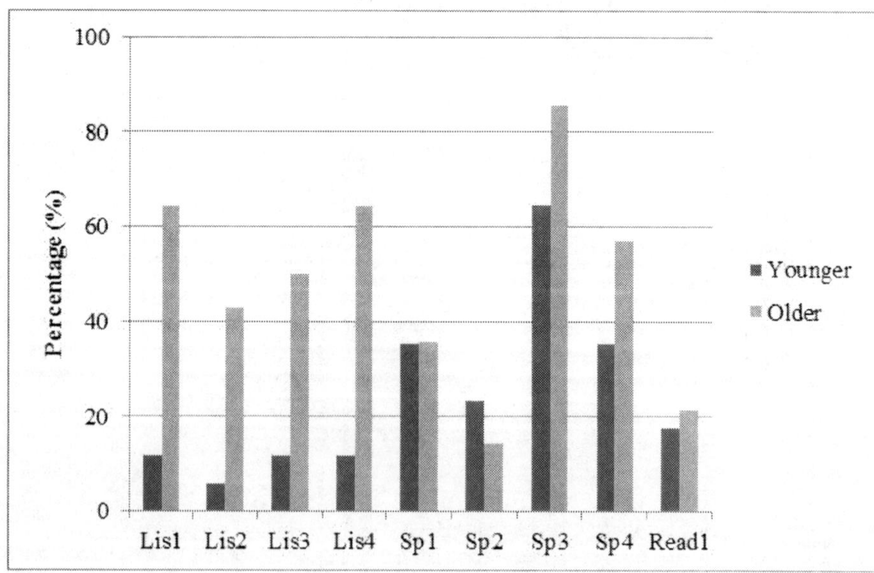

◆ Figure 2.1. *Goals/imagined instances* as a reference point by age group

◆ Table 2.3. Reference points (percentages and frequencies)

	Items								
	Listen				Speak				Read
Reference points	1	2	3	4	1	2	3	4	1
1. Social category	...	...	...	...	...	3.2%(1)	...	3.2%(1)	...
2. Meaningful other	...	6.5%(2)	3.2% (1)	6.5%(2)	6.5%(2)	...	16.1%(5)	3.2%(1)	...
3. Feedback/approval	3.2%(1)	...	...	3.2%(1)	3.2%(1)	3.2%(1)	19.4%(6)	...	...
4. Past performance	...	...	...	...	...	...	...	...	...
5. Recent multiple instances	87.1%(27)	83.9%(26)	61.3%(19)	77.4%(24)	96.8%(30)	96.8%(30)	93.5%(29)	90.3%(28)	45.2%(14)
6. Recent specific instance	6.5%(2)	12.9%(4)	16.1%(5)	32.3%(10)	...	...	3.2%(1)	...	29.0%(9)
7. Goal/imagined instances	35.5%(11)	22.6%(7)	29.0%(9)	35.5%(11)	35.5%(11)	...	74.2%(23)	45.2%(14)	19.4%(6)
8. Unclear/Intuition	3.2%(1)	6.5%(2)	9.7%(3)	9.7%(3)	3.2%(1)	...	3.2%(1)	3.2%(1)	9.7%(3)
9. Others	...	3.2%(1)	19.4%(6)	3.2%(1)	...	6.5%(2)	3.2%(1)	3.2%(1)	29.0%(9)

Note: Multiple entries were possible. Zero frequency is indicated as "...".

understand conversations when people use difficult words or conversations with long and complicated sentences." With respect to the reading item ("I can read a short story"), one child acknowledged that her listening ability is better than her reading ability in English and said, "Reading and listening are connected. I can do listening okay, so I think I should be able to do equally well in reading" (ID#18, age ten). In contrast, as figure 2.2 shows, relying on a recent specific instance was more likely to be observed among children in the younger group, although the frequencies were generally lower and variable across the items. When asked about the same reading item as above, an eight-year-old talked about a time when her teacher gave her a picture book about a butterfly whose color changed many times (ID#4, age eight). When the children did not have much experience with the target activity, they tended to rely on a recent specific instance or intuition.

4. Making an Evaluative Decision

Children often seemed to apply different rationales for self-appraisal between the can-do format and the five-point, Likert-type-item format. Figure 2.3 shows percentages of children who mentioned that they judged differently between the two formats. Of course, just because they did not mention judging themselves differently does not necessarily mean that they had the same rationales for making decisions for the two formats. The observed age difference in making an evaluation decision should be treated as a tentative result. However, children tended to make evaluative judgments heuristically or impressionistically when they completed can-do items, whereas they tended to be more analytical when responding to the scaled items. In responding to the scaled items, the children often reported thinking about more varieties of instances, including both successful and unsuccessful instances,

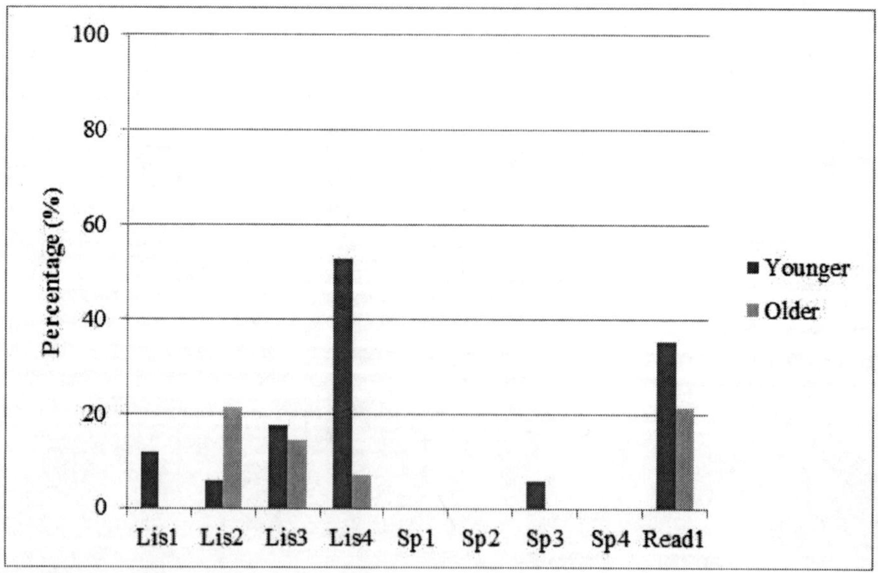

◆ Figure 2.2. *Recent specific instance as a reference point by age group*

and tended to think about ideal or hypothetical situations as well. For example, in answering Listen 3 ("I can follow short stories"), one child (ID#14, age twelve) judged her ability to be "can" in the can-do format, saying "I am usually okay. When I notice words that I already know, I feel like I understand the story" and "Guessing [the rest of the story] is good enough" for responding to "yes" in the can-do item. When she dealt with the same item in the scaled format, however, she said, "I tend to listen to stories without paying much attention. When I listen to stories carefully, I know that I would not understand them perfectly." She debated between 3 and 4 and ended up giving herself 4 on the five-point, Likert-type format. Another child (ID#16, age ten) said, "This [the scaled item] is harder because now I have to think when I can do it and when I cannot do it." Depending on which instances they retrieved and how they set the reference points, the children's judgments for the scaled items varied.

Discussion

In this study, we explored young learners' processes and rationales for responding to SA items. The study found that there was substantial variability in the processes and rationales when young learners responded to the SA across individuals, items, and formats (i.e., can-do and scaled formats). As a result, the young learners' responses to generic SA (decontextualized SA) items are not necessarily a direct reflection of their ability but instead likely reflect a combination of elements, including aspiration and self-efficacy. This result is consistent with a meta-analysis among adult learners in different disciplines, showing that their SA responses correlated better with

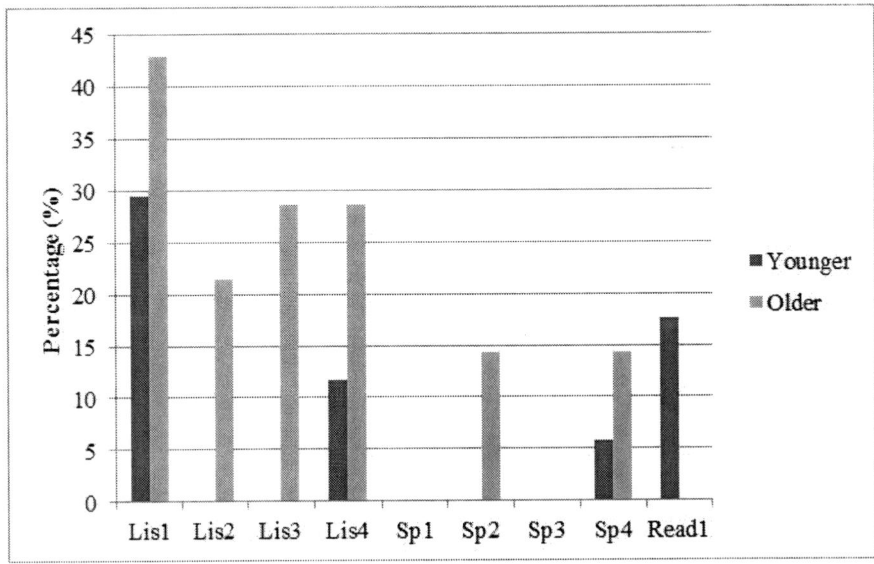

◆ Figure 2.3. Percentage of children who expressed different rationales for responding to the two different formats

affective measures, such as motivation, than with their factual or skill-based knowledge, as measured by objective means (Sitzmann et al. 2010).

First, we found that the children's comprehension of commonly used words, such as "follow" and "understand," in can-do descriptors varied across individuals, and their interpretations of items may differ from what teachers and item writers might assume. This may be caused by a discrepancy between semantic meaning (decontextualized meaning) and pragmatic meaning (contextualized meaning). In many readily available SA items designed to apply to wider contexts, such as the generic can-do descriptors we used in this study, the wording is often purposefully vague. However, the children tried to contextualize the meaning based on their own learning experiences. The aforementioned case of Listen 4 ("I can understand someone else's conversation") exemplifies such efforts. Depending on the situation (conversations carried out between native speakers, between teacher and student, or between students; or the conversations that take place in class or outside of class, etc.), the children recognized that what counts as "understanding" and the expectations for "understanding" might vary. One may interpret "understand" as perfectly accurate comprehension in formal classroom interactions, whereas one may interpret it as reasonably good guesses when listening to two teachers' conversation outside of the class. Accordingly, underlying abilities for "understanding"—not only linguistic abilities but also nonlinguistic abilities—also can differ depending on contexts, and some children seemed to acknowledge this fact. The variability in children's interpretations of pragmatic meaning makes us wonder what generic SA items really capture.

Age emerged as another important factor contributing to the variability. We found that older children tended to more frequently retrieve instances that went beyond their immediate learning experiences and to use acquired guides as reference points (set goals or imagined or hypothetical standards). This result corresponds well with the previous research on human development indicating that one's pursuit of personal performance goals increases with age (R. Butler 2005). In addition, the age differences found in this study might also be attributed to other confounding factors associated with age—such as greater experiences and social-environmental changes—rather than the developmental level of internal mental structures, per se. Indeed, the participating children in this study, regardless of their age, used multiple instances as a reference point. This result suggests that, at least by the age of eight (if not earlier), children have sufficient capacity to handle multiple domain-specific memories and sufficient information to evaluate their own competence. But, as children grow older, they more likely have a greater variety of experiences. As they gain more experiences, it is understood that children become more sensitive to social expectations to demonstrate superior abilities; at the same time, they may become more aware of the social cost of exhibiting inflated self-appraisal. Depending on context, age-related peer pressure may cause children to refrain from demonstrating honest judgments of their own abilities or confidence (R. Butler 2005). How all these age-related factors contribute to young learners' final SA results appears complicated. What we can say with some confidence, however, is that young learners' SA responses are due to a combination of elements and that they vary depending on context.

Relatively low frequencies of reliance on social-environmental factual reference points (social category, meaningful other, and feedback) were unexpected given that previous studies on child development suggest that middle and upper primary-school students should have developed an ability to judge their performance through social comparison or social-based standards. Our result was also different from Moritz (1996). It may be the case that, because the participating children in this study were relatively new to English learning, they had not yet had sufficient experience observing other students' performance in the specific domain (i.e., English learning). The result may also be partially due to the legacy of Japan's recent Yutori Educational Policy (relaxed education policy), which deemphasized social comparisons among children. It would be interesting to see if the same result can be obtained among children who have greater experience with social comparison.

There are some limitations in this study. A major limitation concerns the use of retrospective interviews to understand the process of responding to SAs. A think-aloud technique would have been a more accurate method to access children's cognitive processing (Ericsson and Simon 1993). However, we decided not to use think-aloud techniques in this study because they require substantial training for children in advance, which may in turn greatly guide their cognitive processing and outcome. A pilot trial conducted prior to this study also indicated that some children had a hard time verbalizing their thought processes without any assistance while filling out the SA items. Although efforts were made to increase the validity of the retrospective interview method (e.g., we conducted the interview immediately after the children responded to a short list of SA items), the children still had to retrieve the processes from their memory, and they might have even tried to make sense of their processes rather than simply describe them. We need to be aware that the elicited verbal data was not necessarily a direct reflection of their online thinking processes (Dörnyei 2007).

Conclusion and Implications

This study explored young learners' processes and rationales when responding to generic SA items (decontextualized general items). Despite some methodological limitations, the study provided significant insights into the processes young learners engage in when responding to SA items. The study revealed the complex nature of those processes, which involve multiple individual factors as well as social-environmental factors.

Appendix A: An Example of the Self-Assessment Sheet

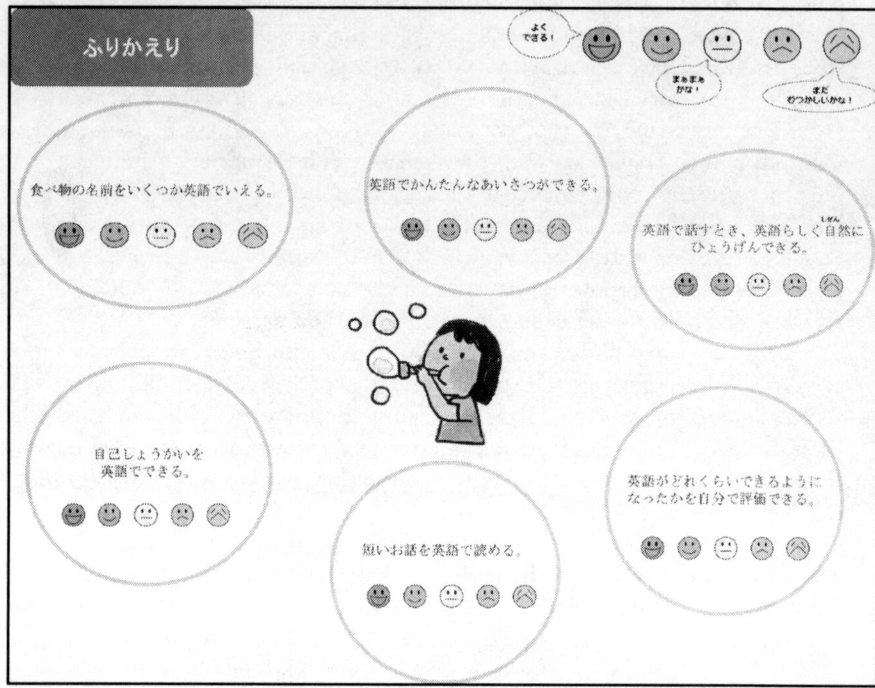

◆ **Figure 2.4.** Example SA Sheet. (*Note:* The original sheet was in color)

Note

1. Note that the assessment originally included an additional metacognitive item: "I can evaluate how much I have improved in English." However, results suggested that students had troubling understanding the item, and thus findings are omitted from this discussion.

References

Bachman, Lyle F., and Adrian S. Palmer. 1989. "The Construct Validation of Self-Ratings of Communicative Language Ability." *Language Testing* 6:14–29. doi:10.1177/026553228900600104.

Bandura, Albert. 1986. *Social Foundations for Thought and Action: A Social Cognitive Theory.* Englewood Cliffs, NJ: Prentice Hall.

Blanche, Patrick. 1990. "Using Standardized Achievement and Oral Proficiency Tests for Self-Assessment Purposes: The DLIFC Study." *Language Testing* 6:14–29. doi:10.1177/026553229000700205.

Blanche, Patrick, and Barbara J. Merino 1989. "Self-Assessment of Foreign-Language Skills: Implications for Teachers and Researchers." *Language Learning* 39:313–40. doi:10.1111/j.1467-1770.1989.tb00595.x.

Butler, Ruth. 2005. "Competence Assessment, Competence, and Motivation between Early and Middle Childhood." In *The Handbook of Competence and Motivation,* edited by Andrew J. Elliot and Carol S. Dweck, 202–21. New York: The Guilford Press.

Butler, Yuko Goto. 2016. "Self-Assessment of and for Young Learners' Foreign Language Learning." In *Assessing Young Learners of English: Global and Local Perspectives,* edited by Marianne Nikolov, 291–315. New York: Springer.

CILT (The National Centre for Languages). 2006. *European Language Portfolio–Junior Version: Revised Edition.* http://www.agtv.vic.edu.au/files/Website%202015/8871-junior-passport.pdf.

Dörnyei, Zoltán. 2007. *Research Methods in Applied Linguistics.* Oxford: Oxford University Press.

Dörnyei, Zoltán, and Tatsuya Taguchi. 2010. *Questionnaires in Second Language Research: Construction, Administration, and Processing.* New York: Routledge.

Ericsson, K. Anders, and Herbert A. Simon. 1993. *Protocol Analysis: Verbal Reports as Data.* Cambridge, MA: Bradford Books/MIT Press.

Heilenman, L. Kathy. 1990. "Self-Assessment of Second Language Ability: The Role of Response Effect." *Language Testing* 7:174–201. doi:10.1177/026553229000700204.

Higgins, E. Tory, Timothy Strauman, and Ruth Klein. 1986. "Standards and the Process of Self-Evaluation: Multiple Effects from Multiple Stages." In the *Handbook of Motivation and Cognition: Foundations of Social Behavior,* edited by Richard M. Sorrentino and E. Tory Higgins, 23–59. New York: The Guilford Press.

Kuno, Yuri, Makiko Aida, and Jun Irie. 2014. *Soki eigo Can-do no kenkyu* [A study on can-do in early English education]. Unpublished technical report submitted to the Eiken Foundation in Japan.

Leach, Linda. 2012. "Optional Self-Assessment: Some Tensions and Dilemmas." *Assessment and Evaluation in Higher Education* 37:137–47. doi:10.1080/02602938.2010.515013.

Moritz, Christine. E. F. 1996. "Student Self-Assessment of Language Proficiency." Paper presented at the 18th AAAL Conference, Chicago, IL, March 23–6, 1996.

National Council of State Supervisors for Languages. 2014. "Lingua Folio'." http://www.ncssfl.org/LinguaFolio/index.php?checklists.

Nikolov, Marianne. 2016. "Trends, Issues, and Challenges in Assessing Young Language Learners." In *Assessing Young Learners of English: Global and Local Perspectives,* edited by Marianne Nikolov, 1–17. New York: Springer.

Oscarson, Mats. 1989. "Self-Assessment of Language Proficiency: Rationale and Applications." *Language Testing* 6:1–13. doi:10.1177/026553228900600103.

———. 1997. "Self-Assessment of Foreign and Second Language Proficiency." In *Encyclopedia of Language and Education: Language Testing and Assessment,* edited by Caroline Clapham and David Corson, 175–87. Dordrecht, Nld.: Kluwer Academic.

Otsuka, Tomomi, and Hiroko Ueda. 2011. "Pronunciation Instruction and Its Achievements in Japanese Junior and Senior High Schools: An Analysis of Results from Check Sheets and a Questionnaire." *Bulletin of Osaka Jogakuin University* 8:1–27. http://hdl.handle.net/10775/2431.

Pajares, Frank, and Ellen L. Usher. 2008. "Self-Efficacy, Motivation, and Achievement in School from the Perspective of Reciprocal Determinism." In *Advances in Motivation and Achievement: School Psychological Perspectives,* edited by Martin L. Maehr, Stuart A. Karabenick, and Timothy C. Urdan, 391–423. Bingley, Eng.: Emerald.

Piaget, Jean. 1929. *The Child's Conception of the World.* New York: Harcourt, Brace & World.

Ross, Steven. 1998. "Self-Assessment in Second Language Testing: A Meta-analysis and Analysis of Experimental Factors." *Language Testing* 15:1–19. doi:10.1177/026553229801500101.

Sitzmann, Traci, Katherine Ely, Kenneth G. Brown, and Kristina N. Bauer. 2010. "Self-Assessment of Knowledge: A Cognitive Learning or Affective Measure?" *Academy of Management Learning & Education* 9:169–91. doi:10.5465/AMLE.2010.51428542.

Stefani, Lorraine. 1994. "Peer, Self and Tutor Assessment: Relative Reliabilities." *Studies in Higher Education* 19:69–75. doi:10.1080/03075079412331382153.

Sullivan, Keith, and Cedric Hall. 1997. "Introducing Students to Self-Assessment." *Assessment and Evaluation in Higher Education* 22:289–305. doi:10.1080/0260293970220303.

Suzuki, Yuichi. 2015. "Self-Assessment of Japanese as a Second Language: The Role of Experiences in the Naturalistic Acquisition." *Language Testing* 32:63–81. doi:10.1177/0265532214541885.

Zimmerman, Barry J. 2002. "Becoming a Self-Regulated Learner: An Overview." *Theory into Practice* 41:64–70. doi:10.1207/s15430421tip4102_2.

Chapter 3

◆ The Impact of Self-Assessment on Learning and Teaching in Technology-Mediated Language Education

User Perceptions of the Teletandem Tracking Sheet

VIVIANE BAGIO FURTOSO
State University of Londrina, Brazil

MICHAEL J. FERREIRA
Georgetown University

HOW DO WE ASSESS the progress of students who practice languages through teletandem-type online interactions? Do students learn in autonomous ways? If so, what is the teacher's role? This paper explores the role of assessment within a particular technology-mediated language-learning environment from conceptualizing assessment, to shedding light on the way we can approach assessment in telecollaborative projects, to analyzing and discussing the implementation of a self-assessment tool in a course for English-speaking learners of Portuguese at a US university.

Following discussions about washback on language testing (Alderson and Wall 1993), this study contributes to the discussion of assessment impact on language learning and teaching by explaining key concepts for understanding assessment "as a means to an end, or better, to a variety of carefully articulated ends" (Norris 2006, 579).[1] It is known that assessment impact can be either positive or negative, and being aware of this should be the first step toward ensuring positive assessment consequences and uses.

This study focuses on an online collaborative and autonomous context for foreign language learning, teletandem, in which two learners take turns helping each other learn their language. By its collaborative and autonomous nature, teletandem has used evaluation to improve its implementation (see Telles 2009, 2015; Benedetti, Consolo, and Vieira-Abrahão 2010), but little is known regarding the use of assessment to promote learning and teaching in teletandem learning environments (see Furtoso 2011; Consolo and Furtoso 2015). Therefore, three overarching assessment-oriented research concerns guided this study:

1. Are some theoretical assessment perspectives more appropriate than others for teletandem-type instruction?
2. Why should we use self-assessment in teletandem?
3. What is the impact of using the teletandem tracking sheet (TTS) on both learners and teachers within a blended course of Portuguese language?

These questions are addressed as follows: First, the chapter discusses literature on a telecollaborative project—namely, teletandem—and the roles for assessment within the project. Next, the use and purpose of assessment in this project will be elaborated to explain theoretical assessment perspective(s) that might be used for teletandem-type instruction and, in particular, the use of self-assessment as a way of providing both students and teachers with information about student learning in support of teaching and learning. Following this, the design of the study is presented, including the research paradigm, the teletandem context and framework, TTS and participants, and data collection and analysis procedures. The paper then presents the findings and discusses the impact on the learning and teaching process when the focus is on *using* assessment instead of *doing* assessment (Norris 2006). The study also illustrates some of the challenges and lessons learned in initiating such an experience.

Telecollaboration through Teletandem

As a result of the ongoing development of communication technologies, the distance between language learners and opportunities to talk to other speakers of the target language has ceased to be a constraint on language education as social practice (Furtoso and Ferreira 2016). From a perspective of language in use, online exchanges can support a more contextualized mode of learning since they can support second language learners' development of pragmatic competence and intercultural communicative competence (Chun 2011). The benefits of the telecollaborative projects stem from the social dimension they add to language education (Belz 2002). Furthermore, as Gonçalves points out, "new information and communication technologies are an excellent tool for engaging students in a personalized way, allowing each student to explore their individual interests" (2012, 46).

Representing an initiative for promoting foreign language learning, the Teletandem Brasil Project began in 2006 (Telles 2009). As mentioned previously, teletandem—a type of technology-mediated communication or telecollaboration—is an online collaborative and autonomous context for foreign language learning in which two learners take turns helping each other learn their native language or language of proficiency,[2] since one may be highly proficient in a nonnative language.

Brammerts (2003) proposes three key principles of foreign language learning—autonomy, reciprocity, and equally shared time—each of which guided the Teletandem Brasil Project in promoting linguistic and intercultural exchanges between Brazilian- and English-speaking partners. In addition, through online conversations, partner feedback during conversational breakdowns is essential to contextualize and promote the progress of interactions as well as to provide the required support to acknowledge and give attention to the interlocutor's speech (Furtoso 2011).

A model of teletandem presented by Mompean and Cappellini (2015) allows for the exploration of the different ways telecollaboration can be implemented. The authors distinguish five key notions of teletandem: (1) environment (physical and technical conditions provided), (2) integration (the way teletandem practice is or is not integrated into curriculum), (3) bilaterality (the elements recognized in both institutions), (4) pedagogical paradigm (both human and material resources provided), and (5) evaluation.

The approach to evaluation, important in this study, encompasses the following dimensions: (a) the modalities for assessment (grade or credits), (b) the tools available for assessment (recording of teletandem sessions, portfolio, final exam, oral interview, or self-evaluation), and (c) the criteria for assessment.

Assessment-Oriented Learning and Teaching

Traditionally, teachers (and students) think about learning assessment most frequently in terms of grading. However, the approach to assessment taken in this project was to integrate learning and teaching and to take the view that assessment fundamentally helps students to learn and teachers to better understand how best to teach (Ramsdem 1992). Therefore, assessment is a fundamental driver of what and how students learn (Ross and Siegenthaler 2006).

In addition, the approach to evaluation and assessment in this project was informed by key distinctions among the terms *measurement*, *assessment*, and *evaluation* proposed by Norris:

> "*Measurement* is the consistent elicitation of quantifiable indicators of well-defined constructs via tests or related observation procedures; it emphasizes efficiency, objectivity, and technical aspects of construct validity. *Assessment* is the systematic gathering of information about student learning in support of teaching and learning. *Evaluation* is the gathering of information about any of the variety of elements that constitute educational programs, for a variety of purposes that primarily include understanding, demonstrating, improving, and judging program value" (2006, 579).

As we can see, these terms cannot be used interchangeably (though they often are) since they are not neutral. What does this mean? To us, it means that we must recognize the differences in meaning so that we can choose the most appropriate term to describe our educational aims. The main characteristic that helps stakeholders in an educational context distinguish among them is their function in relation to the specific goals and needs of a program development project; that is, for what purpose, why, and by whom the information gathered about learning is needed. Being aware of—and explicitly stating—the intended function or uses of an educational innovation will direct the process of collecting and interpreting information. In order to undertake any such project productively and usefully, stakeholders must be clear on what specific investigatory activities are needed given project aims. From this perspective, assessment is understood in this study as a means to an end—not the end itself. Assessment, then, is a tool to help both teachers and students do a better job. In this sense, assessment is more than judging students' or teachers' performance; it is using information to improve both learning and teaching. Thus, the assessor or teacher should act—not react—and intentionally *use* assessment toward specific educational aims, rather than *do* assessment for unspecified or routine institutional purposes (as emphasized by Norris 2006).

Formative Assessment in Teletandem

The role of assessment has been mostly captured in traditional distinctions between formative and summative assessment: "Formative assessment provides instructors and learners with information about how learners are learning in order to help both improve performance. Summative assessment occurs when instructors gather evidence [only] to assign grades" (Diaz, Brown, and Salmons 2010, 2).

As noted by Diaz, Brown, and Salmons, formative assessment is more appropriate in an educational context if there is a focus on the learning process, since formative assessment, conventionally, monitors student work on a regular basis; ascertains the need for additional resources, guidance, or revisions; determines whether all participants are contributing; and determines whether the timeline is being observed (Diaz, Brown, and Salmons 2010). Formative assessment allows us to find out what needs to change during the process of instruction while there is still time to intervene.

Within this framework, it is imperative to bear in mind that teletandem is an online collaborative and autonomous context for foreign language learning. The collaborative dimension is, therefore, one of the elements that defines the concept of assessment in teletandem. In a collaborative environment, the participants are expected to work together, giving and receiving feedback, which can help them negotiate both sociocultural and linguistic meanings, in order to use the language. Regarding appropriate assessment tools in the telecollaboration literature, then, we highlight those that seem most appropriate to teletandem: recording of teletandem sessions, portfolios, blogs, logbooks, journals, text writing, and mutual correction between partners, as well as a reporting on evaluation of the student partnership and the learning that took place.

Given the variety of tools presented here, there are as yet few initiatives or reported examples of using assessment in teletandem learning experiences. Most of the studies (e.g., Telles 2015) have examined data collection and related tools for the purpose of evaluating the telecollaboration course or program itself. Of the few assessment-oriented studies, we highlight Furtoso (2011) and Aranha and Cavalari (2015), each reporting on complementary use of individual and collective formative assessments targeting different areas of language learning and programmatic development.

As this study aims at increasing disciplinary knowledge of the benefits of assessment for the learning and teaching process, we support formative assessment to deal with the autonomous and collaborative dimensions in teletandem and, specifically, the use of self-assessment to follow up on teletandem practice and to develop sociocultural and linguistic proficiency.

Self-Assessment within Autonomous Learning Environments

Just as it is crucial to divorce assessment from its common association with measurement (Norris 2006), so too is it important to question a belief in the incompatibility between assessment and autonomy. Within teletandem, "a kind of control, such as regular attendance and activities with graded assignments, and assessment procedures … in a sense calls into question the participants' levels of autonomy" (Ramos 2015, 699). On the other hand, a complete lack of control can produce chaos. Mompean and Cappellini summarize the principle of autonomy as described by Holec (1981): "Learners are responsible for their learning, since they establish contents, decide how to learn and evaluate their learning, therefore taking an active posture in the process" (Mompean and Cappellini 2015, 636). We can see from this comment that the assessment dimension can play an important role in an autonomous learning environment. What should be deepened is the learners' participation in the process of establishing a connection between the reasons for and the benefits of assessment.

Since learners can also be responsible for their learning by sharing this task with teachers, we believe that learner-centered assessment encourages students to reflect on their own learning processes. So, it is, in fact, key to fostering learning and to helping students develop autonomy. Previous studies have focused on the contribution of assessment to increased autonomy, responsibility, and compromise in teletandem (e.g., Cavalari 2009; Furtoso 2011). Looking at teletandem in the light of assessment, Furtoso (2011) proposed a first version of the self-assessment tool investigated in the current study. Although Furtoso's study indicated the necessity of reformulating the tool, the preliminary results showed that such a tool had the potential to provide teletandem partners with more formative feedback on language learning, as well as support the teacher's feedback and scaffolding as a mediator of the students' construction of knowledge.

As the version of the tool proposed by Furtoso has not yet been analyzed systematically outside the context where it was originally piloted, this study highlights its potential for self-assessment in telecollaborative projects. We believe that to be valuable, the tool needs to be carefully planned, moderated and assessed, as McNamara and Brown (2008) point out. Therefore, the following section details ways in which self-assessment is used within a particular technology-mediated learning environment and how the authors gathered information to explore the impact of that use on both learning and teaching.

Methodology

In this section, we address the design of the study as it responds primarily to the third research concern of this chapter: What is the impact of using the TTS on both learners and teachers within a blended course of Portuguese language? To this end, we describe (a) the adopted research paradigm, (b) the teletandem context and format, (c) the TTS and participants, and (d) data collection and analysis procedures.

Research Paradigm

Qualitative research paradigms involve generating results in a contextual framework accessible to the researcher and study participants, without the intention of generalizing to participants or situations beyond the study. The researcher, who also takes part in the investigated context, conducts their observations in the natural environment where people live, work, or study. Therefore, the current study follows a fitting qualitative approach, embodied in the notion of action research, since it seeks to improve practice, the understanding of practice by its practitioners, and the situations in which practice is located (Carr and Kemmis 1986).

Teletandem Context and Format

The study took place in an advanced Portuguese conversation course over one semester at a US university. The course met twice a week, and the online interactions were integrated with contact classes as an example of institutionally integrated teletandem (Aranha and Cavalari 2015). On Mondays, the students attended in-person classes and were required to work both individually and in groups with an instructional emphasis on oral presentations. On Wednesdays, students participated in one-hour teletandem sessions, during which they freely discussed, for half an hour, themes regarding Brazilian and US culture and daily life with a student from a Brazilian university. During the other half hour, partners were expected to do the same in English.

As part of the assignments for the teletandem sessions, students were expected to send notes on language and culture to their instructor via e-mail after each synchronous meeting. The quality of the note-taking would be weighed according to the following criteria: (a) richness of information in terms of vocabulary, structures, and cultural points; (b) organization of vocabulary input by semantic fields; and (c) submission punctuality of note-taking. They were also required to post a blog entry for each session and compare the first and last recordings of their teletandem sessions. All online exchanges were recorded at the university language lab and students had access to the recordings. Considering the scope of this study, we will focus on investigating the tool used to follow up on student note-taking on their language learning.

Teletandem Tracking Sheet

In order to organize the note-taking assignment for both students and the teacher, we adopted the Teletandem Tracking Sheet (Furtoso 2011) and monitored its implementation for this study. The TTS is a can-do self-assessment tool that focuses on oral comprehension (item 1 in figure 3.1), fluency (items 6, 7, 8), vocabulary (items 2, 3), grammar (item 4), pronunciation (item 5), interactional competence (items 9, 10), cultural knowledge (item 12), feedback on partner's oral production (item 13), and awareness of linguistic aspects from the partner's speech (item 11). The TTS also allowed students to enter notes on their ratings in a text box next to every self-assessment item. Many of the criteria have guided the assessment of oral proficiency in foreign languages in other studies (Furtoso 2011) and were adopted in this study (and past studies by Furtoso) based on the assessment grid of face-to-face interaction of Celpe-Bras.[3] Students used the version of TTS in Portuguese, which was translated into English to be included in this paper (see figure 3.1).

Participants

Eleven English-speaking learners of Portuguese filled out the Excel-format TTS and sent it via e-mail to their instructor after each synchronous meeting. Each student filled out 10 TTSs during the online exchanges, which took place over a ten-week period from September to December. The advanced Portuguese conversation course consisted of fifteen students; however, only eleven completed the task, which left us with a set of 110 TTSs.

Surname:		YES	NO	MORE or LESS	Notes
	In this session I was able to				
1	understand my partner's speech without asking him/her to repeat slowly very often.				
2	hold a conversation on a daily topic.				
3	give my opinion about unfamiliar topics. Was there a more complex topic? If so, what?				
4	use adequate grammar to express my ideas. Any difficulty? What kind?				
5	pronounce the words clearly. Any difficulty? Which words?				
6	speak clearly.				
7	keep the flow of conversation in a given rhythm without interrupting abruptly. If not / more or less, why?				
8	use appropriate fillers in Portuguese. (For example: ahn ahn, uhn uhn, sei, exato, others)				
9	explain words and/or expressions when I didn't know the exact ones in Portuguese. Which one(s)?				
10	use stock phrases in Portuguese in order to save time while thinking about what to say.				
11	become aware of unknown words, grammar aspects and/or pronunciation through my partner's speech. Which one(s)?				
12	fill the cultural gaps without reinforcing stereotypes. Which cultural aspects did you discuss in this session?				
13	satisfactorily provide feedback to my partner on questions.				
14	Other(s):				

◆ Figure 3.1. English version of Teletandem Tracking Sheet (TTS)

As an instance of action research, the class instructor and the visiting postdoctoral researcher were also considered participants of this study. They both played fundamental roles in the implementation of the self-assessment tool, since they were in charge of analyzing the students' notes to inform the design of follow-up activities and for providing them with feedback both in class and via e-mail between the teletandem sessions.

Data Collection and Analysis Procedures

The compilation of the information from the TTS during the semester was carried out using a software developed by a graduate student to gather individual as well as collective data. In this way, it was possible to access notes from a given student as well as notes for the whole group for each session (i.e., the collective notes of all students). The visiting researcher was responsible for analyzing the data and preparing feedback, which was given to students during Monday meetings, following each teletandem session. The instructor contributed during in-class feedback. It is important to highlight that the in-class feedback happened during the first half of the course. During the second half of the course, the students received feedback in a collective, compiled version of the notes, by e-mail.

Data in this study were collected from the TTS instrument and an online questionnaire asking for feedback on the TTS instrument. The online questionnaire ("Teletandem Tracking Sheet – Feedback") was administered at the end of semester and completed by the fifteen third-year Portuguese students. The questionnaire was answered in English. The purpose of the questionnaire was to get information from learners about the impact of using a self-assessment tool. The questionnaire had nine items: five dichotomous yes/no questions (items 1, 2, 3, 4, and 7; see table 3.1), and three open-ended questionnaire items (items 5, 6, and 8; see table 3.2).

◆ **Table 3.1.** Results of students' perceptions about using self-assessment in teletandem (N = 15)

Question	Answer	
	% Yes	**% No**
1. Did filling out the tracking sheet influence the way you perceive your own learning in the teletandem sessions? Why?	86.7	13.3
2. Did having access to the compilation of remarks help you during your interactions with your partners? Why? How?	73.3	26.7
3. Did you notice that you incorporated knowledge acquired from your tracking sheet and/or form your classmates during your interactions with your partners? Why? How?	80	20
4. Which approach helped you the most to notice aspects of the Portuguese language in greater detail: when the compilation was discussed in class and then sent via e-mail or when the compilation was just sent via e-mail?	Discussed and emailed	Email only
	100	0
7. Do you think the instructor could have made more in-class observations regarding the remarks brought up in the compilation of the teletandem tracking sheets? How?	53.3	46.7

◆ **Table 3.2.** Open-ended response questions from the Teletandem Tracking Sheet — Feedback questionnaire

5. What aspects of your proficiency improved the most through teletandem practice (vocabulary, grammar, pronunciation, fluency, cultural knowledge, or others)? Why?

6. Did you sense a difference between the teletandem tracking sheet and the blog? What did you notice? Answer completing the following phrases: The teletandem tracking sheet helped me ... The blog helped me ...

8. Do you have any suggestions to improve the implementation of the teletandem tracking sheet so that it may contribute to learning Portuguese? Which ones?

Findings

Findings suggest evidence not only of learning but also of aspects of teaching that impacted the learners' progress. Starting with responses from the "Teletandem Tracking Sheet – Feedback" questionnaire, the quantitative results show positive perceptions about self-assessment in teletandem (see table 3.1).

The TTS was shown to be useful to support learners in perceiving their own learning in the teletandem sessions (item 1); it helped learners during the interactions with their partners, since they had access to the compilation of remarks from the previous sessions (2); and it provided the students with linguistic and cultural knowledge from their tracking sheet and from their classmates, which was incorporated during the interactions with their teletandem partners (3). Respondents unanimously agreed that all the benefits were provided when the compilation was discussed in class and then sent via e-mail, as compared to when the compilation was just sent via e-mail (4).

These findings are elaborated by learner comments from each of the yes/no questions, as well as from three open-ended items asking about learning (item 5), the relative helpfulness of the blog compared to the tracking sheet (6), and overall suggestions for improving the tracking sheet (8; see table 3.2). In addition, a final item (9) asked for any final, additional comments.

Results from open-ended questionnaire items show a number of benefits of TTS self-assessment including awareness of strengths and weaknesses, self-monitoring of progress, and ownership of the learning process.

The impact of the self-assessment tool on learners' awareness of strengths and weaknesses in learning Portuguese is captured in the following comment and reflects comments offered by other students as well.

Comment 1

By recording notes and answering questions on the tracking sheet, I became aware of the mistakes I was making. After consciously writing out these mistakes on the tracking sheet, I felt as though I made an effort to stop making the same mistakes in conversation with my teletandem partner.

Comment 1 shows the way in which filling out the self-assessment tool, and, in turn, receiving immediate feedback on the content, can help learners be aware of their mistakes and make decisions about their learning. We can relate this to learner autonomy, since the respondent felt as though they made an effort to stop making the same mistakes in conversation with their teletandem partner.

In addition to promoting awareness, comment 2 highlights how the TTS helped the learner identify characteristics of their speech.

Comment 2

Filling out the tracking sheet made me think about the way in which I speak. It was a great way to reflect upon tendencies I have when speaking Portuguese, and to note these tendencies. Without the tracking sheet, I don't think I would have realized that I have certain habits. It also made me conscious of how many times I say "um" and use fillers when speaking.

It is challenging for either learner or teacher to be aware of the appropriateness of using fillers without some kind of follow-up activity. In this sense, we acknowledge that recording the teletandem session could also be an extra tool to support learners when filling out the TTS, as learners could listen to the recorded interactions again in order to fill it out. By listening to their interactions, learners would be provided with a much more complete record of their speaking, which could help them avoid the difficulty mentioned in comment 3, for example:

Comment 3

The problem is that we did it after the session so it was hard to reflect back on these specific topics.

The following comment also demonstrates the usefulness of self-assessment to promote awareness of learning in teletandem:

Comment 4

The Excel sheet helped visualize change over time both in terms of the proportion of YES / MORE OR LESS / NO responses given, and also to be able to quickly compare comments in individual sections across the overall sections.

Comment 4 reflects another important aspect regarding the use of the TTS; that is, the benefits of reviewing accumulated group notes as the sessions take place. As noted above, the TTS was available individually (each learner could see and manage their own notes by session) or by session (the notes were grouped and both teacher and researcher could see all learners' notes by session). Only the instructor and the visiting researcher had full access to student notes, and every Monday, in order to discuss the notes collectively, learners had access to a compiled version of all notes.

The next comments show how self-assessments are useful to help learners foster their learning as they monitor their progress, which fosters autonomy as well.

Comment 5

I really liked filling out the tracking sheet because I thought it was a good way of tracking our progress and looking for ways to improve in each session. By looking over our tracking sheets we were also able to look at the things we learned in each session and the things we should revise and work on (maybe vocab, expressions, etc.) before the next session.

Comment 5 captures the tracking role of the self-assessment tool. As learners become aware of their strengths and weaknesses, they can monitor their progress in future interactions. Students monitored their vocabulary, grammar, fluency, and pronunciation, as exemplified by the following comment.

Comment 6

I would say that the aspects I feel improved the most are, in order: 1. fluency (I feel far more comfortable speaking, even when I do not know a specific word I can usually still express the intended thought); 2. pronunciation (it is very important to me to try to speak accurately, so I ask about pronunciation a lot); and 3. vocabulary (I have learned a lot of slang to which I likely would not have had access otherwise).

From Comment 6, we can also recognize the utility of the TTS in enhancing teletandem since learners are expected to develop communication strategies to talk to each other and not switch to their L1 when they do not know a word or expression in the target language. Furthermore, feedback plays an important role, as emphasized in the respondent's comment on asking about pronunciation. The third benefit of teletandem noted in the respondent's comment is the opportunity to learn informal language such as slang from the interactions for daily conversation.

In teletandem, one of the main benefits is increasing cultural knowledge and intercultural competence. From the following comment, we can also see how the TTS helps learners to be aware of and monitor their cultural learning.

Comment 7

Cultural knowledge, vocab, and fluency all improved the most. Cultural knowledge simply because it was direct and helpful having a Brazilian partner who could describe cultural themes/aspects, vocab because a native-speaker in the same age-range has access not only to general vocab, but also slang, and fluency because talking for 30 minutes a week without interruption is productive toward that goal.

Another point highlighted by learners was their conscious effort in using language from the compiled TTS notes in their next teletandem practice session, as shown in comment 8.

Comment 8

I really tried to listen to the Portuguese idiomatic expressions and incorporate them into my own speaking. I don't think I would have done this as much if it weren't for the sheet.

I tried to incorporate the new words that I saw in the compiled sheet.

The collective discussion about notes from the TTS in face-to-face meetings was also useful to promote a sense of ownership.

Comment 9

The topics that my classmates talked about with their partners gave me ideas about what to talk about with my partner.

On the other hand, a few learners did not have the same perception about the diversity of topics and linguistic and cultural aspects discussed in the teletandem interactions, as reflected in the following comment.

Comment 10

I feel that it would be more useful if the teletandem sessions would have a task-essentialness (a completion goal), or that all of the students had similar topics/even better, rotated topics, so that at one point or the other during the semester, all of the students would actually have a need for the specific lexicon and/or grammatical structures in the feedback sheet. For example, student A did Topic 1 the first week, and student B might do the same topic on week 3. He would therefore have prior knowledge of that sheet and its contents, which would help him use it for his session.

We shift now to discuss the impact of self-assessment on teaching and teachers and implications for planning instruction. The way the topics are chosen in teletandem can vary according to the specific groups of learners involved, which has been an object of investigation in previous research (e.g., Telles 2015). Noting again comment 10, we agree that teachers should consider the possibility of proposing some common topics at such a time. However, we also believe this decision has to be made collectively in order to take into account learners' interests from both sides and to respect the collaborative nature of teletandem.

Another suggestion for teacher planning, this time related to the frequency of filling out the TTS, again relates to the use of the recordings to help learners become aware of their strengths and weaknesses. The possibility of working on a set of recorded interactions can avoid learners' negative perceptions, such as the one in comment 11.

Comment 11

It is hard to reference back to the remarks while simultaneously talking to someone. At times, it seemed like the tracking sheet was redundant and I felt like I was writing the same things every week.

We note, however, that the perception of writing the same things every week was from a single student. Most other respondents highlighted the helpfulness of the TTS because of the discussion about the compiled notes between teletandem sessions. We assume that another scheme of implementation, more periodically for example, has to be adopted and investigated in order to understand whether the usefulness of the TTS is shown to be the same as when it is filled out after each teletandem session. The helpfulness of the in-class discussion of the compiled notes after each session is supported by the following comment.

Comment 12

Having [the notes] in class allowed us to discuss them in person and ask follow-up questions if necessary. Having classmate input and questions was also helpful for the same reason as above, namely, because they would often be something that I personally would not have thought of on my own.

Next, we turn to helpfulness of feedback from the TTS. Feedback is fundamental during the learning process, since there is time to act and react in order to improve. It can promote learners' awareness, monitoring, and decision-making (as in comment 12) and provide teachers with information that enables them to intervene during the learning process. In addition, immediate feedback is considered essential and learners' perceptions showed that. Since students had in-class feedback on the teletandem tracking sheet during the first half of the course only, some respondents wanted more in-class feedback in the second half of the course as well.

Another example that underscores the importance of feedback were the explicit requests for feedback on the blog assignment.

Comment 13

I wish that we got some feedback on our blogs to make sure that we were also improving our writing skills.

We can infer from this comment that the expectation for assessment for students is to support both learners and teachers in the learning process, and it is useful for enhancing such processes.

In addition to the various benefits of the TTS described above, we draw attention to areas of improvement, such as the length of the TTS and its content, as captured in comment 14.

Comment 14

Do not have so many questions. Maybe have 8–10 important questions. The more questions given the harder it is for a student to track their progress. With fewer questions it is easier to keep track of the growth. You do not want these sheets to become extra work and no fun for students.

Although the learners' comments can be taken into consideration for future modification, we note that the statements on the TTS were developed from oral evaluation rubrics from international proficiency exams. Sometimes questions that may look identical can be focusing on different linguistic and cultural aspects of language learning.

Finally, we note comments from participants on how the blog offers assessment feedback to teachers and learners that helpfully supplements the TTS and improve language skills.

Comment 15

The teletandem tracking sheet seemed to be a tracker of form and structure of conversation, whereas the blog centered more around vocabulary and content. They were complementary of each other, which I found helpful.

Both tools appear to help students learn in teletandem since they seem to complement one another, though additional studies will be needed to confirm this finding. Meanwhile, we assume that the TTS is useful in promoting oral skills since it helps learners raise analytical awareness of linguistic and cultural aspects in spoken communication.

As we can see from the findings presented in this section, assessment can provide both learners and teachers with information to improve their participation in technology-mediated language-learning environments. This claim is reinforced by O'Dowd's (2015) model of competencies for enhancing telecollaboration. According to O'Dowd, effective telecollaborative exchanges in classrooms require that instructors (1) support students in follow-up classroom discussions, (2) integrate appropriate assessment procedures that accurately reflect the activities carried out during interaction, (3) integrate the content and themes of the telecollaborative exchange into contact classes (when they exist), and (4) provide learning support either through scaffolded guidance (in the classroom or in online tutorials) or through the provision of reflective tools (such as logs or journals). To these tools we can now also add the proposed TTS designed for teletandem exchanges.

Discussion

Based on the literature review and the findings of this study, assessment seems to add much to language learning within telecollaboration, insofar as it is understood as a means to a well-defined, articulated goal shared among the participants.

Regarding our first research concern, the most appropriate theoretical assessment perspective for teletandem-type instruction should be one that accommodates the collaborative and autonomous nature of language learning. The way students learn must guide the ways in which we both teach and assess. It is important to underscore, then, the usefulness of the formative assessment perspective in teletandem, since assessment is aimed at diagnosing strengths and weaknesses, to better address them during the learning process. The findings show that self-assessment supports formative assessment, since it provides the necessary information on student learning to help improve both teacher's and learner's performance.

In response to our second research concern (why use self-assessment in teletandem), students' perceptions support positive impacts on both learning and teaching when TTS is integrated as a self-assessment tool within teletandem practice during contact classes.

Regarding our final research question on the impact of the TTS on learners and teachers, the benefits to language learners are: enhanced awareness of strengths and weaknesses, ability to self-monitor progress, and a sense of ownership of the process. We conclude that self-assessment helps learners foster their learning as they monitor their progress, which consequently fosters autonomy.

The impact of assessment on teachers relates to: providing insights for planning teletandem practice; gathering information about linguistic and intercultural learning, which can be addressed in contact classes to help students improve oral proficiency; and recognizing the essential role of immediate feedback.

The findings from this study broaden the usefulness of the TTS as previously discovered in Furtoso (2011) since they suggest how the tool was used to impact both learning and teaching. Equipped with these assessment conclusions, learners and teachers can better understand the roles they play in particular telecollaboration language-learning environments, such as teletandem.

Final Words

It does not matter if you have no idea *how* to do assessment in teletandem. Rather, what you should know is *why* you should use assessment. Do not forget: Without feedback during the process, assessment itself may be useless in helping students learn.

Acknowledgements

The authors would like to acknowledge that the study reported in this paper was carried out with the funding support of both the Fulbright Commission and CAPES (Government of Brazil). We would also like to express our gratitude to our third-year advanced Portuguese conversation course at Georgetown University as well as Jonggun Park for designing the software used for this study. Also, a grant from the Initiative on Technology-Enhanced Learning (ITEL) permitted us to extend the use of teletandem practices to eight modern languages within the faculty of languages and linguistics at Georgetown College. Finally, we would like to thank the anonymous reviewers and John Davis, who provided valuable insight and suggestions in their reviews of earlier drafts of this paper.

Notes

1. Impact and washback effect (or backwash effect) are used as synonyms in this study, although some authors distinguish them.
2. This study follows the notion of proficiency as defined by Scaramucci (2000, 14) in which proficiency is seen as a relative concept, not an absolute one, that takes into consideration future language use. The scale is seen as degrees of proficiency, not as proficient/not proficient. The degree of proficiency depends on the specificity of language use in a particular situation.
3. Celpe-Bras is the Certificate of Proficiency in Brazilian Portuguese for Foreigners, developed and administered by the Brazilian Ministry of Education (MEC).

References

Alderson, John C., and Dianne D. Wall. 1993. "Does Washback Exist?" *Applied Linguistics* 14:115–29.

Aranha, Solange, and Suzi M. S. Cavalari. 2015. "Institutional Integrated Teletandem: What Have We Been Learning about Writing and Peer Feedback?" *D.E.L.T.A.* 31 (3): 811–28.

Belz, Julie A. 2002. "Social Dimensions of Telecollaborative Foreign Language Study." *Language Learning & Technology* 6 (1): 60–83. http://llt.msu.edu/vol6num1/pdf/belz.pdf.

Benedetti, Ana M., Douglas A. Consolo, and Maria H. Vieira-Abrahão. 2010. *Pesquisas e Ensino no Teletandem Brasil*. Campinas, Bra.: Pontes Editores.

Brammerts, Helmut. 2003. "Autonomous Language Learning in Tandem: The Development of a Concept." In *Autonomous Language Learning In-Tandem*, edited by Tim Lewis and Lesley Walker, 27–36. Sheffield, Eng.: Academy Electronic Publications.

Carr, Wilfred, and Stephen Kemmis. 1986. *Becoming Critical: Education, Knowledge and Action Research*. Geelong: Deakin University Press. https://enotez.files.wordpress.com/2011/09/becoming-critical.pdf.

Cavalari, Suzi. M. S. 2009. "A Auto-Avaliação em um Contexto de Ensino-Aprendizagem de Línguas em Tandem Via Chat." PhD diss., Universidade Estadual Paulista. http://repositorio.unesp.br/handle/11449/103514.

Chun, Dorothy M. 2011. "Developing Intercultural Communicative Competence through Online Exchanges." *CALICO Journal* 28 (2): 392–419.

Consolo, Douglas A., and Viviane B. Furtoso. 2015. "Assessing Oral Proficiency in Computer-Assisted Foreign Language Learning: A Study in the Context of Teletandem Interactions." *D.E.L.T.A.* 31 (3): 665–89.

Diaz, Veronica, Malcolm Brown, and Janet Salmons. 2010. "Unit 4: Assessment of Collaborative Learning Project Outcomes." EDUCAUSE Learning Initiative (ELI). http://net.educause.edu/ir/library/pdf/ELI80084.pdf.

Furtoso, Viviane B. 2011. "Desempenho Oral em Português para Falantes de Outras Línguas: Da Avaliação à Aprendizagem de Línguas Estrangeiras em Contexto *Online*." PhD diss., Universidade Estadual Paulista. https://repositorio.unesp.br/bitstream/handle/11449/103505/furtoso_vab_dr_sjrp.pdf?sequence = 1.

Furtoso, Viviane B., and Michael J. Ferreira. 2016. "Nem Cá, Nem Lá, Nem Acolá: O Português Falado em Espaços de Aprendizagem Desterritorializantes." In *O Mundo do Português e o Português no Mundo Afora: Especificidades, Implicações e Ações*, edited by Maria Luisa O. Alvarez and Luis Gonçalves, 525–61. Campinas, Bra.: Pontes Editores.

Gonçalves, Luis. 2012. "O Ensino de Português Como Segunda Língua nos EUA: Desafios Antigos e Recursos Inovadores." In *Ensino de Português nos Estados Unidos: História, Desenvolvimento, Perspectivas*, edited by José F Luna, 43–56. Jundiaí, Bra.: Paco Editorial.

Holec, Henri. 1981. *Autonomy and Foreign Language Learning*. Oxford: Pergamon Press.

McNamara, Judith, and Catherine Brown. 2008. "Assessment of Collaborative Learning in Online Discussions." In *ATN Assessment 08: Engaging Students in Assessment*. Adelaide, Aus.: University of South Australia. http://citeseerx.ist.psu.edu/viewdoc/download?doi = 10.1.1.536.4167&rep = rep1&type = pdf.

Mompean, Annick R., and Marco Cappellini. 2015. "Teletandem as a Complex Learning Environment: Looking for a Model." *D.E.L.T.A.* 31 (3): 633–63.

Norris, John M. 2006. "The Why (and How) of Assessing Student Learning Outcomes in College Foreign Language Programs." *Modern Language Journal* 90:576–83.

O'Dowd, Robert. 2015. "Supporting In-Service Language Educators in Learning to Telecollaborate." *Language Learning & Technology* 19 (1): 64–83.

Ramos, Karin A. H. P. 2015. "Interactants' Beliefs in Teletandem: Implications for Teaching of Portuguese as a Foreign Language." *D.E.L.T.A.* 31 (3): 691–709.

Ramsdem, Paul. 1992. *Learning to Teach in Higher Education*. London: Routledge.

Ross, Pauline M., and Susan L. Siegenthaler. 2006. "Assessment for Learning and Motivation." In *UniServe Science Symposium Proceedings: Assessment in Science Teaching and Learning*, 120–25. Sydney: UniServe Science. http://science.uniserve.edu.au/pubs/procs/2006/ross.pdf.

Scaramucci, Matilde V. R. 2000. "Proficiência em LE: Considerações Terminológicas e Conceituais." *Trabalhos em Linguística Aplicada* 36:11–22.

Telles, João A. 2009. *Teletandem: Um Contexto Virtual, Autônomo e Colaborativo para a Aprendizagem de Línguas Estrangeiras no Século XXI*. Campinas, Bra.: Pontes Editores.

———. 2015. "Learning Foreign Languages in Teletandem: Resources and Strategies." *D.E.L.T.A.* 31 (3): 603–32.

Chapter 4

◆ An Integrated Approach to Foreign Language Instruction and Assessment

KEIKO KODA
Carnegie Mellon University

JUNKO YAMASHITA
Nagoya University

THIS CHAPTER DESCRIBES AN approach to foreign-language (FL) instruction and assessment that integrates three skill domains: language learning, knowledge acquisition, and communication. The integration of the three domains was achieved within a single unified framework built around reading-to-learn. As a multifaceted construct, reading-to-learn entails interlinked operations through which a learner builds text meanings based on sequences of graphic symbols on the page and then internalizes text information to incorporate it into their knowledge bases. Assessment plays a pivotal role in the approach as the primary means of monitoring student learning and as the basis for designing and evaluating instructional materials intended to enhance learning.

Project Overview

The setting for the project was three English classes at a large university in Japan. The instructor of these classes was one of the authors of the chapter. The goal of the project was to implement an approach that integrates assessment and instruction for the purpose of promoting the concurrent development of language learning, knowledge acquisition, and communication. The approach is assessment-driven in that assessment tools were developed directly from the learning objectives and used to guide and monitor instructional effectiveness and learning progress. The intended users of the assessment were the instructors and students of the courses in which the approach was implemented. The intended uses of the assessment included: conveying the learning objectives and expected outcomes to students, monitoring their learning, helping them learn to monitor their own progress, guiding instruction, and making decisions about each student's achievements in the course.

The Conceptual Framework: Reading-to-Learn

Three fundamental assumptions underlie the current approach. First, content understanding occurs during reading when text information is connected with learners' personal experiences and prior knowledge. Second, second language (L2) reading development builds on what learners have previously acquired in their first language (L1; Hulstijn 2015; Nakamura, Koda, and Joshi 2014). Third, complex mental activities, such as comprehension and learning, are incomplete until content information is conveyed to others. The sections that follow describe how these assumptions are built into the assessment framework.

Reading-to-Learn as a Meaning-Construction Operation

Reading-to-learn in this study is conceptualized as the process entailing three interlinked operations, including text meaning building, personal meaning construction, and knowledge refinement (Koda 2016).

Text meaning building involves converting printed words into their phonological and morphological information, retrieving their meanings, and assembling word meanings into larger text segments, such as sentences and paragraphs. The operation relies heavily on the knowledge of the language used in the text and the skills to use the knowledge efficiently for building local text meanings.

Personal meaning construction is important for achieving deeper text understanding. To do so, text meanings must be personalized at both local and global levels. At the local level, leaners must draw on their prior knowledge to fill semantic gaps in a text created by unstated information. At the global level, personalization is needed for learners to make out how text information fits with their real-life experiences. Through this process, locally assembled text meanings are connected with relevant information stored in long-term memory.

The third operation, knowledge refinement, involves the incorporation of personal text meanings into learners' knowledge bases. According to Britton (1994), new understanding emerges when text information induces a change in a relationship, or a set of relationships, among stored concepts. Learning during reading only occurs when learners recognize any such restructuring in their existing knowledge bases as a result of reading. Knowledge acquisition thus is dependent on, and restricted to, what learners already know. In short, reading-to-learn entails the simultaneous utilization of language skills and content knowledge for the purpose of text meaning construction, content analysis, and reflection. As such, our central contention is that reading-to-learn is an ideal construct for fostering the concurrent development of language skills and knowledge acquisition in the FL classroom.

The Role of Communication in Knowledge Acquisition

Reading-to-learn, as noted above, entails continual interactions between input information and stored knowledge of the learner. Communication plays an integral role in monitoring such interactions and clarifying what emerges as their outcomes. According to the Boyer Commission on Educating Undergraduates in the Research University, a critical commitment colleges and universities have to their students is to provide "maximal opportunities for intellectual and creative development" (1998, 8). On the assumption that learning occurs through knowledge construction, rather than mere transmission of information, the commission promotes inquiry-based learning that engages students in active knowledge construction through self-discovery and experience as a way of enhancing the growth of their intellectual and creative capacities. In general, inquiry-based learning entails three major steps, including formulating a question, obtaining evidence that supports an answer to the question, and evaluating the answer (Banchi and Bell 2008). These steps correspond roughly to the three phases of knowledge acquisition proposed by Sternberg (1999): (1) selective encoding (distinguishing relevant from irrelevant information about the question addressed), (2) selective combination (putting together relevant information for the purpose of answering the question), and (3) selective comparison (relating new information to relevant information already stored in memory).

The Boyer Commission (1998) underscores the centrality of communication in learning through self-discovery as the primary means of monitoring and regulating the mental activities involved in knowledge construction. Since learning is incomplete until learners convey mastery to others, instruction, aiming to promote knowledge construction, must be committed to fostering strong communication skills that support learning.

Within the constructivist view of learning, the current approach incorporates communication as a vital component of reading-to-learn. Besides its primary function as the means of monitoring and regulating mental activities, we intend to use communication for two additional purposes: (1) promoting students' productive use of language in multiple modalities and (2) collecting assessment information for monitoring their progress in acquiring reading-to-learn skills.

Reading-to-Learn Skills

To capture reading-to-learn skills (see next section) and enable the various assessment uses mentioned above, a system of assessment tools was developed within the framework. The system consists of three types of assessment that differ in the frequency of administration and content specificity. At the course level, two versions of curriculum-independent, researcher-made assessments were administered twice, once at the beginning and once at the end of the course. Each version comprised a source text (about 450 words) and three sets of tasks designed to engage students to use distinct reading-to-learn skills for task completion. The purposes of this assessment were threefold: conveying the expected learning outcomes to students at the outset of the course, collecting the baseline information on the focal skills, and estimating gains in those skills at the end of the semester. At the unit level, curriculum-dependent, teacher-designed performance assessments were used. Assessment information was used to monitor progress in learning the focal skills and provide feedback and scaffolding if needed. At the lesson level, classroom formative assessments were used in conjunction with lesson plans. Because this form of assessment is continuous and fluid, it is fully integrated into instruction. Assessment information was used to create and modify lesson plans, worksheets, and homework assignments. It was also used to monitor teaching against the learning objectives at various instructional levels, including course, unit, and lesson. For diverse assessments to fulfill their functions individually and jointly, it is essential that they be parts of a complex whole. We used the specifications of the construct in creating the course-level assessments so that assessment outcomes can be interpreted by reference to the focal construct. In what follows, the skills each reading-to-learn operation entails are defined.

Text Meaning Building Skills

Text meaning building entails a set of skills necessary for converting graphic symbols to word meanings and then to local text meanings that correspond to the learner's real-life experiences and knowledge stored in memory. These skills include

- Integrating individual word meanings into local text meanings,
- Inferring the meaning of unfamiliar words and phrases based on local text meanings and prior knowledge,
- Identifying the main idea in each paragraph or section,
- Integrating local text meanings into a coherent whole, and
- Identifying the author's view on the topic.

Personal Meaning Construction Skills

Personal meaning construction involves making links between text information and the stored knowledge of the learner, ranging from memory of an isolated experience in a single instance to more general information abstracted from all related experiences. The operation involves

- Comparing text information with the learner's personal experiences,
- Comparing text information with what the learner knows about the topic, and
- Comparing the author's view with the learner's own view on the topic.

Knowledge Refinement Skills

Knowledge refinement occurs when the learner recognizes conceptual restructuring induced by constructed text meanings. The operation relies on

- Reflecting on similarities between the author's view and what the learner knows about the topic,
- Reflecting on differences between the author's view and what the learner knows about the topic, and
- Reflecting on changes, however subtle they might be, in the learner's view on the topic after reading and personalizing the input source passage.

In the project, assessment development was guided by the constructivist principle that underscores the importance of the alignment between assessment and learning (Caccamise, Snyder, and Kintsch 2008). Following the principle, each assessment was designed to provide authentic learning experience by immersing students in the actual reading-to-learn processes.

The Project

In a larger project, the approach was implemented in four universities in Japan. Five experienced EFL instructors participated in the project. Within the framework, two versions of course-level assessment were developed and given at the beginning and end of the course to estimate gains in the focal skills (Test 1 and Test 2, respectively). Each version was based on a passage (about 450 words) that compared cultural perspectives on particular educational issues in Japan and the United States. The content appropriateness for student participants was approved by all the instructors in the project. The texts, originally located on an internet website, were modified to create the source passages in the two versions of the course-level assessment. Each version consisted of three sections corresponding to the three reading-to-learn operations.

In the first section, students were expected to demonstrate their text meaning building skills. They were first presented with a passage with a series of questions requesting the information that could be found by using one or more text meaning building skills. The section contained twelve multiple-choice and three short-answer items.

The second section posed twelve multiple-choice questions that asked students to describe how text information related to their personal experiences and prior knowledge. These questions were designed to engage students in personalizing text information they built through reading the source passage and answering the questions in the first section. Cronbach's alpha for the first two sections in the two assessments was as follows: .70 (section 1) and .78 (section 2) in Test 1, and .68 (section 1) and .79 (section 2) in Test 2.

In the third section (knowledge refinement), students were asked to write a short essay to express how their understanding of the topic had changed by comparing the information presented in the source passage with their personal experiences, knowledge, and views they had held before the assessment. The rubric for essays in section 3 consisted of six categories (organization, analysis, content, reflection, language use, and impact) with each being scored on a four-point scale from 0 to 3. *Organization* refers to the overall coherence of the essay with ideas logically connected. *Analysis* is about the choice of topic (e.g., its scope and relevance to the source material) and analysis of the phenomena discussed in the passage (e.g., similarities and differences between the cultures). *Content* is pertinent to the explanation of the analyzed phenomena (e.g., how the phenomena relate to cultural features). *Reflection* concerns further development of the student's thoughts and insights, connecting observed phenomena to underlying cultural values and biases. *Language use* has to do with accuracy and appropriateness of the language used. Finally, *impact* refers to the effective use of discourse and other devices to make an impact on audience (e.g., good opener/closure, evidence, and examples). The essays were scored by the instructors and trained doctorate students. Interrater reliability (the mean correlation among the raters) was .82.

Implementation: A Case Study

In this chapter, we describe a single case from the project where the second author was the instructor and provide detailed documentation of how the approach was implemented and what impacts it had on the instructor and students together with limitations of this implementation in this specific case. The study used a mixed-methods design; thus, the instructor's observation and self-reflection are reported largely in a narrative format.

Setting

The university is one of the major research universities in Japan. It adopts a two-semester system with one semester being fifteen weeks. The university's EFL program offers four semesters of academic English training to all freshman and sophomore students. Credits from EFL courses are required for graduation of all the students. Thus, every year, a large number of first- and second-year students enroll in EFL courses.

The overarching goal of the EFL program is to promote academic skills in English. Since students from various academic backgrounds enroll in the EFL courses, the curriculum does not specify any content area to foster through the EFL program; rather, it emphasizes the mastery of general academic language skills. The focal competencies are paragraph reading and writing skills in the first semester, essay reading and writing skills and basic oral communication skills in the second semester, oral presentation skills in the third semester, and understanding of cultures in English-speaking countries in the fourth semester. An EFL class meets once a week for ninety minutes in each semester.

There are several recommended textbooks for instructors. Many, though not all, instructors select their textbook from among those recommended. However, they have freedom and responsibility in deciding how to use the textbook of their choice.

The current approach was implemented in three sections of a third-semester course. The course objective was to integrate language skills, both written and spoken, and ultimately cultivate oral presentation skills. The students were all in their second year, had studied basic academic discourse structures, received training in reading and writing paragraphs and essays, and engaged in a range of activities to improve their listening and speaking skills in the first year's program at the university. As summarized in table 4.1, the students' majors included economics, science, and literature. On average, students started studying English at the age of twelve. This means that they had studied English for six years through secondary school education prior to the university. None of them had any experience studying or living in English-speaking countries. Their exposure to English outside the class was limited to the occasional viewing of English Internet pages.

◆ Table 4.1. Characteristics of participants

| Department | Participants | | | Start age[a] |
	Male	Female	Total	
Economics	15	4	19	11.8
Science	15	6	21	12.4
Literature	4	16	20	11.7
Total	34	26	60	12.0

a. Average age at which students started studying English.

Additional Assessments

In addition to the course-level assessments, described in the preceding section, multiple assessments were employed to promote the focal skills and monitor students' progress in acquiring them.

Oral presentations were used as intermediary, unit-level assessments for the purpose of monitoring progress in the focal skills with particular reference to the specific type of presentation practiced in the unit.

Formative assessment information on self-monitoring and reflection was collected through open-ended questionnaires. An instructor questionnaire prompted the instructor to reflect on changes in her beliefs and thoughts about instructional design, assessment, and their alignment with the learning processes. The questionnaire for students asked them about how they prepared their oral presentations, what aspects of presentation they paid special attention to, and what opinions they have about the integration of language and content in the assessments in the course.

Instructional Design

The instructor selected one of the recommended textbooks designed to teach various oral presentation skills. It has six units that are built around specific types or topics of presentations to practice. A unit contains a model presentation on DVD, warm-up introductory exercises, listening comprehension tasks, lists of key English expressions, and activities to help organize ideas. The instructor chose three units from the textbook for the course, which she thought would help students prepare for academic presentations. The units cover survey reports, news article summaries, and argumentative presentations. As mentioned, three oral presentations, each of which corresponds to a unit in the textbook, were used as intermediary unit-end assessments in the course: a warm-up group presentation followed by two individual presentations.

The instructor had taught this course in previous years using the same textbook. The fundamental instructional design was the same as before. The model presentation in each unit was used as source material, the class was divided into four to five groups, and the group work was the basis for class activities. However, some changes were made in class activities to foster reading-to-learn skills. Based on the two versions of course-level assessments, the instructor created a series of worksheets for instructional activities and homework assignments for the course. The worksheets consisted of three sections of questions, with each section corresponding to one of the three reading-to-learn operations. For instance, based on the model presentation that reported survey results on eating habits, the students engaged in the understanding of the source material (i.e., text meaning building) by answering questions such as "Do the survey participants think they have healthy eating habits?" and "Why does the speaker think that most university students do not have healthy eating habits?" At the level of personal meaning construction, the students were guided to connect local and global meanings of the source material to their personal experiences by pondering questions such as "How often do you eat healthy foods and unhealthy foods?" and "Do you think you have healthy eating habits?" Finally, for knowledge refinement, they were prompted to reflect on the topic and content by discussing questions such as "If you were conducting a survey on the same topic, what else would you like to ask?" and "What do you think is a healthy eating habit?"

With some variations, each unit was completed following the same general procedures. The instruction started with an explanation of the unit goal followed by a variety of pedagogical activities using the worksheets and textbook resources, which included introductory warm-up tasks (e.g., sharing opinions about controversial issues, such as whether watching TV harms young people, in the unit on argumentative presentation) to prepare students for the target form of the presentation, listening comprehension exercises, studying key English expressions, and watching the model DVD. The students answered worksheet questions by discussing them in small groups. Their answers were shared with the whole class and the instructor gave feedback.

The instruction was designed to be assessment-driven within the reading-to-learn framework. To this end, at the beginning of the course the instructor explained what skills and abilities students were expected to learn and how progress in their learning was to be assessed. Although it was a common practice for her to explain about the course assessments, this time she was able to provide much more concrete and systematic information about the assessments because the specific skills to be taught and assessed are clearly specified in the framework. Specifically, the instructor explained the three reading-to-learn operations, distributed a copy of the essay rubric, and delineated its six assessment categories, one by one, to show how their products (oral presentations and essays in the course-level assessments) were to be assessed. It was especially emphasized that the content and English language skills were both important, and thus, the students were expected to demonstrate content-learning skills stemming from the three reading-to-learn operations. It was hoped that the explicit presentation of the framework, assessment instruments, and evaluation criteria would help students understand the learning objectives of the course and motivate them to meet the expectations.

Administration

The reading-to-learn skills and assessment instruments were explained in the first week, and one version of the course-level assessment (Test 1, a pretest) was administered in the second week. The other version (Test 2, a posttest) and the student questionnaire were given in the last week of the semester. Both versions of the course-level assessment had time limits: thirty minutes for section 1 (text meaning building), fifteen minutes for section 2 (personal meaning construction), and thirty-five minutes for section 3 (knowledge refinement). Dictionary use was allowed only in section 3. On the part of the instructor, she responded to the instructor questionnaire twice, once before and once after the semester.

Learning Outcomes
Gains in Reading-to-Learn Skills
To estimate gains in the reading-to-learn skills, answers from the multiple-choice and short-answer questions that were scored dichotomously and ratings from the essay rubric from forty-eight students, whose scores on the two versions of the course-level assessment were available, were submitted to Bonferroni-adjusted Wilcoxon signed ranks tests ($p < .006$). We opted for the nonparametric test because essay scores are not on a continuous scale and test scores deviated from a normal distribution. Tables 4.2 and 4.3 summarize descriptive statistics and Wilcoxon test results, including effect sizes (r). Overall, section score means were improved, but gains were more pronounced in the text meaning building and personal meaning construction skills. Ceiling effects were observed in sections one and two in Test 2. Especially, the section two scores reached the complete ceiling in Test 2. Three categories of the essay scores showed significant gains (organization, language use, and impact), but the other three did not reach statistical significance. Effect sizes (r) were large in sections one and two (.72 and .68, respectively), and medium in the total, section-three score (.47, ranging from small to medium in its sub-scores by category).

◈ Table 4.2. Descriptive statistics and t-test results

	Test 1				Test 2			
	$\bar{X}$	SD	95% CI	% $\bar{X}$	$\bar{X}$	SD	95% CI	% $\bar{X}$
Text-meaning building	10.96	1.76	[10.45, 11.47]	.73	13.33	1.87	[12.79, 13.88]	.89
Personal meaning construction	10.23	1.89	[9.68, 10.78]	.85	11.88	.61	[11.70, 12.05]	.99
Knowledge refinement (essay)	10.31	3.1	[9.41, 11.21]	.57	12.33	2.95	[11.48, 13.19]	.69
Organization	2.10	.72	[1.90, 2.31]	.70	2.50	0.55	[2.34, 2.66]	.83
Analysis	1.63	.67	[1.43, 1.82]	.54	1.88	0.82	[1.64, 2.11]	.63
Content	1.60	.96	[1.33, 1.88]	.53	1.77	1.04	[1.47, 2.07]	.59
Reflection	1.46	.71	[1.25, 1.67]	.49	1.75	0.84	[1.51, 1.99]	.58
Language use	2.17	.72	[1.96, 2.38]	.72	2.52	0.55	[2.36, 2.68]	.84
Impact	1.35	.89	[1.10, 1.61]	.45	1.92	0.85	[1.67, 2.16]	.64

◆ **Table 4.3.** Results of Wilcoxon signed-ranks tests and effect sizes

	Z	p	r
Text-meaning building	−5.39	.000	0.72
Personal meaning construction	−4.91	.000	0.68
Knowledge refinement (essay)	−3.34	.001	0.47
Organization	−2.92	.003	0.43
Analysis	−1.54	.124	0.24
Content	−0.97	.332	0.13
Reflection	−1.95	.051	0.28
Language use	−2.81	.005	0.40
Impact	−3.54	.000	0.51

The mean section 2 score was already high on Test 1 and reached the complete ceiling in Test 2 (85% and 99% accuracies, respectively). A possible explanation is that the multiple-choice format may not be a suitable method for assessing personal meaning construction skills. This format may have unduly limited the ways the students could demonstrate their capacity and involvement in the process of personalizing local and global text meanings. Other means, such as brief, constructive responses with an appropriate rubric and think-aloud protocol analysis, may be better windows through which to observe the development of the personal meaning construction skills.

Text meaning building heavily relies on L2 linguistic knowledge. The significant increase in the mean section 1 scores is likely attributable to the approach implemented in this course.

Differential impacts of the instruction on the six categories of the essay rubric may be explained at least partially by the students' conscious efforts prompted by the implemented approach. On the whole, it seemed that the students demonstrated progress in what they were expected to pay attention to. As detailed below, students were seriously concerned about communicating their message to the audience. They reported on the questionnaire that they had made conscious efforts to improve the logical flow of the message, the organization of presentations, and the effective use of language to make impacts on their audience. These attempts match the three categories of the rubric (organization, language use, and impact) in which a statistically significant difference was found in the mean rating scores between the two course-level assessment versions. The significant improvement in language use corroborates the results of section 1 scores as well.

On the other hand, a statistically significant difference was not observed in the other three rubric categories pertinent to content analysis and reflection. An explanation may lie in different content areas in the assessments and the class activities. As mentioned above, the reading passages of the assessments were on the cross-cultural comparisons, but this topic was not explicitly covered in the textbook. Thus, the students received scant training in making cross-cultural comparisons and reflecting on cultural issues. We may need more sustained efforts over multiple semesters to ensure that the reading-to-learn skills fostered in one content domain transfer to and are manifested in a new content domain to a measurable degree.

Observations by the Instructor

The instructor implemented the integrated approach by (a) making the course objectives and assessment criteria clear and explicit at the beginning of the semester; (b) bringing consistency to class activities, formative assessments, and feedback within the reading-to-learn framework; and (c) aligning instructional contents with all forms of formative and summative assessments. All these were manageable adjustments for her. These relatively small changes, however, led to considerable differences in students' motivation, attitudes, and resulting performance in their first group presentations compared with what she had observed in the past. The improved performance described below may be caused by the explicit specifications of the construct in the framework and the instructor's emphasis on the dual instructional foci on content learning and academic language use.

The group presentations utilize survey projects. The process involved in the task activates the reading-to-learn skills: comprehending the model presentation that serves as a point of reference, devising original survey questions, collecting and understanding source information (survey data gathered by the group members), interpreting the survey outcome and reflecting on it through group discussion, and communicating their discovery to the audience. The general topic of the survey project in the unit is young peoples' habits and opinions. Each group decides their topic and makes several survey questions. Some class hours are spent on interviewing classmates to collect information. In previous classes, most groups finished their survey in the class hour despite the instructor's encouragement to expand it beyond the classroom; if they did, they simply added several responses from friends readily available to them. Thus, the mini-surveys in the past classes were highly limited in sample size, findings, and students' reflections. However, under the current approach, all groups extended their surveys outside of the classroom. For instance, a group used a social networking service and collected responses from over one hundred participants. Another group added data by calling their friends studying in distant universities. Clearly, the students' motivation and engagement in the task were higher than those of the past students. It was not only the scope of the survey but also the analysis of collected information and overall quality of the presentations that favorably differed from those in previous years, according to the instructor's observations. The students discovered interesting facts through various analyses, presented persuasively with evidence and examples, and demonstrated deep reflections on their findings. For instance, a group who conducted a survey on the topic of "university students and music" presented their findings from multiple perspectives, including favorite genres of music, devices used to listen to music, sources of music (CD, internet, etc.), when and where to listen to music, and relationships between academic majors and music preferences. Their conclusion was that diversity existed in the way university students enjoy music in their lives. This may not be a surprising discovery, nor was their survey comparable to real academic research, but the presentation was persuasive because it was based on close analyses of a large dataset and delivered efficiently using graphs and diagrams. The group presentation was conducted only after two weeks of instruction at the beginning of the course. It is unlikely that this short period of instruction had such strong impacts on boosting the students' performance. Rather, the explicit framework given in the first class may have made students aware that they had learned many of the reading-to-learn skills in their L1, and this led them to capitalize on those skills whenever and wherever they could. Performances beyond expectations were commonly observed in all three classes. It was truly impressive to observe presentations of high quality early in the semester, even with her long career of EFL teaching.

The students sustained their motivation and engagement in class activities throughout the semester, and on the whole, continued showing high engagement in the subsequent presentations. Progress was consistently observed in delivery, confidence, and discourse organization through class activities. Despite this, however, differences emerged when they started working on their presentations individually. There was a tendency for those who showed an excellent performance in the first presentation to score well in their second presentation also. They were able to demonstrate interesting and thought-provoking discussions based on their text meaning building, personalization, and knowledge refinement skills on two different topics. On the other hand, it seemed hard for some students to improve their higher-order skills, such as building arguments and arriving at deep reflections leading to knowledge refinement. It is not clear how these skills differed in Japanese among the students who were enrolled in the course in the semester when the approach was implemented. To be accepted by one of the top-level universities, their fundamental academic competencies are assumed to be high among the undergraduate population in the country. Even so, individual variations in those skills in their L1 are likely to have existed prior to enrollment. English language proficiency may be another factor underlying performance differences. Some students may not have been able to display their content-learning skills because of their insufficient language abilities or weak regulatory skills that adjust the way to express their content with their limited English language resources. For such students, longer instructional engagement appears necessary to enhance the knowledge refinement skills in English outlined in the reading-to-learn framework.

From students' responses to the student questionnaire, the instructor learned that they were sensitized to the communicative nature of their presentations by the instructor's introduction of the course at the beginning of the semester. They have kept their audience in mind and tried to use different linguistic and discourse devices to convey their ideas and messages effectively. They referred to every aspect of the presentations that was to be evaluated in the assessments. It was clear that they understood the reading-to-learn framework, grasped the descriptors in the rubric well, and used them to guide their efforts in preparing their oral presentations administered as the unit-end performance assessments. Interestingly, the students did not use phrases like "to improve my presentation" or "to make a good presentation" but instead said "to communicate my ideas" or "to make the audience understand what I want to say." It might be the case that, although the instructor did not explicitly mention it, the students received the implicit message that communication is a vital component of meaning construction and knowledge acquisition and used it as the guiding principle in their preparation for presentations.

Another interesting observation was that many of the students stated that they attempted to make their English as plain as possible to assist comprehension by the audience. A sizable number of such responses made a sharp contrast to the attitude of some students the instructor had encountered in the past, who simply copied low-frequency words and phrases from a dictionary with little consideration for the audience.

Finally, from students' responses, the instructor learned that students support the dual-focused approach that takes both content learning and language use into account in assessing their performances. With some variations in their opinions, the students seem to prefer to have their performance assessed with equal emphasis on their content and language skills in EFL courses. A noteworthy point was brought up by a student: They have learned basic English by the end of secondary school and want to do more intellectually challenging activities in English at the university level.

Instructor's Self-Reflection

The most impressive impact that this instructor witnessed came from the assessment-driven aspect of this approach. Not only were there relatively immediate impacts on students but the approach also had an influence on the instructor. Being a long-term EFL teacher, she had thought she was well aware of the importance of assessment. Indeed, she had always explained her assessment policy and methods to students and acted accordingly. However, in retrospect, she had to admit that her assessment ideas were somewhat general and had virtually no influence on guiding the design and delivery of instruction. By contrast, a clear conceptual framework was used in this project, based on the reading-to-learn operations, which the instructor found offered a useful point of reference to plan pedagogical activities and provide feedback. She was able to be consistent in what she offered to and expected from students in her classes. In other words, the framework guided the instruction powerfully and consistently.

Through her experience, the instructor identified four key words that captured the elements needed for successful assessment-driven language instruction: concrete, explicit, consistent, and iterative. Concrete descriptions of the focal skills (i.e., learning objectives) and assessments in the framework should be made explicit to students and should be consistently used throughout class activities iteratively until the framework becomes an internal template for students that guides and supports their self-regulation.

The experience of using this approach has changed the instructor's view on assessment in EFL courses. Prior to the implementation of the integrated approach, the instructor believed that linguistic knowledge and language skills were the main focus in EFL instruction, and therefore did not give content a fair amount of weight in her assessments. However, she has seen that integrating content learning in assessments motivated the students and made them work harder in improving their language to communicate their messages. Coupled with the questionnaire results mentioned above, the instructor decided to change her assessment policy and integrate content learning and language use in her future assessment practices.

The instructor has realized that the reading-to-learn framework is applicable to any topic, communication modality, and content area. As mentioned earlier, the textbook she used is skills based; its units are built around different topics and contents, and the students' presentations were made on a wide variety of topics. In spite of this, she was able to design her instruction and conduct assessments consistently in alignment with the framework. It is worth emphasizing that the reading-to-learn framework represents cognitive processes underpinning learning in any content domain that students can personally relate to. Thus, the framework is flexible enough to allow instructors to select any topic and incorporate the conceptual components in their language instruction and assessment. The instructor believes that the reading-to-learn framework offers a potent way of responding to students' desires for more intellectually challenging activities in college-level EFL classes while simultaneously enhancing their communication skills in a FL.

Summary and Reflections

In this chapter, we have described the framework for an integrated approach built around the concept of reading-to-learn. Reading-to-learn entails three interlinked meaning-construction operations that engage students in using their language skills purposefully as tools for learning, reflecting on, and communicating content information. The motivation behind the approach is to promote the academic use of language skills by capitalizing on college students' cognitive maturity, academic learning experiences in their L1, and the extensive conceptual knowledge they have accumulated in their lives.

The approach was implemented in three sections of an EFL course at a university in Japan. The instruction was assessment-driven and dual-focused. The reading-to-learn skills the students were expected to learn were explicitly and concretely explained at the beginning of the course. The instruction was delivered in alignment with the conceptual framework by emphasizing the importance of both language skills and content-learning skills as specified in the framework. The instructor observed that the students' motivation, engagement, and classroom performances were higher than those in past classes. These observations seem to suggest that the assessment-driven design, the clear specifications of the focal skills, and consistent adherence to the framework during instruction may have helped students clearly understand what to learn and how to learn it. In response to the questionnaire, students indicated that knowing what they were expected to do did motivate them to work harder toward the goal. The course-level assessments given at the beginning and end of the course showed general improvements in all reading-to-learn skills specified in the framework with some variations in categories of the knowledge-refinement skills. The students responded favorably to the dual-focused approach, supporting the inclusion of content-learning skills in EFL instruction and assessment.

Utility of the Approach in FL Instruction

One of the noteworthy changes observed by the instructor was more active and deeper engagement of students in learning, in general, and content generation and analysis, in particular. We attribute the changes to the approach's heavy emphasis on the personalization of input information. As described above, the instructor made it clear that knowledge acquisition and the conveyance of knowledge are equally important in the course. She also underscored the importance of personalizing content information in knowledge acquisition. As shown by the students' comments, their understanding of "content learning" in language courses seems to have been substantially refined during the semester. Personal meaning construction is a naturally occurring process during reading in college students when reading in their L1. This is not always the case, however, in FL reading when students are not expected to achieve deeper text understanding for analysis and reflection. If the incorporation of content learning in language instruction triggered the realization that "learning" in the language classroom involves more than transmitting information in the target language, this and other dual-focused approaches could potentially empower college students to engage in a discovery mode of learning in a FL.

Effectiveness of Assessment-Driven Instruction

The positive changes in student engagement seem attributable to the assessment-driven design used in this approach. As shown above, the instructor clarified the course objectives, assessment procedures, and evaluation criteria at the beginning of the course. She also reminded the students of the procedural details of the assessments and outcome expectations throughout the semester. The instructor used each round of clarification as a basis for adjusting and refining her instruction and feedback. Student questionnaire responses indicate that the initial clarification helped them understand what they were expected to do, and that motivated them to work hard to meet the expectations. Clearly, the assessment-driven design raised students' metacognitive awareness, and heightened awareness led to a notable increase in their motivation and engagement. According to students, the frequent feedback the instructor provided during the class helped them monitor their progress. The instructor's reflection also suggests that the assessment-driven design reinforced her understanding of the framework, which allowed her to maintain procedural consistency in planning and delivering instruction and assessment activities.

It should be noted, however, that the instructor is knowledgeable about the theoretical underpinnings of the approach. It is not clear to what extent her research expertise played a role in the successful implementation. As mentioned earlier, the approach has been implemented in other EFL courses in Japan. It might be useful to compare learning outcomes, student engagement, motivation, and other related changes across diverse EFL courses and programs.

Multiple Integrations

The implementation of the integrated approach, as its name might suggest, requires multiple integrations of diverse curricular elements. The approach's dual foci demand a seamless integration of the two instructional goals—language development and knowledge acquisition. The assessment-driven design requires careful alignment of assessment with the construct, reading-to-learn, as well as with instruction. A system of assessments implemented in the project also entails another layer of integration to bring together various types and forms of assessment given at the lesson, unit, and course levels. Without integration and alignment, none of the key elements of success (i.e., concrete, explicit, consistent, and iterative) could have occurred in this implementation. We also underscore the value of the specifications of the focal construct in joining all the elements together; they allowed us to clarify the learning objectives and use them as the basis for designing and adjusting the rest of the curricular elements.

Intellectual Challenges

A striking reaction to the approach shared by students was their appreciation of and satisfaction with the intellectual challenges they experienced in the approach implemented in the course. Recall that the instructor did not change the textbook and used a subset of passages from the textbook as the input source in the course. Apparently, the instructional material does not explain the sense of fulfillment expressed by students. One possible explanation is that a self-discovery mode of learning through personal meaning construction and knowledge refinement may have led students to deeper levels of conceptual engagement. If so, a clear implication is that we could intellectually stimulate collegiate FL learners through conceptually challenging tasks with linguistically level-appropriate input source materials and sufficient linguistic scaffolding.

In closing, in today's world, there have been growing demands for individuals with high levels of proficiency in a foreign language (American Council on the Teaching of Foreign Languages [ACTFL] 2015). It is vital for the language teaching community to address such needs through innovative approaches to FL instruction and assessment. This chapter has described a framework built around the concept of reading-to-learn as the basis for designing an assessment-driven approach that utilizes assessments in creating, monitoring, and modifying materials intended to enhance learning. The observed improvements in the focal skills, as well as the heightened motivation reported by students, seem indicative of the approach's potential for maximizing the utility of assessment as the primary means of promoting deeper learning and understanding through sustained engagement.

References

American Council on the Teaching of Foreign Languages. 2015. *World-Readiness Standards for Learning Languages*. New York: American Council on the Teaching of Foreign Languages.

Banchi, Heather, and Randy Bell. 2008. "The Many Levels of Inquiry." *Science and Children* 46:26–9. http://www.miscagrant.umich.edu/lessons/files/2013/05/The-Many-Levels-of-Inquiry-NSTA-article.pdf.

Boyer Commission. 1998. *Reinventing Undergraduate Education: A Blueprint for America's Research Universities*. Washington, DC: US Department of Education.

Britton, Bruce. 1994. "Understanding Expository Text: Building Mental Structures to Induce Insights." In *The Handbook of Psycholinguistics*, edited by Morton Ann Gernsbacher, 641–74. San Diego: Academic Press.

Caccamise, Donna, Lynn Snyder, and Eileen Kintsch. 2008. "Constructivist Theory and the Situation Model." In *Comprehension Instruction: Research-Based Best Practices*, edited by Cathy Collins Block and Sheri R. Parris, 80–97. New York: Guilford.

Hulstijn, Jan H. 2015. *Language Proficiency in Native and Non-native Speakers*. Amsterdam: John Benjamins Publishing Company.

Koda, Keiko. 2016. "Development of Word Recognition in a Second Language." In *Reading in a Second Language: Cognitive and Psycholinguistic Perspectives*, edited by Xi Chen, Vedran Dronijc, and Rena Helms-Park, 70–98. London: Routledge.

Nakamura, Pooja R., Keiko Koda, and R. Malatesha Joshi. 2014. "Biliteracy Acquisition in Kannada and English: A Developmental Study." *Writing System Research* 6:132–47.

Sternberg, Robert J. 1999. "Intelligence as Developing Expertise." *Contemporary Educational Psychology* 24:359–75. doi:10.1006/ceps.1998.0998.

Chapter 5

◆ Using Assessment to Promote Learning

Clarifying Constructs, Theories, and Practices

CONSTANT LEUNG
King's College London

with

CHRIS DAVISON
University of New South Wales

MARTIN EAST
University of Auckland

MICHAEL EVANS and YONGCAN LIU
University of Cambridge

LIZ HAMP-LYONS
University of Bedfordshire

JAMES E. PURPURA
Columbia University

THE USE OF ASSESSMENT to promote learning has gained considerable traction in second or additional language education in the past twenty years. Terms such as 'assessment for learning,' 'dynamic assessment,' 'embedded assessment,' 'formative assessment,' 'learning-oriented assessment,' and 'teacher assessment' appear in research and professional journals regularly. The common theme that unites these pedagogically linked assessment approaches is their commitment to embed assessment in the teaching-learning process. The key question is: Do these different terms refer to a common underlying concept, or do they represent diverse conceptualizations and epistemologies in terms of learning, teaching, and assessment? In this chapter we present four accounts of actual and proposed innovations in the assessment of additional or foreign language learning. All the contributing authors have been, in one way or another, directly engaged with the development of the ideas and practices that they discuss; their voice is that of the experienced researcher and teacher educator reflecting on their own work.

Together, these four accounts, covering concrete professional experiences and theoretical issues, provide illustrations of the kinds of conceptual, theoretical, and implementational challenges that pedagogically linked assessments have to face. It is hoped that, by shining a light on these issues, we will be in a better position to address them in the future.

New Zealand

Embedding Assessment for Learning into a High-Stakes Assessment System

MARTIN EAST

At the turn of the century, New Zealand's high-stakes assessment system for high school students underwent a major transformation. The largely summative, norm-referenced, examination-dominated model was substantially refocused. The widespread introduction of internal (teacher-created and teacher-graded) assessments was intended to support "a standards-based approach, the emphasis on reporting more than on scoring, constructive alignment of learning and outcomes, peer collaborative assessment, learning intentions and success criteria, and the realization of the power of feedback" (Hattie 2009, 259). This was, in Hattie's words, a "revolution" that related to assessment for learning (AfL). The new régime—the National Certificate of Educational Achievement (NCEA)—was introduced in 2002. The NCEA operates at three levels (1, 2, and 3), aligned to the final three years of secondary schooling (Years 11, 12, and 13) and measuring increasing subject-relevant knowledge and understanding as students progress.

A key position paper (Ministry of Education 2011) underscores New Zealand's commitment to AfL. It encourages a move "beyond a narrow summative ('end point' testing) focus to a broader focus on assessment as a means of improving teaching and learning" (4). In this regard, "the design of the NCEA is such that it provides potential for assessment to be used formatively and to be an integral part of teaching practice" (14). Through internal assessments, teachers provide feedback on students' ongoing work in relation to the expectations of the assessment with a view to improving subsequent performances.

In practice, and emerging from a traditional model, the high-stakes nature of the system meant that principles such as accountability, validity, and reliability are still viewed as important. Consequently, external examinations remain a key part of the system and teachers' internal assessments are subject to review. Labeled 'quality assurance systems,' this review includes internal moderation of assessment tasks to make sure that all classes in the same school undertake comparable tasks (New

Zealand Qualifications Authority [NZQA] 2014b) and external moderation of samples of work to check that both tasks and awarded grades are in line with the national standard (NZQA 2014a).

These processes set up genuine tensions within the system. Essentially, a theoretical argument that the purpose of assessment is to enhance individual learning (assessment *for* learning) is potentially in conflict with an argument that the purpose of assessment is to measure performances in a standardized and uniform way (the assessment *of* learning). Teachers, who bring to classrooms their own beliefs and understandings about the aims of assessment, shaped by their own experiences, end up caught between two conflicting perspectives on what assessment should be about. In this kind of situation, they allow their own understandings to shape practice in ways that may run counter to AfL intentions.

Interact

A useful illustration of the tensions is a new learning-oriented assessment of foreign language (FL) students' spoken proficiency, called *interact*. Proposed as a consequence of the recent standards-curriculum alignment exercise, *interact* replaced a summative teacher-led interview test (*converse*) that had often led to largely rote-learned responses. *Interact* emphasizes authentic and unrehearsed student-initiated peer-to-peer interactions as they take place in the context of ongoing classroom work. In the course of the academic year, and as students deal with different themes or topics in class, teachers may set up opportunities for students to talk spontaneously with each other on issues related to the theme or topic, and students may record these interactions for assessment purposes. Feedback on students' interactions is designed to enhance their interactional proficiency (also referred to as interactional competence). At the end of the year, students submit what they and their teachers regard as their two best pieces of interactional evidence, and teachers provide an overall summative grade.

Theoretically at least, deliberate attempts were being made via this reform to move away from the artificiality imposed by a summative interview test and toward assessment evidence emerging from and aligned to teaching and learning goals, given the specified assessment use of improving teaching and learning. In practice, accountability requirements (e.g., moderation of assessment tasks) have meant that naturally emerging evidence of learners' interactional proficiency in the context of teaching and learning becomes overshadowed by a tendency to separate out the assessment from the teaching and learning as a means of standardizing and controlling the evidence collection. Thus, attention is drawn to the assessment as a separate event (tantamount to a test). A tension is set up between assessment for learning and the assessment of learning.

Tensions in Theory and in Practice

A recent research project drawing on survey and interview data (East 2016) brings out the tensions when seen from an AfL perspective. A summary of key emerging issues is provided below.

On the positive side, survey respondents noted that *interact* represented a movement toward more authentic use of the FL between students in contrast to students simply responding to their teacher's prepared questions. For example, students were encouraged and supported to use the kinds of language that would sustain real-world conversations with first-language speakers (such as interjections, asking questions, and making requests for clarification), and to employ these strategically to demonstrate a level of genuine and spontaneous interaction. Interactions targeted at a lower level of proficiency (NCEA level 1) might be about weekend plans or subject options, providing students with opportunities to share and justify different choices. At a higher proficiency level (NCEA level 3), interactions might require students to discuss opposing viewpoints on an issue of controversy (for example, the gay marriage debate in France and New Zealand; the relevance of the popular Japanese cat café concept for New Zealand). In respondents' words, it was anticipated that, as a consequence of the new assessment, students would come to see the FL as "a living language spoken by millions of people around the world" (East 2016, 113). The assessment compelled students to interact more authentically and "think what it would really be like" (116) in the target country. This made the assessment "a more accurate measure of the student's ability to respond to an interaction in a real-life situation" (116).

However, two key challenges indicated a perceived mismatch between assessment for learning and a more static assessment of learning perspective. There was evidence to suggest that both teachers and students interpreted the requirements of *interact* through a more traditional end-point testing lens. For example, since this was "still an examination after all and they want to do well," it could be "hard not to have students scripting speaking tasks" because "they [found] it almost impossible to do this in unrehearsed situations" (East 2016, 129). This led to a perception that an emphasis on spontaneity was unworkable. Also, when viewing each interaction as a test, perceptions of impracticality loomed large: workload was seen to have increased because what was once a single snapshot, end-of-year, interview test was now being replicated across the year as teachers and students worked to collect appropriate evidence. It was perceived as "unrealistic to expect the busy teachers to do this!" (127).

Interview data corroborated survey findings. One teacher (Janine) comments, "with our girls it's very hard to get them to be spontaneous because they are nervous and they want to script it, they want to write it down and … just keep doing it until it's perfect." She concludes, "it's a pity—but I can understand because at the end of the day you do have criteria to meet for excellence" (East 2016, 139).

It seemed that genuine spontaneity was hindered by conditions of assessment that required both internal and external moderation of assessment tasks, thereby calling attention to the assessment as a distinct event. In turn, the assessment was being compromised. In Peter's words, the original idea was "to record students talking to one another rather than to their teacher, off the cuff and unrehearsed, and like you would actually do if you were in the country." In practice, *interact* was "not turning into that." When students know that the interaction contributes to assessment, "they prepare everything and they basically learn scripted things, and then they add in a few minor phrases or hesitation phrases or whatever to make it sound more authentic." Peter concludes, "it turns into an assessment circus" (East 2016, 139). In this context, a perception of impracticality was not surprising.

It seems the assessment authorities, while in *theory* encouraging samples of authentic language use, in *practice* encourage a testing model. This is not necessarily deliberate, but is a consequence of the assessment conditions. These conditions emphasize accountability and measurement perspectives more aligned with assessment *of* learning. A conceptual mismatch emerges between what the authorities *say* they want to happen and what happens *in practice*. Consequently, when teachers, who bring to the assessment their own understandings based on past experiences, are still often perceiving the interactions through a testing lens, the evidence of spoken proficiency derived from *interact* assessments, and therefore the usefulness and learning potential of the assessment, are arguably compromised.

Australia (national, initially Victoria/New South Wales)

Tools to Enhance Assessment Literacy for Teachers of English as an Additional Language (TEAL)

CHRIS DAVISON

The Australian approach to AfL is best captured by the New South Wales (NSW) Board of Studies (NSW Assessment Resource Centre [ARC], n.d.), which argues that AfL has had worldwide success in enhancing teaching and improving student learning: "Assessment for learning gives students opportunities to produce work that leads to development of their knowledge, understanding and skills. Teachers decide how and when to assess student achievement, as they plan the work students will do, using a range of appropriate assessment strategies including self-assessment and peer assessment" (NSW ARC, n.d.). In this approach, AfL highlights the interactions between learning and manageable assessment strategies that promote learning; it clearly reflects a view of learning in which assessment helps students learn better (i.e., assessment should not just be about pushing students to get a higher mark). It also provides ways for students to use feedback from assessment, encourages students to take responsibility for their own learning, and above all it is inclusive of all learners.

However, for such an assessment paradigm to make a difference to learner achievement, especially for students from linguistically and culturally diverse backgrounds, schools and teachers need to be granted a high degree of trust and autonomy in the design, implementation, and timing of assessment tasks. Students also need to be given sufficient time and support in order to demonstrate their best—to show what they *can do*—and for teacher-assessors to be able to confidently assess their output, and even more importantly, 'test' their own informal judgments of students' language levels and achievements. Also necessary are more formal summative and formative assessment tasks that encourage the teacher to stand back and reflect on their implicit or explicit assumptions about individual students' capacities, compare those assumptions with careful analysis of examples of students' actual performance, and then subject their judgments to explicit scrutiny and challenge, or confirmation, by others. Research shows that such teacher assessment is never objective; the teacher always has preconceived ideas or assumptions about a student's level, and perhaps more importantly, their potential (see Lantolf and Poehner 2004). However, such assumptions must be made explicit and open to discussion with fellow teachers and the learners themselves. Trustworthiness comes from this process of expressing disagreements, justifying opinions with reference to criteria, work samples, and peer benchmarking. As Wiliam argues, "in order to maintain trust communities will have to show that their procedures for making judgments are fair, appropriate and defensible (i.e., that they are valid), even if they cannot be made totally transparent" (2001, 173–74). So a key goal for educational systems is to improve the ability of all key stakeholders to draw inferences or derive judgments from data, especially those who are meant to be doing the improving (i.e., students, parents, teachers, and policymakers). This can be achieved by establishing common understandings of the task, publicly agreed and explicit assessment criteria, and strong moderation processes as well as constructive feedback and concrete recommendations for improvement. Because there will always a problem of interpretation, professional dialogue and interaction have to be central to the decision-making process. These are inherent strengths, not weaknesses, of teacher-based assessment for learning systems.

The TEAL Project

Drawing on these AfL principles and a Vygotskian theory of learning, the Tools to Enhance Assessment Literacy for Teachers of English as an Additional Language (TEAL) project was funded for use in all Victorian schools as an online assessment source of guidance and toolkit (http://teal.global2.vic.edu.au/). The intent was to help more than forty thousand teachers assess the stage of development of EAL students in speaking and listening as well as reading and writing, and to improve learning and teaching. As the project originated in Victoria, all tools are aligned against the Victorian EAL Standards (VELS) and the EAL Developmental Continuum (Department of Education and Early Childhood [DEECD], n.d.), with potential for alignment to other standards by other jurisdictions in Australia.

The online EAL assessment resources, launched in mid-2015, attract more than ten thousand page views per month from over twenty countries. The website includes four main components: (1) a set of sequenced teacher professional learning resources about EAL and AfL, including self-assessments, designed for small groups or self-directed study; (2) an assessment tool bank containing a range of assessment tools and tasks organized around the three broad macro-skills (oral, reading, and writing), three macrofunctions (informative, persuasive, imaginative), three stages of schooling (early elementary, middle to upper elementary, and secondary), and a range of EAL proficiency levels; (3) a range of AfL and teaching exemplars, including a selection of annotated units of work across a range of subject areas and year levels, showing assessment tasks with formative feedback embedded within a teaching-learning cycle; and (4) an online teacher discussion forum, including a password-protected area for teachers to share problems and strategies and to moderate or benchmark work samples. As part of the toolkit, there is an assessment system for the collection and analysis of student oral and written language samples and exemplars aligned with the EAL continuum to provide information on students' English language and literacy development, including strategies for evaluating students' L1 and literacy development. There is also a bank of reading and vocabulary items linked to texts used in a computer adaptive testing system aligned with the EAL continuum to provide information on students' L1 and English language and literacy development at four age-related assessment points (grades 3, 5, 7, and 9). Within each component, the project has drawn on the specific professional knowledge of EAL teachers in collecting, evaluating, and developing exemplar school-based assessment materials, tasks and strategies, writing, and critical review of assessment tasks items, and in providing feedback on existing and recommended assessment practice.

Tensions in Theory and in Practice

The success of the TEAL resource, which has been used in more than two thousand schools and with more than a hundred thousand students at all age levels, demonstrates that with support and collaboration, teachers and researchers can build an assessment system that puts the learners and their learning at the center of the assessment process. External validations have found the system to be theoretically and philosophically coherent, capable of modeling desired outcomes and scaffolding and supporting sustainable improvements in assessment, learning, and teaching. For these reasons the system is contributing to the building of an assessment-literate community of not just teachers, but also students, parents, and other key stakeholders. Results of backwash studies and other external evaluations show that the resources help teachers adopt differentiated, contextualized, tailor-made assessment practices that also have commonality, consistency, and public confidence.

However, even in such a supportive EAL and assessment environment, there continue to be a number of challenges (Davison and Leung 2009). One key challenge is the need to consolidate the place of multilingualism as the central assumption of the TEAL assessment tools; that is, to build recognition of the fact that all EAL learners come to English in and through a huge range of other languages. This affects every aspect and stage of the process of assessment, including

- communicating the role and purpose of assessment to students and parents in their dominant language;
- assessing all the students' languages and literacies at point of entry into an EAL program;
- evaluating how they draw on and use their first and additional languages in learning and using English;
- drawing on their first language skills and competencies to understand and explain some characteristic features of their English language development; and
- ensuring feedback to parents and students is provided in languages which they know and can understand, so that they can make sense of and actually use the assessment information they have been given to improve.

Another key challenge is to maintain the balance between the measurement and formative feedback or feed-forward functions of the tools, so that neither assessment purpose dominates nor undermines the other. Given that each of these functions is enhanced by the presence of the other, it is important to maintain a system that provides high quality information to all stakeholders in a form that is tailored for their needs. For example, educational systems generally want more backward-looking, quantitative, aggregated data about a large range of language learners to account for their expenditure of public resources, whereas the individual student or teacher needs highly contextualized and individualized data that they can use to feed forward to improve the language and literacy of one particular language learner. A conceptual challenge has been educating all stakeholders about the needs and perspectives of the other, in order to build an assessment system that integrates the two functions so the same data can be used for the two different purposes. This raises the related but more practical concerns of how to provide access for all stakeholders to upload and retrieve information that is useful for them (that is, not just administrators but teachers and students), and how to ensure sustainability for the assessment system through building a cohesive and collaborative community of practice that will continually evaluate and enhance the tools. Other challenges will undoubtedly emerge as more and more students, teachers, and systems use TEAL to improve their assessment processes and practices, and thereby enhance EAL learning and teaching.

The United Kingdom

PEST Principles at Play in Assessment Innovation Contexts

LIZ HAMP-LYONS

All education innovation is subject to external conditions or constraints that, as a generalization, are often referred to as PEST—political, economic, social, and technological—principles (Alderson 2000; Collins 2001). This account briefly describes two projects that attempted assessment innovation, in order to illustrate the reality that even attempts at change designed to be humanistic and empowering may appear threatening to some stakeholders.

Context 1. Hong Kong: The School-Based Assessment of English Project

Chris Davison and Liz Hamp-Lyons developed a teacher-assessed component of student speaking for the senior secondary school system for the Hong Kong Examination and Assessment Authority (HKEAA) in 2006 (Davison and Hamp-Lyons 2010; Hamp-Lyons 2016). The HKEAA wanted to improve Hong Kong students' ability to use spoken English (as a second language) with confidence and accuracy through school-based assessment for learning (SBA). At the same time the authority also wanted the SBA component to have a summative aspect.

Initially Chris Davison and Liz Hamp-Lyons worked with forty teachers for a year, designing teaching and assessment materials, developing scoring structures, trialing the materials, and holding feedback meetings with teachers. The SBA component consists of a reading or viewing program where students read or view three texts (print, digital, fiction, and nonfiction material) over two years, keep a log book of comments and personal reflections, and then take part in a video-recorded discussion with classmates or make an individual presentation on the books, videos, and films that they have read or viewed. The assessment is focused on the student's speaking performance; the content of the reading or viewing is not directly assessed. The assessment criteria vary slightly for the two task types, but broadly cover pronunciation, communication strategies, vocabulary and language patterns, and ideas and organization. These speaking tasks take place in class within the teaching program, and are assessed by the class teacher supported by the subject team in school, and by SBA coordinators in their school district. The criteria were empirically derived and included some issues relating to language use in context, such as voice projection, making eye contact, and using body language to signal interest.

The forty teachers proved to be enthusiastic early adopters, and in the first year of implementation they were joined by a group of teachers from other schools, who were the "early majority" in Rogers's (1962, 2004) terminology. Other schools and teachers joined the initiative in the following two years until all Hong Kong schools were using this SBA component for English. After six years, follow-up studies of nearly seven thousand teachers undertaking professional development courses showed that there was growing adoption and acceptance of the underlying philosophy. Yet many teachers remained unconvinced or partial and reluctant adopters, not yet fully comfortable with applying SBA.

Tensions in Theory and in Practice

After six years of implementation, with steady official policy endorsement, the SBA still appeared to need further support. What were the reasons for this? Among the PEST principles probably most dominant were the sociocultural issues: Hong Kong families are heavily acculturated to "Confucian Heritage" values (Carless and Lam 2014), and are very aware of the power exams exert in a society where exam results are the major socioeconomic commodity for young people. There is, of course, also an economic factor: the dominant 'cram school' system in Hong Kong pressures families to invest in their children's exam preparation (Bray 2012). At the same time, teachers are severely overworked and underpaid. Politically, all aspects of education are organized by government, and within schools power lies with principals, not with teachers. For many teachers any test is an instance of the exertion of higher force and therefore a potential threat. Thus, a small technological innovation—the introduction of video-recording of students speaking—was initially seen as a threatening intrusion and as demanding new skills.

Context 2. Introducing Learning-Oriented Language Assessment within a Formal Standardized Test

Liz Hamp-Lyons and Tony Green (2013) introduced the term LOLA—learning-oriented language assessment—to acknowledge the special qualities and opportunities when the subject being assessed is language. Language should be readily assessable because learners are, at least in theory, performing their knowledge and skill in that subject continually in the classroom. However, as the PEST principles suggest, learning-oriented, interactional language assessment cannot be expected to succeed in the classroom unless conditions at wider levels—the school, the education system, the society—are sympathetic. With funding from Cambridge English Language Assessment, Hamp-Lyons and Green's study focused on whether a learning-oriented approach could be built into a formal test of spoken English. We developed a model for LOLA and road-tested it with one Cambridge English test (Cambridge English: First).[1] We studied a small sample of video-recorded speaking test events within this test and considered the extent to which a LOLA approach was evident in teacher-examiners' spoken interaction with exam candidates, and in teaching materials for Cambridge English: First preparation.

Figure 5.1 provides an overview of the key principles of LOLA, contrasted with the traditional practices and principles of large-scale testing.

We worked with a sample of ten fifteen-minute video recordings in which two test candidates of similar level were interviewed and given tasks by one interlocutor examiner in the presence of one observer-examiner. Paying special attention to the interlocutor-examiners, we found that speaking examiners are trained to avoid engaging in interaction with the candidates, which from some perspectives (particularly measurement perspectives) is appropriate for ensuring objectivity and consistency in scoring. But our analysis of the videos showed that examiners also seemed to avoid some good, effective interactional behaviors that facilitate test-takers' conversational engagement, such as making eye contact, smiling, and nodding, as well as inviting follow-on responses. Adhering to the rubrics, speaking examiners often seemed reluctant to manage turn-taking; and in test phases where candidates were

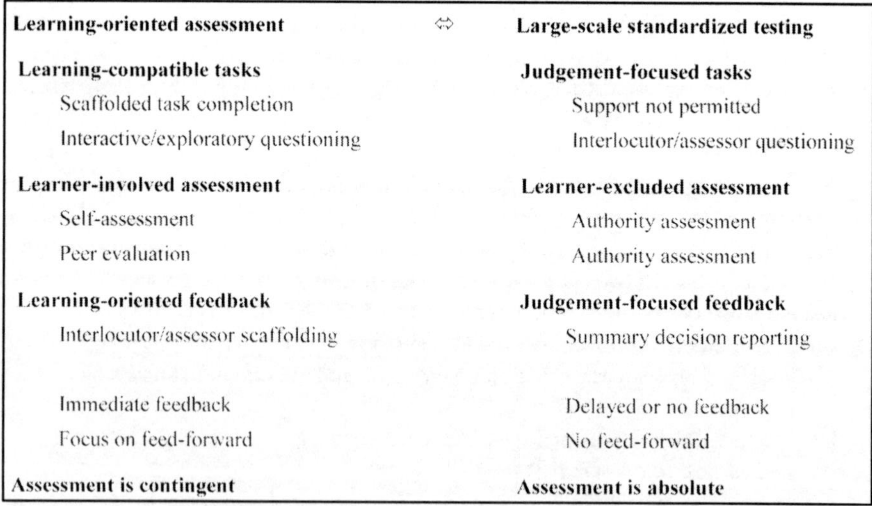

<table>
<tr><td>Learning-oriented assessment</td><td>⇔</td><td>Large-scale standardized testing</td></tr>
<tr><td>Learning-compatible tasks</td><td></td><td>Judgement-focused tasks</td></tr>
<tr><td>Scaffolded task completion</td><td></td><td>Support not permitted</td></tr>
<tr><td>Interactive/exploratory questioning</td><td></td><td>Interlocutor/assessor questioning</td></tr>
<tr><td>Learner-involved assessment</td><td></td><td>Learner-excluded assessment</td></tr>
<tr><td>Self-assessment</td><td></td><td>Authority assessment</td></tr>
<tr><td>Peer evaluation</td><td></td><td>Authority assessment</td></tr>
<tr><td>Learning-oriented feedback</td><td></td><td>Judgement-focused feedback</td></tr>
<tr><td>Interlocutor/assessor scaffolding</td><td></td><td>Summary decision reporting</td></tr>
<tr><td>Immediate feedback</td><td></td><td>Delayed or no feedback</td></tr>
<tr><td>Focus on feed-forward</td><td></td><td>No feed-forward</td></tr>
<tr><td>Assessment is contingent</td><td></td><td>Assessment is absolute</td></tr>
</table>

◆ Figure 5.1. An emergency model of learning-oriented language assessment and its contrasts with large-scale testing required to interact with each other, interlocutor-examiners avoided initiation of the interaction.

At the same time, we also felt that we could see a number of learning-oriented assessment micro-behaviors that speaking examiners could be trained to consciously practice in order to set up a "bias for the best" environment just before a formal assessable moment. Even the small matter of making eye contact with a candidate can make a difference: Candidates appeared to respond faster and more confidently when they had already seen the examiner's gaze on them before the test prompt was spoken. Our analysis also suggested that the interlocutors could use prejudgment time for LOLA purposes: For example, between the presentation of task and a judgment being made, a task could be reformulated if the interlocutor-examiner sees that the candidate is unclear; the assessable moment can begin after the reformulation.

We also looked at current teacher support resources (test prep materials) promulgated by Cambridge, and found them good in many ways, but having relatively few LOLA features. Although the related learning-oriented assessment (LOA, as opposed to LOLA) literature calls for assessment tasks that are authentic representations of real-world task types (Turner and Purpura 2016), we found little guidance for teachers on how the speaking tasks can embody features of tasks from contexts other than the examination room. Other central concerns in LOLA, such as the provision and use of feedback or engaging learners in evaluating their own performance, were also given very limited attention. However, there was no pedagogic incompatibility between preparing for these tests and LOLA. Learner engagement and effective feedback could be presented as essential tools for the test preparation classroom, by emphasizing links to local curriculum, learner needs, and longer-term learning goals, and by providing more guidance to teachers on feedback mechanisms. Moving toward a LOLA approach in test prep would make it easier to incorporate LOLA into the speaking test event itself.

Tensions in Theory and in Practice

In terms of PEST issues, there would seem to be few financial obstacles to a learning-oriented language assessment ethos in the materials and the tests, since the Cambridge tests are bought by many thousands of test-takers every year. That said, perhaps even small changes to the test might jeopardize the income stream. Change is always challenging for big test agencies since huge numbers of teachers, institutions, families and even countries are invested in the status quo. In fact, following research by Lazaraton (1996) on Cambridge examinations and by Brown (2000) on the IELTS, a more tightly scripted format using interlocutor "frames" was introduced to constrain examiner variations in interviewing behaviors. A follow-up study by Brown (2003) shows that the revised frames had the desired effect, and since then the interlocutor frame approach has been added to the Main Suite tests. Brown (2003) wonders whether the changes may have gone too far, and our study suggests that may be the case.

We do not know whether Cambridge Assessment intends to introduce our recommendations, and our report has not appeared so far in the internal Research Reports, though we have spoken to examiners who do favor such changes. One might argue that, since the current Cambridge model is economically successful—why change it? But Cambridge Assessment does have a history of gradual, careful but positive change.

Adjusting examiner behavior would inevitably involve some technological challenges and financial consequences, especially in terms of retraining all speaking examiners. But among the PEST issues, technological issues are probably the least difficult to solve. The proposals we made in our full report included many elements that could be piloted and introduced gradually. The main issues seem to be sociopolitical: a potential for a clash between entrenched expectations about what an assessment system should look like, and the research-led perceptions of language and assessment experts about what a valid speaking assessment should aim for.

This project suggests that innovative assessment initiatives are unlikely to be successfully introduced, unless more attention is given to teacher assessment literacy in pre-and in-service teacher education and examiner training, and unless innovative initiatives are integrated into a learning oriented assessment environment. It also suggests that those who create and deliver the big tests need to have the courage to try out new approaches, and view these trials as part of developing an assessment use case within test validation.

UK (England)

Dynamic Assessment for English as an Additional Language

YONGCAN LIU AND MICHAEL EVANS

Among many pressing issues in relation to English as an additional language (EAL) in the schooling provision, assessment remains the most significant one due to its immediate and long-term impact on EAL children's achievement. A recent survey of schools we conducted in the East of England suggested a wide diversity of EAL assessment practices and considerable eagerness for external support and direction on this issue (Evans et al. 2016). Surprisingly, however, given the high-stakes consequences of educational attainment, there is no national assessment framework for EAL in England (although a set of English-language proficiency descriptors have been introduced recently to screen newly arrived students: see UK Department for Education 2016), and teachers have been using a wide range of disparate materials for this purpose. Yet, these assessment tools are usually based on the conceptualization of competence as a fixed ability and one that focuses on determining the students' past achievement. Understandably, schools are keen to know what newcomer migrant children have achieved academically prior to arrival and how ready they are linguistically for mainstreaming in the host school. For EAL children from a disadvantaged background in particular, however, what really matters is not past achievement, but a recognition of their potential and the opportunities for future development. To realize these goals, we need to, first and foremost, have faith in the modifiability of human capabilities (Feuerstein, Feuerstein, and Falik 2010). On that basis, we can further explore the following questions:

1. Where does the potential of EAL children with different social, cultural, and linguistic backgrounds lie?
2. How can we modify their capacities in order to develop their potential?

We argue that these questions can be addressed through dynamic assessment (DA), which is essentially a structured program of learning during assessment through teaching.

Feuerstein's Dynamic Assessment Model

One of the most successful DA programs so far is perhaps that of Reuven Feuerstein and his colleagues, originally developed in the 1970s (Feuerstein, Rand, and Hoffman 1979; Feuerstein et al. 1980). Feuerstein's methods focus on redevelopment of the cognitive capacities in interventions through providing the conditions deprived of them, and it has two core components. The first is the Learning Propensity Assessment Device (LPAD), which includes a battery of adapted tests of intelligence and cognitive ability that can be used in a dynamic and interactive way with the affected children. The examiner or teacher, by providing prompts and dialogic instruction, is enabled to identify the domains with potential for development based on the amount of assistance the children need to complete the tasks. The second component is Feuerstein's Instructional Enrichment (FIE) program. This is a structured learning program that targets the specific domains identified as showing potential for development. In this program, students are coached by their examiner or teacher to use learning strategies to complete a series of tasks intended to reinforce the structural change in their cognitive capacities. Through more than half a century's work, a considerable amount of empirical, clinical, and classroom evidence has been gathered, which demonstrates a statistically and qualitatively important effect of DA on the affected children.

Dynamic Assessment for EAL

DA is based on the fundamental principle of sociocultural theory, which argues that the human mind is mediated (Vygotsky 1978). Language development, as a kind of higher mental functioning, can thus be seen as emerging as a result of cultural mediation (see Lantolf and Poehner 2014; Poehner 2008). As discussed before, prior to arrival in the host country many EAL children will not have shared access to the same sources of cultural mediation as their peers in the new school, because their lives and school experiences are severely disrupted before arriving in the United Kingdom. In other words, they are deprived of the normal experiences that enable them to develop, cognitively and linguistically. In DA terms, they lack the "mediated learning experience" (MLE; Feuerstein, Feuerstein, and Falik 2010) that is needed to succeed in the English school system. It is therefore reasonable to argue that we are not in a position to identify EAL children's potential for development unless we understand accurately to what extent their learning capacities can be modified when the MLE conditions are provided through the DA for EAL program and how well they can respond to different cultural stimuli in the intervention.

In this program, we seek to develop a specific Language Propensity Assessment Device for Reading (LPAD for R) and the companion Instructional Enrichment Program for Phonological Awareness (IEP for PA), which can be seen as the application of the two core components in Feuerstein's DA model in the context. More specifically, we propose a focus on raising the level of phonological awareness in the reading of new arrivals who have limited English, and we argue that the acquisition of phonological awareness skills will lead to early reading development (Bialystok 2001), which is best achieved through DA. The DA framework provides a practical structure for assessing and scaffolding the development of such skills, including, for example, rhyme production and recognition, word and phoneme discrimination, and phoneme and syllable segmentation. In LPAD for R, we will draw upon a range of existing instruments of phonological awareness that are widely used in literacy and early reading. These assessment instruments will be piloted and validated to suit the specific needs of EAL children. For IEP for PA, we will adapt some reading instruction materials widely used in the professional community with a particular focus on the scaffolding of phonological awareness.

In summary, the DA for EAL program aims to achieve two goals: (1) to identify the domains of phonological awareness in relation to reading that are susceptible to modifiability (Stage 1), and (2) to (re)develop EAL children's structural change in language awareness, which can be transferred to other learning reading tasks (Stage 2).

Epistemologically DA differs from traditional norm-based and standardized assessment which highlights the direct relationship between independent learning and human development. Rather, it embraces a sociocultural epistemology which argues that the relationship between learning and development is not direct but mediated by external cultural tools. In the DA for EAL program, this MLE is reflected in the fact that there are two stages in the program. The first stage aims to identify the domains with the potential for development as well as the cultural tools that can stimulate this development, while the second stage aims to develop self-regulated learners who can fully control the cultural tools provided and use them independently and autonomously in similar or more complex situations. It is this transition from explicit awareness to fluency of practice that has hitherto been a weak point in the DA perspective but which in the EAL domain can be addressed through the mediating process targeting learner self-regulation of the language to be learned.

Internal and External Tensions
Internal Tensions

While Feuerstein's model of DA is predicated on the principle of selective use of the strategy in particular contexts and with particular groups of learners, especially refugee children who suffer from extreme social, cultural, cognitive, linguistic, and health disadvantages, its application in the EAL context involves an extension of scope and interacts with bilingualism-related factors of reading development, which is considered an important skill in early learning. This additional dimension is very likely to trigger unforeseen conceptual and diagnostic issues.

While DA focuses on potential, there is still a need to take account of what is to be achieved in the mainstream school curriculum. As the mainstream school curriculum specifies both content- and age-related attainments, the scope for individual-oriented DA for EAL is likely to be highly constrained. This will call for research and curriculum development related to the different ways of using and learning English in different curriculum activities so that individual learner needs are met.

External Tensions

The implementation of a DA system of EAL support in schools entails overcoming practical considerations which condition the introduction of an intensive pedagogical scheme based on assessment-intervention-practice within the mainstreaming context of the schooling of EAL children in England. Potential external constraints are, on the one hand, lessened by the current absence of a centralized policy on EAL assessment and provision in schools. On the other hand, recent reforms granting greater financial and educational autonomy to state schools, accompanied by an absence of accountability for the expenditure and provision, has led to an unevenness of provision across schools, the closure of related local authority services, and the employment of fewer suitably qualified professionals to coordinate policy and practice in schools. Within such a policy context, this will inevitably raise the issue of teacher training, which plays an important role in dynamic assessment in terms of providing appropriate mediation for EAL students in an ethical way.

Concluding Remarks

It is quite clear that a complex web of conceptual, educational, and epistemological considerations underlies the four accounts of for-learning assessment presented above. Perhaps this is not surprising. Unlike the one-off, stand-alone nature of large-scale assessment in the form of externally produced standardized examination and tests, for-learning assessment is embedded in pedagogic practice involving a large number of stakeholders working in particular institutional and policy environments. Diversity of approaches and practices seems to be the norm. Nevertheless, it would be useful to try to identify the underlying distinguishing themes or features if we are to achieve some analytic purchase on this complex phenomenon. Firstly, context is important. All four accounts of development and innovation are situated in particular educational and sociocultural environments. They have all emerged as a response to an existing assessment regime in different ways. The introduction of new ideas has to be worked into the available affordances and opportunities within the existing professional cultures and practices, with varying levels of success (in the case of the proposed DA, probabilities of success). Secondly, unlike the much greater control on what is to be assessed (i.e., construct) by standardized test developers, teachers involved in for-learning assessment have to grapple with ambiguities and diverse student needs, as well as curriculum expectations. For instance, in the case of TEAL, teachers themselves are arrayed along different positions when assessing student work; in the case of *interact*, teachers appear to struggle with what counts as 'authentic' language use; and in the case of DA, the focus on individual learner needs may be incompatible with the specifications of a mandated curriculum. Thirdly, there are different conceptualizations of learning. DA (the type adopted by Liu and Evans), for example, is undoubtedly cognitive in orientation, whereas the LOLA principles are unquestionably interactionist in approach. Fourthly, the attention to language, or more precisely the conceptual and structural features of language, varies a good deal. The DA approach in the present account is clearly linguistically oriented whereas situated language use is valued in *interact*. The TEAL experience points to an additional issue—namely, the monolingual conceptualization of language and language use—potentially leading to under-recognition of students' multilingual repertoires and their diverse language learning trajectories (also see Turner and Purpura 2016 for a related discussion).

In sum, the four accounts of for-learning language assessment here offer much food for thought. There are many other conceptual aspects of these attempts at innovative practice that can be discussed. The four themes identified here—context, construct, learning, and linguistic focus—can be seen as a set of interlocking issues that can begin to help us explore the diversity in for-learning assessment in a systematic inquiry in relation to the nature of the knowledge being assessed, the practices being adopted, and the assumptions underlying what counts as learning.

Note

1. Cambridge English: First, formerly the First Certificate in English (FCE), is an English-language test widely administered internationally for educational and workplace decision-making.

References

Alderson, J. Charles. 2000. "What Does PESTI Have to Do with Us Testers?" In *Discourses and Development in Language Education*, edited by Joseph Hung, Vivien Berry, Vernon Crew, and Chris Davison, 215–34. Hong Kong: Chinese University Press.

Bialystok, Ellen. 2001. *Bilingualism in Development: Language, Literacy and Cognition*. Cambridge: Cambridge University Press.

Bray, Mark. 2012. "Wolves Lurking in the Shadows of Education." *South China Morning Post*, July 19.

Brown, Annie. 2000. "An Investigation of the Rating Process in the IELTS Oral Interview." In *IELTS Research Reports*. Vol. 3, edited by Robyn Tulloh, 49–84. Canberra: IELTS Australia.

———. 2003. "Interviewer Variation and the Co-Construction of Speaking Proficiency." *Language Testing* 20 (1): 1–25.

Carless, David, and Ricky Lam. 2014. "Developing Assessment for Productive Learning in Confucian-Influenced Settings." In *Designing Assessment for Quality Learning*, edited by Claire Wyatt-Smith, Valentina Klenowski, and Peta Colbert, 167–79. Dordrecht, Nld.: Springer.

Collins, James. 2001. *Good to Great: Why Some Companies Make the Leap... and Others Don't*. Glasgow: HarperCollins.

Davison, Chris, and Liz Hamp-Lyons. 2010. "The Hong Kong Certificate of Education: School-Based Assessment Reform in Hong Kong English Language Education." In *English Language Assessment and the Chinese Learner*, edited by Liying Cheng and Andy Curtis, 248–62. New York: Routledge.

Davison, Chris, and Constant Leung. 2009. "Current Issues in English Language Teacher-Based Assessment." *TESOL Quarterly* 43 (3): 393–415.

Department of Education and Early Childhood. N.d. "The EAL Developmental Continuum P-10." Melbourne: DEECD.

East, Martin. 2016. *Assessing Foreign Language Students' Spoken Proficiency: Stakeholder Perspectives on Assessment Innovation*. London: Springer.

Evans, Michael, Claudia Schneider, Madeleine Arnot, Karen Forbes, Linda Fisher, and Yongcan Liu. 2016. *Language Education and Educational Achievement: The Opportunities and Challenges in the Education of EAL Students*. Cambridge: Bell Foundation.

Feuerstein, Reuven, Rafael Feuerstein, and Louis Falik. 2010. *Beyond Smarter: Mediated Learning and the Brain's Capacity for Change*. New York: Teachers College Press.

Feuerstein, Reuven, Ya'acov Rand, and Mildred Hoffman. 1979. *The Dynamic Assessment of Retarded Performers: The Learning Potential Assessment Device (LPAD)*. Baltimore: University Park Press.

Feuerstein, Reuven, Ya'acov Rand, Mildred Hoffman, and Ronald Miller. 1980. *Instrumental Enrichment: An Intervention Program for Cognitive Modifiability*. Baltimore: University Park Press.

Hamp-Lyons, Liz. 2016. "Implementing a Learning-Oriented Assessment in Hong Kong." In *Assessing Chinese Learners*, edited by G. Yu and Y. Jin, 17–37. London: Palgrave Macmillan.

Hamp-Lyons, Liz, and Anthony Green. 2013. "Seeking Opportunities for a Learning-Orientation in the Context of a Large Scale Speaking Test. Final Research Report Submitted to Cambridge English Language Assessment." Unpublished manuscript.

Hattie, John. 2009. "The Black Box of Tertiary Assessment: An Impending Revolution." In *Tertiary Assessment and Higher Education Student Outcomes: Policy, Practice and Research*, edited by Luanna Meyer, Susan Davidson, Helen Anderson, Richard Fletcher, Patricia M. Johnston, and Malcolm Rees, 259–75. Wellington: Ako Aotearoa.

Lantolf, James P., and Mathew E. Poehner. 2004. "Dynamic Assessment of L2 Development: Bringing the Past into the Future." *Journal of Applied Linguistics* 1 (1): 49–74.

———. 2014. *Sociocultural Theory and the Pedagogical Imperative in L2 Education: Vygotskian Praxis and the Research/ Practice Divide*. New York: Routledge.

Lazaraton, Anne. 1996. "Interlocutor Support in Oral Proficiency Interviews: The Case of Case." *Language Testing* 13 (2): 151–72.

Ministry of Education. 2011. *Ministry of Education Position Paper: Assessment (Schooling Sector)*. Wellington: Ministry of Education.

New South Wales Assessment Resource Centre. N.d. "Assessment for Learning in the Years 7–10 Syllabuses." https://arc.nesa.nsw.edu.au/go/9-10/afl.

New Zealand Qualifications Authority. 2014a. "External Moderation." http://www.nzqa.govt.nz/ providers-partners/assessment-and-moderation/managing-national-assessment-in-schools/ secondary-moderation/external-moderation/.

———. 2014b. "Internal Moderation." http://www.nzqa.govt.nz/providers-partners/assessment-and-moderation/managing-national-assessment-in-schools/secondary-moderation/ external-moderation/internal-moderation/.

Poehner, M. E. 2008. *Dynamic Assessment: A Vygotskian Approach to Understanding and Promoting L2 Development*. New York: Springer.

Rogers, E. 1962. *Diffusion of Innovation*. London: Simon and Schuster.

———. 2004. "A Prospective and Retrospective Look at the Diffusion Model." *Journal of Health Communication* 9 (S1): 13–19.

Turner, Carolyn, and James E. Purpura. 2016. "Learning-Oriented Assessment in Second and Foreign Language Classrooms." In *Handbook of Second Language Assessment*, edited by Dina Tsagari and Jayanti Baneerjee, 255–72. Boston: De Gruyter, Inc.

UK Department for Education. 2016. *School Census 2016-2017*. London: UK Department for Education.

Vygotsky, Lev Semenovich. 1978. *Mind in Society: The Development of Higher Psychological Processes*. Cambridge, MA: Harvard University Press.

Wiliam, Dylan. 2001. "An Overview of the Relationship between Assessment and the Curriculum." In *Curriculum and Assessment*, edited by David Scott, 165–81. Westport, CT: Ablex Publishing.

Winke, Paula. 2011. "Evaluating the Validity of a High-Stakes ESL Test: Why Teachers' Perceptions Matter." *TESOL Quarterly* 45 (4): 628–60.

Part Two

Innovating, Framing, and Exploring Assessment in Language Education

Chapter 6

Linguistic Correlates of Proficiency (LCP)

At the Intersection of Testing and Teaching

SVETLANA V. COOK, SHAUNA J. SWEET, ALIA LANCASTER, NICHOLAS B. PANDŽA, SCOTT R. JACKSON, ERIC PELZL, KIRA GOR, and CATHERINE J. DOUGHTY
University of Maryland

LANGUAGE PROFICIENCY ASSESSMENT PLAYS an important role in a wide range of contexts related to foreign language learning, from relatively low-stakes evaluation and placement applications to high-stakes applications such as job requirements or eligibility for incentive pay. Proficiency itself is a broad construct, but typically focuses on the idea of *functional* ability, in the sense that certain levels of proficiency are aligned with the ability to function in certain broad capacities in the language.

Three commonly used functional proficiency scales include the Interagency Language Roundtable (ILR) scale, the American Council on the Teaching of Foreign Languages (ACTFL) scale, and the Common European Framework of Reference (CEFR) scale. Each of these scales provides a global description of learners' speaking, listening, reading, or writing proficiency in a target language in terms of discrete levels, on a scale of 0–5 (ILR), Novice to Superior (ACTFL), or Basic User (A1) to Proficient User (C2; CEFR). Each of these scales is designed to be functionally equivalent across languages, such that someone earning an ILR rating of 3 in Speaking in Persian and someone earning that same rating in Spanish demonstrate the same level of functional proficiency: both learners are "able to speak the language with sufficient structural accuracy and vocabulary to participate effectively in most formal and informal conversations in practical, social and professional topics" (ILR 2011). The ILR scale was developed prior to the other scales, and development of both ACTFL and CEFR has drawn many insights from it and also inherited many of its limitations.

Because they are language agnostic, an inherent limitation of these scales is that they lack detailed linguistic descriptions of each proficiency level. To accommodate a variety of language typologies, descriptions of functional proficiency have to be sufficiently broad. To illustrate, in the description of speaking proficiency at ILR 0+ we read: "Most utterances are telegraphic; that is, functors (linking words, markers and the like) are omitted, confused or distorted" (ILR 2011). This statement covers a wide range of linguistic phenomena, which have different realizations in different languages with different implications for instruction. For example, in Persian, the above descriptor could refer to a learner's inadequate grasp of the grammatical system (e.g., object marking) and for Mandarin Chinese, it could be referring to a lexical problem (e.g., a learner's difficulty with classifiers). In addition to being vague this descriptor is potentially inaccurate: research demonstrates that it is not the case that all linking words, markers, and "the like" are expected to pose an equal challenge to learners at a given stage of development (Dulay and Burt 1974; Larsen-Freeman 1995). Moreover, omission and distortion of the same functors can signal different learning challenges, each of which may require a different instructional approach to remediation (e.g., Pienemann 1998).

If a scale is to be used diagnostically as guidance for future pedagogical interventions, then the level of description in these language-agnostic scales offers minimal insight to instructors or to learners. Standardized assessments of functional proficiency, such as Oral Proficiency Interview (OPI) protocols or the Defense Language Proficiency Test (DLPT), use functional tasks, such as carrying out certain kinds of conversational tasks on different topics, or answering comprehension questions about different kinds of texts. The resulting score from these assessments, however, is not readily interpretable in an instructional context. The score locates the test-taker on a standardized scale, but simply knowing that a learner is currently a 2 or an Intermediate High does not provide any information as to what they are struggling with linguistically, or what they need to improve in order to advance to the next level. The problem is exacerbated at higher levels, because of the breadth of expectations for learner performance at those levels. Is a learner struggling to achieve an ILR 3 (professional proficiency) due to a lack of appropriate high-level vocabulary, or do they have significant gaps in their grammar such that they struggle with constructions typical of higher-level texts, or are they oblivious to important pragmatic aspects such that they completely misread tone or communicative intent? These are all things that could prevent a learner from reaching higher proficiency levels, but a score of 2 or 2+ on an OPI or DLPT does not provide any indication of the problems a particular learner faces, or even what problems are typical for learners in that language at that level.

Although a language-agnostic approach to functional proficiency level descriptors may be insufficient to usefully inform instruction, it does not mean that functional proficiency scales should be abandoned altogether. They provide linguists, instructors, and learners alike with a common and standardized metric for comparing language proficiencies across typologically diverse languages. What the current systems lack, however, is a direct mapping of the language-independent skill descriptors to language-specific features, which can inform classroom practice and future refinement of proficiency assessment criteria. This is precisely the gap the Linguistic Correlates of Proficiency (LCP) batteries aim to fill, through the identification and empirical testing of appropriate sets of language-specific linguistic features, and how performance on these features aligns with different functional proficiency levels. Performance on these batteries may provide more fine-grained evidence for learners' individual learning trajectories and identify possible gaps in their language knowledge and use.

The currently developed LCP batteries aim to assess knowledge, skills, and abilities that are relevant for and distinguish between learners with functional proficiency at levels 2, 2+, and 3 on the ILR scale,[1] which is roughly equivalent to Advanced Low/Mid, Advanced High, and Superior on the ACTFL scale.[2] Learners within this proficiency range are mostly self-sufficient in meeting routine social demands and can function in a professional environment with varying degrees of support, understand most everyday conversations and written texts, and demonstrate an emerging ability to understand nonliteral aspects of meaning such as implication, speaker attitude and intent, and "reading between the lines."

In the development of the LCP batteries, there are two main challenges in providing diagnostic information on more detailed linguistic features while aligning with global proficiency scales. The first challenge is essentially a challenge of sampling—identifying the best subset of linguistic features to test for a given language. The second challenge is to make battery development parallel across languages in a meaningful way, despite the fact that all features tested are inherently language-specific.

It is practically, and perhaps even theoretically, infeasible to test *all* of the linguistic features of any given language. The question is how to select a useful subset of features to be included in a test battery. Linguistic features included on an assessment must be theoretically motivated and empirically justified, and must reliably measure learners' abilities. Test items need to target a sample of features that is sufficiently broad to be representative of advanced proficiency without resulting in an unnecessarily long instrument that overwhelms the test-taker. Study 1 below summarizes preliminary results of research examining the performance of sampled items.

Assessment of learners in this higher range of proficiency also presents some unique challenges. Advanced learners have already acquired, at least to some degree, many aspects of grammar, morphology, and vocabulary being tested, and in order to differentiate between learners at these higher levels, measures that go beyond simple accuracy may be useful. Second language acquisition (SLA) research suggests that the mastery of a linguistic feature is reflected in the automaticity of performance in using this feature (e.g., DeKeyser 2007), which means that cognitive performance measures, such as processing speed in certain kinds of tasks, could potentially aid in differentiating between degrees of mastery over a feature. To this end, we have included some tasks that integrate reaction time (RT) measures as well as accuracy. We discuss an examination of a potential application of RT measures in Study 2.

A broad goal of this research is not merely to develop batteries for specific languages, but to also build a framework for developing additional LCP batteries in new languages, especially under-resourced or less commonly taught languages (LCTLs). This is important work particularly since it is not possible to align assessments across languages on a feature-by-feature basis, precisely because languages differ at this level of description. Put another way, achieving high levels of functional proficiency in languages that are typologically diverse does not necessarily require a command of the same linguistic features.

We have therefore begun to develop an approach that frames language-specific features as belonging to a set of linguistic domains that *are* common across different languages. As shown in table 6.1 and described in the following paragraphs, several subdomains are identified within each of these major domains, and tasks are developed which measure learners' proficiency with respect to each of these subdomains. Instead of developing tasks that are parallel at the features level, in the current LCP framework, the parallel structure is at the level of measured knowledge, skills, and abilities (KSAs). These KSAs are common across languages, though the selection of linguistic features used to assess them are necessarily language-specific. The composition of these KSAs and their organization into domains and subdomains with different processing levels offers a new, and arguably more tractable, approach for achieving a parallel structure across language batteries, which nevertheless complements the description of language-agnostic functional abilities that characterizes traditional proficiency scales such as the ILR and ACTFL scales. We propose that this structure is particularly promising for the investigation of crosslinguistic patterns in the alignment of linguistic development and functional language proficiency.

The process of selecting linguistic features to be tested as well as designing the particular tasks best suited to measure ability in these features is a complex and multistep process. Before a representative sample of features can be selected, a broad selection of candidate features relevant to a particular domain and subdomain for the target language need to be identified. Furthermore, the sampled features must distinguish between learners within a targeted proficiency range, which requires that there be some theoretical or empirical rationale identifying such features as being relevant to the developmental trajectory in L2 learners for a particular language. Within each domain or subdomain, the construct being measured is that of the test-taker's *linguistic ability*, where the performance of a native speaker of the language represents the end-point or maximum of this scale.

This means that there are two basic criteria to establish whether a particular measurement of a particular feature is appropriate for inclusion in an LCP battery. First, the measurement of a feature must track with another assessment of global proficiency. Otherwise, the feature is either irrelevant for progression through the proficiency range being tested, or it is simply too unreliable or variable between learners at these levels. Second, because we are measuring detailed linguistic features and not functional proficiency directly, a typical native speaker of the language is identified as the top of the dimension being measured in the LCP. Therefore, any feature measurement in which native speakers (NSs) do not consistently test close to ceiling performance is not a good candidate for inclusion. In short, the LCP batteries are intended to measure a construct that is *distinct* from functional proficiency (i.e., native-like linguistic ability), but nevertheless *correlates* with functional proficiency in a useful way, in order to provide additional diagnostic information regarding learners' developmental path to higher proficiency.

◆ **Table 6.1.** Mapping of LCP features to linguistic domains and subdomains

KSA* Domains	Processing Level	Subdomains	Language-Specific Features
Phonological Perception	Phonemic/Syllabic Level	Segmental Type	
		Suprasegmental Type**	
	Word Level	Segmental Type	
		Suprasegmental Type**	
	Phonotactics		
Vocabulary	Word Level	Vocabulary Breadth	
		Vocabulary Depth	
		Word Formation**	Derivational Morphology
			Compounding Morphology
	Phrase Level	Collocations	
Morphosyntax	Word Level	Word Form Generation**	Inflectional Morphology
			Nonconcatenative Morphology (Introflection)
	Phrase Level	Local Dependencies**	Agreement
			Government
	Sentence Level	Contextualized Dependencies	Construction
			Comprehension

Note: * KSA = Knowledge, Skills, Abilities; ** denotes subdomains that may not be robust in some languages

The purpose of the studies described below is to test whether the framework we have developed for selecting and measuring candidate features leads to measures that satisfy these basic criteria. The first study focuses on a grammaticality judgment task (GJT) in which accuracy is assessed, and the second study explores the use of a RT or processing-based measure.

Study 1

In this section we describe an attempt to apply the principles of feature selection outlined earlier. The main research goal of the feature selection process can be formulated in a question: Did the selected tasks measure linguistic ability within the target domain? Answering this question is comprised of three parts: for each task it was important to demonstrate that NSs perform uniformly well, as well as to show that learners who are not yet native-like perform consistently below the native threshold, but also that there is sufficient variation in scores across the proficiency ranges (e.g., there are no severe floor or ceiling effects for particular tests). The results below are from a Russian GJT and demonstrate that even theoretically sound and pedagogically supported features can deliver unexpected results.

Participants

Participants in the study included forty-eight L2 learners of Russian who were English NSs (twenty-three male), and thirty-one native Russian speakers (ten male). The mean age of the L2 learners was 23.50 years ($SD = 5.33$); the mean age of the NSs was slightly older, 30.84 ($SD = 8.84$). Russian learners were recruited from Russian language programs at various universities in the United States. All L2 learners began learning Russian as adults, with an average age of onset for learning of 18.21 years ($SD = 3.44$), average classroom learning of 3.2 years ($SD = 2.13$), and an average immersion experience in the country of the target language of 2.2 years ($SD = 1.71$). L2 participants' language proficiency was measured via an officially administered ILR OPI. Those included in the analysis were identified as advanced learners of Russian, with four learners at an ILR level of 2, fourteen learners at ILR 2+, twenty-six learners at ILR 3, and four learners at ILR 3+. Consistent with the official testing protocol, interview scores were double-blinded.

Testing Protocol

The Russian GJT consisted of 150 items in each of two counterbalanced lists. Each participant saw one version of each item (grammatical or ungrammatical), but not both. Items were designed to test eleven grammatical structures, including aspect, gerund construction, numeral inflections, verbs of motion, and reflexives. For this study, difficulty of the items was rated by language experts and experienced instructors who ensured that the selected grammatical structures ranged in difficulty; that is, some features were expected to be fully acquired even at the lower end of the tested proficiency range, while others were expected to be only partially acquired or not acquired at all. Each item on the GJT consisted of a sentence that was either grammatical or ungrammatical, which the test-taker needed to read and assess. The experiment was programmed in DMDX (Forster and Forster 2003). Each sentence was presented on the screen in four clearly numbered regions, all displayed at once. The participants were asked to press the number 5 key to indicate if the sentence was grammatical and had no errors, or the number keys 1–4 to identify which region (1, 2, 3, or 4) contained an error. Participants were given 15,000 milliseconds (ms) to respond to each item, after which the screen automatically advanced to the next item. On average, participants completed the GJT in 30 minutes.

Methods

Analyses presented in this section examine response data collected on L2 learner's performance on tasks targeting reflexives, verbs of motion, and numeral inflections. Because of the unique structure of the LCP, whereby each participant responds to multiple trials (or isomorphs) of the same target item (yielding a repeated measures structure), we analyzed the response data using logistic multilevel models (MLMs) in order to appropriately account for variance in the likelihood of producing an accurate response both within and between subjects and trials.

Separate MLMs were estimated predicting accuracy on tasks featuring reflexives, verbs of motion, and numerical inflections. In each case, the dependent variable was the likelihood of learners' producing an accurate response to each trial. Models featured fixed effects to capture the impacts of grammaticality and proficiency on learners' accuracy. Tasks were either coded grammatical or ungrammatical; ILR proficiency scores were coded "2" for ILR 2, "2.6" for ILR 2+, and "3" for ILR 3. A two-way interaction between proficiency and grammaticality was also included in the model, as well as cross-classified subject and item random effects, both intercepts and slopes (Baayen, Davidson, and Bates 2008; Linck and Cunnings 2015). All analyses were performed using the lme4 package in R (Bates et al. 2015; R Core Team 2015).[3]

Reflexives. Model-based estimates of the impacts of grammaticality and proficiency on performance are shown in table 6.2 below.

Table 6.2. Results of the logistic multilevel model for reflexives on the Russian GJT

Fixed effects	*b*	exp(*b*)	*SE*	*p* value
Intercept (grammatical, ILR 3)	1.53	4.62	0.20	<.001[*]
Grammaticality (ungrammatical)	−0.98	0.38	0.16	<.001[*]
Proficiency	1.13	3.09	0.36	.002[*]

Random effects		Variance	SD
Intercepts	Subject	.57	.75
Intercepts	Item	.20	.44

Grammaticality is significant, indicating that, controlling for proficiency, participants were about three times less likely to correctly reject an ungrammatical sentence compared to a grammatical one. Proficiency is significant, indicating that, controlling for grammaticality, participants were almost three times more likely to correctly respond to an item with each one-point increase in ILR (e.g., from ILR 2 to 3 or from ILR 2+ to 3+). Our analyses suggest that this effect of proficiency is consistent across both grammatical and ungrammatical conditions. We note descriptively that learners were performing near ceiling, at above 90% accuracy. Descriptive results of accuracy are displayed in figure 6.1 with NSs' performance on the task represented graphically for comparison.

Verbs of Motion. Model results are shown in the table 6.3 below. Descriptive results of accuracy are displayed in figure 6.2 alongside NSs' performance for comparison.

Of the effects tested, our results suggest that only grammaticality is significant, meaning that controlling for whether a sentence is grammatical or ungrammatical, proficiency has no effect on learners' accuracy on tasks featuring verbs of motion. Specifically, our analyses suggest that learners were about five times less likely to

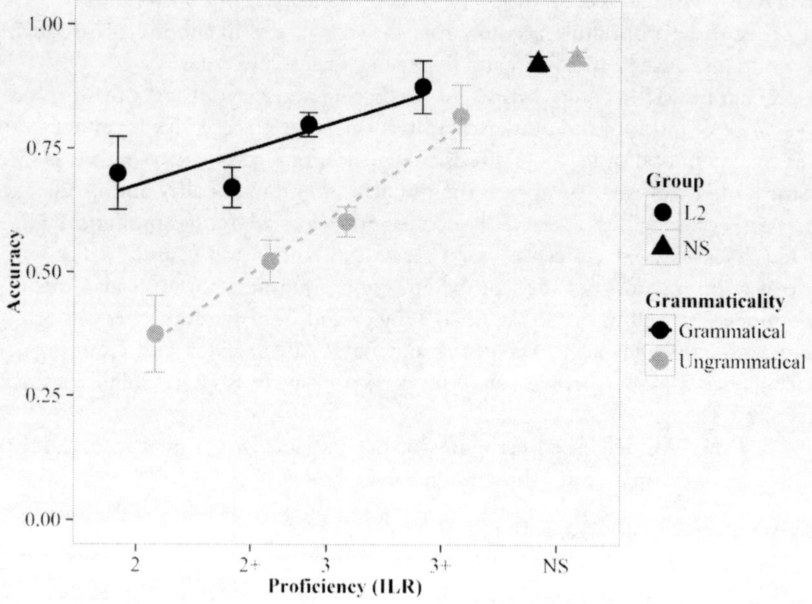

◆ Figure 6.1. Accuracy on reflexives from the Russian GJT

◆ Table 6.3. Results of the logistic multilevel model for verbs of motion on the Russian GJT

Fixed effects	b	exp(b)	SE	p value
Intercept (grammatical)	1.62	5.04	0.21	<.001*
Grammaticality (ungrammatical)	−1.57	0.21	0.16	<.001*

Random effects		Variance	SD
Intercepts	Subject	.87	.93
Intercepts	Item	.15	.39

correctly reject an ungrammatical sentence compared to a grammatical one. We also note that NSs only performed with approximately 80% accuracy on these tasks, as shown in figure 6.2 below.

Numeral Inflection. Model estimates predicting learners' accuracy are reported in table 6.4 below; and descriptive results of learners' and NSs' accuracy on these tasks are displayed in figure 6.3.

As shown in table 6.4, there is a significant interaction between grammaticality and proficiency. Results of these analyses reflect an interesting pattern in which higher proficiency learners perform less accurately on grammatical sentences, while at lower proficiencies, participants respond in the expected direction: less accurately to ungrammatical than grammatical sentences. As shown in figure 3, this pattern is driven primarily by the performance of learners with ILR 2. Further, we note that NSs are performing only at about 80% accuracy on both grammatical and ungrammatical sequences.

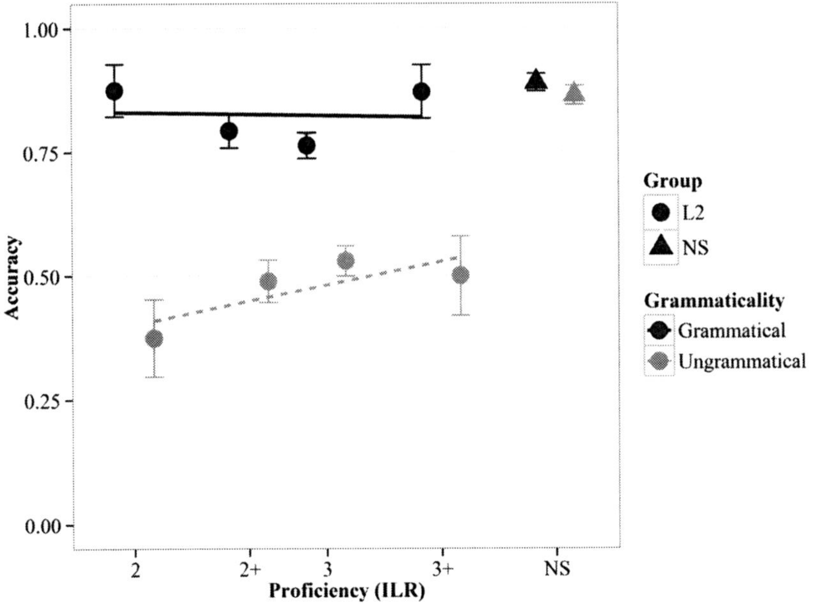

◆ Figure 6.2. Accuracy on verbs of motion from the Russian GJT

◆ Table 6.4. Results of the logistic multilevel model for numerals on the Russian GJT

Fixed effects	b	exp(b)	SE	p value
Intercept (grammatical, ILR 3)	0.55	1.73	.26	.03*
Grammaticality (ungrammatical)	0.30	1.35	.17	.08^
Proficiency	0.76	2.14	.40	.06^
Grammaticality × Proficiency	0.98	2.67	.44	.02*

Random effects		Variance	SD	
Intercepts	Subject	.47	.68	
Intercepts	Item	.84	.92	

Discussion

As noted above, in addition to having a theoretical rationale for inclusion, there are two initial empirical criteria that must be met by items on the LCP in order for those items to be considered candidates for inclusion in the battery: (1) items targeting sampled features must distinguish between learners within the targeted proficiency range such that performance accuracy is aligned with functional proficiency, and (2) NSs of the language must perform reliably with near-perfect accuracy on the task. Our results illustrate the ways in which some items targeting certain features met the required criteria for inclusion in future versions of the LCP (reflexives), while other sets of items did not (numeral inflection, verbs of motion), despite there

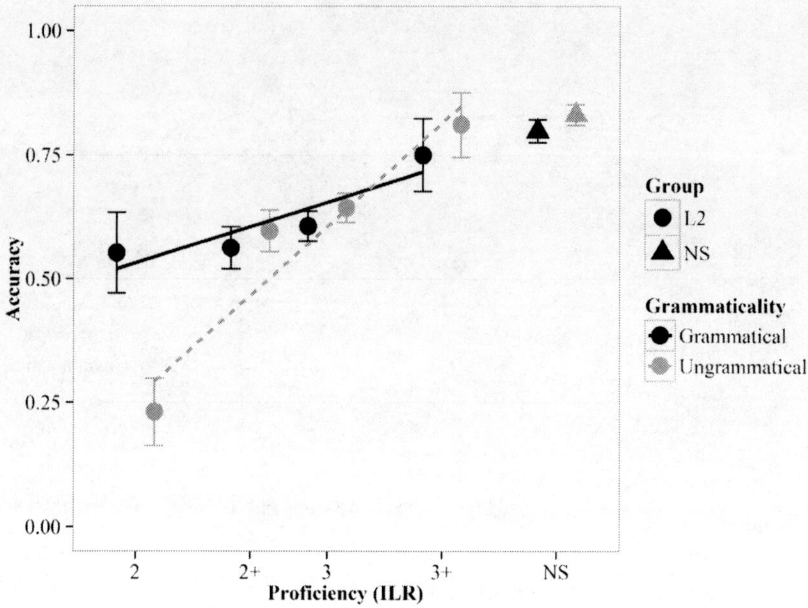

◆ **Figure 6.3.** Accuracy on numerals from the Russian GJT

being a strong theoretical rationale for their inclusion. Out of the three features, reflexives were the most successful and met both criteria for test inclusion. Native speakers performed near ceiling, and the L2 participants demonstrated stepwise increases in the accuracy of performance, which was consistent and reliable.

Although the relationship between proficiency and performance accuracy was still as we would expect for the numerical inflection items, the items failed to meet the second criterion: on average we found that the NSs made incorrect judgments of grammaticality on one in five trials. Because the LCP is ultimately measuring learners' linguistic ability, NSs are expected to be close to ceiling in accuracy; however, as we see with the numerals, this is not the case. The most likely explanation for the low accuracy in NSs is the fact that inflected numerals, though a grammatically complex domain of Russian language, are being phased out of the Russian language and are often avoided by NSs. Items targeting verbs of motion also failed to meet the first empirical criterion: increases in L2 speakers' proficiency was not associated with higher accuracy on GJT items targeting fluency with verbs of motion. Overall, L2 speakers' accuracy when judging ungrammatical items was very low, and accuracy on these tasks was highly variable even among learners who tested at an ILR 3+.

As we illustrate in this study, many theoretically motivated and proficiency matched grammatical features do not meet the criteria for inclusion in the test. One of the main challenges of the language proficiency tests like LCP is to identify a limited subset of features that are sufficiently difficult for learners of the targeted proficiency, but are also able to reveal consistent gains from one level to the next toward native-like performance. As we have demonstrated, grammatical features that meet both criteria in a particular language—relative difficulty and consistent gains—can be extremely challenging to identify.

Study 2

The inclusion of a broad range of linguistic features on the LCP batteries is motivated by the stated goals of the assessment to provide a more fine-grained assessment of advanced learners' developing language abilities and skills. There are, however, practical limits to how many features can be included effectively in a battery. Utilizing cognitive performance measures, such as latent response times, are one way to accumulate stronger evidence of test-takers' language proficiency with targeted features without adding more test items.

While the utility of cognitive performance measures for proficiency assessment is still an open question, there is a large body of evidence that suggests that their use deserves further consideration. Reaction time studies (see Posner 1978 for a review) have consistently demonstrated that response times are sensitive to linguistic factors, such as lexical frequency, complexity of grammatical patterns, and number of similar patterns or words (for reviews, see Brysbaert et al. 2011; Ellis 2002). Second language research has further expanded the utility of RT studies by examining additional (nonlinguistic) factors that may contribute to individual differences in response latencies, including test-takers' working memory capacity or attentional control. Studies have shown that when these factors are controlled for, there is sufficient variability in test-takers' reaction times to support inferences about test-takers' automaticity of control over the linguistic structure(s) being targeted by a task. Reaction times are therefore correlated with second language proficiency (Jiang 2004; Keating and Jegerski 2015; Phillips et al. 2004; Segalowitz, Segalowitz, and Wood 1998). In addition to recording the accuracy of learners' performance, many tasks on the LCP are therefore designed so that reaction times are captured, in order to provide evidence of how efficiently linguistic knowledge is applied in real-time language processing—a critical component of advanced language proficiency (e.g., DeKeyser 2007; Favreau and Segalowitz 1983; Segalowitz, Segalowitz, and Wood 1998). The following section discusses an analysis of test data from an Arabic lexical decision task (LDT) to illustrate how RT measures complement accuracy measures to provide a more complete picture of advanced language learners' abilities.

Testing Protocol

Items that make up the LDT within the LCP are designed to assess learners' phonemic sensitivity to problematic, or "confusable," L2 contrasts when they are embedded in words. There are certain types of consonants that are particularly difficult for second language learners of Arabic whose native language is English. Gutterals are one such type, because they are produced relatively far back in the oral cavity (e.g., pharyngeal fricatives) and are unlike any sounds produced in the English language. Emphatics are another set of consonants that are typically problematic, because they have secondary pharyngeal articulation and are difficult to distinguish from their nonemphatic counterparts (e.g., /s/ vs. /sˤ/). The LDT evaluated how well, during auditory speech perception, L2 learners resolved challenges of phoneme identification and discrimination when listening to sequences of nonsense sounds (nonce words) and to actual words. Success with this task required that learners successfully evoke bottom-up phonological representations to distinguish between problematic contrasts with top-down lexical access processes to simultaneously accessing lexical representation, a skill which is believed to correlate with the increases in overall language proficiency (Darcy, Daidone, and Kojima 2013; Cook et al. 2016).

At the beginning of the LDT, test-takers were instructed to listen to Arabic words and other sounds sequences (i.e., nonce words). They were informed that some stimuli sounded like Arabic words, but did not exist as such, and were instructed to indicate if each stimulus was a real Arabic word or not as quickly and as accurately as possible. Seventy items examined the perception of confusable phonemes in Arabic words, comprising a portion of the critical conditions in LDT (other conditions not reported here); the task took participants approximately twenty minutes to complete. Each trial began with a fixation point, "*," which appeared when the audio stimuli begin to play. Participants were instructed to press the right response button if the sound combination was a real word, or the left response button if it was a nonce word. If no response was given after 4,000 ms, the next trial began automatically.

Real word stimuli were selected due to the presence of confusable phonemes, such as emphatic /sˤ/, which NSs of English often confuse with the nonemphatic version /s/, both of which exist in Arabic. Nonce word stimuli were created by replacing one confusable phoneme with another, and all were judged by an NS not to be words in the Arabic lexicon. For example, we replaced the emphatic phoneme in /fasˤl/ (class) with the nonemphatic /s/ to create the nonce word /fasl/. Accurate identification of the lexicality of both the real and nonword, requires that learners be able to accurately perceive these problematic phonemes in Arabic words. In addition to confusable phonemes, we also presented real and nonce words with control phonemes (i.e., those that exist in both Arabic and English). For instance, the /r/ in /buruz/ (prominence) was replaced with /l/ to create the nonce word /buluz/. Two lists were created such that one participant would hear either a real word (e.g., /fasˤl/) or a nonce word (e.g., /fasl/) of the same pair.

Actual words included in this task were selected from a frequency dictionary of Arabic that lists the top five thousand most frequent words in Modern Standard Arabic (Buckwalter and Parkinson 2011), to ensure the words would be those with which advanced L2 learners would be familiar. The ratio of actual words to nonce words presented during the task was 1:1 in order to deter participants from adopting a response strategy. All stimuli were produced by one male native Arabic speaker. Each production was normalized in loudness to 73.6 dB and had a 50 ms silent buffer prior to and following the stimulus.

It was expected that learners would be more accurate and faster when reacting to real word targets than to nonce targets with confusable phonemes, but that this difference would be smaller for control phonemes (i.e., nonce words with control phonemes would be easily classified as nonce words by the learners). The goal of these analyses was to determine the extent to which reaction times could be used to complement accuracy information as evidence of learners' Arabic proficiency.

Participants

Study participants included forty-two L2 learners of Arabic (nineteen male) who were English NSs, and fourteen Arabic speakers (eight male). The mean age of the L2 learners and the NSs was comparable, with the learners' at an average of 23.5 years ($SD = 5.33$), and NSs at a mean age of 26.57 ($SD = 6.74$). Study participants were recruited from Arabic language programs at various universities in the United States. L2 participants spent on average 3.70 years ($SD = 2.41$) in the classroom, and 0.67 years ($SD = 1.05$) in a language immersion environment in an Arabic-speaking country. The average age of onset for learning Arabic was 17.64 years ($SD = 5.78$) for the L2 learners.

For this study, L2 learners' proficiency was measured using a cloze test. Twenty words were deleted from a shortened version of an authentic text (i.e., written for native speakers by a native speaker), and learners were instructed select one of three options for each blank. Deletions and response options were carefully selected to assess learners' fluency with a variety of morphological, lexical, and grammatical features. The shortened text and response options were checked by a NS for comprehensibility. Learners' cloze scores ranged from 3 to 18 out of maximum possible score of 20 with a mean of 13.6 ($SD = 3.78$), and were approximately normally distributed ($W = 0.97, p = 0.239$).

Methodology

Similar to the analysis of the Russian GJT data, a multilevel modeling approach was utilized to examine the relationships between (1) learners' proficiency and accuracy and (2) learners' proficiency and reaction times to tasks on the Arabic LDT.[4] For models predicting accuracy, a logistic MLM was utilized; for models predicting RT, log-transformed RT data was used. RT data was also trimmed to exclude responses with times equal to 0 ms or 3,000 ms, where 3,000 ms indicates the response timed-out. Response times exceeding three standard deviations of each participant's individual response time variation were also excluded, eliminating 2.56% of total observations. For the purposes of this chapter, we present a series of models from our analyses that regress the likelihood of learners' accuracy on proficiency and task conditions, including lexicality of the target (real or nonce word), phoneme status of the phonemes contained in the target (confusable or control), and cloze (continuous and centered), as well as those interactions between conditions that were determined to be significant via backward testing of fixed effects. The models also feature cross-classified random person and item intercepts to account for the particular design of the LCP battery. These models discussed here were selected to have adequate model-data fit to support interpretation of parameters as well as answer specific questions about task performance.

Results

Table 6.5 indicates that nonce words containing confusable phonemes were more likely than not to be incorrectly identified as real words by L2 speakers of average proficiency. A significant three-way interaction between lexicality, phoneme status, and cloze suggests that the difference in likelihoods of correctly identifying

◆ **Table 6.5.** Arabic LDT results of logistic multilevel modeling for accuracy

Fixed effects	b	exp(b)	SE	p value
Intercept (confusable phoneme, nonce word)	−0.54	0.58	0.21	.012*
Lexicality (real word)	1.66	5.24	0.30	<.001*
Phoneme Status (control)	1.64	5.14	0.30	<.001*
Cloze	0.04	1.04	0.03	.197
Lexicality × Phoneme Status	−1.49	0.22	0.43	.001*
Lexicality × Cloze	0.12	1.12	0.04	.003*
Phoneme Status × Cloze	0.10	1.10	0.04	.012*
Lexicality × Phoneme Status × Cloze	−0.12	0.89	0.06	.036*
Random effects	**Variance**	**SD**		
Intercepts	Subject	0.91	0.96	
Intercepts	Item	0.06	0.24	

Note: *Significant at $p < .05$; ˆMarginal at $p < .10$.

confusable nonce- and real-word targets is different than that of control real- and nonce-word targets, and that the magnitude of that difference is affected by proficiency. As proficiency increases, accuracy in identifying confusable nonce words remains low, while accuracy for all other target types increases. Thus, as Arabic L2 learners become more proficient, they are better able to recognize real-word targets containing control and confusable phonemes as real words and are better able to correctly reject nonce-word targets containing control phonemes. However, rejecting nonce words with confusable phonemes remains a challenge. Descriptive results of accuracy are displayed in figure 6.4 with proficiency grouped into low ($n = 15$), mid ($n = 14$), and high ($n = 13$) proficiency according to cloze score for ease of interpretation, but cloze scores were entered continuously into the MLM.

As shown in table 6.6, cloze score did not significantly influence participants' RT to the confusable nonce targets ($b < 0.01$, $SE = 0.01$, $t = 0.18$), but cloze did influence the difference in reaction times between real and nonce words with confusable phonemes ($b = −0.02$, $SE = 0.01$, $t = −1.96$).[5] As illustrated in figure 6.5, lower proficiency learners have similar reaction times among all target types, but higher proficiency learners tend to have a slower RT to nonce targets containing confusable phonemes.[6]

Discussion

Results from the analysis of accuracy and RT complement one another to provide a more complete picture of L2 learners' developing proficiency. Models of accuracy suggest that as their proficiency increases, learners are more likely to recognize real words and correctly reject nonce words with control phonemes. However, results also suggest that higher proficiency learners are no more likely than their peers to accurately discriminate between confusable phonemes in nonce word targets. But

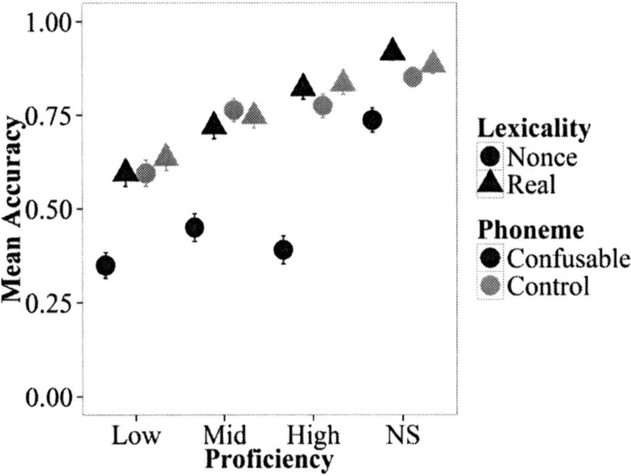

◆ **Figure 6.4.** Arabic LDT mean accuracy. Error bars represent +/− 1 SE

◆ **Table 6.6.** Arabic LDT results of linear multilevel modeling for reaction time

Fixed effects	b	SE	t-value
Intercept (confusable phoneme, nonce word)	6.15	0.07	88.68*
Lexicality (real word)	−0.05	0.05	−0.88
Phoneme Status (control)	−0.07	0.05	−1.34
Cloze	0.00	0.01	0.18
Lexicality × Cloze	−0.02	0.01	−1.96^
Random effects	**Variance**	**SD**	
Intercepts	Subject	0.04	0.21	
Intercepts	Item	0.10	0.32	

Note: *Significant at $p < .05$; ^Marginal at $p < .10$.

while proficiency does not impact accuracy under these conditions, there is an effect of proficiency on RT. Higher-proficiency learners are slower than lower-proficiency learners to respond to nonce words containing confusable phonemes. This pattern is consistent with information-processing theories of language learning whereby higher proficiency learners with greater knowledge and understanding of the language are sensitive to and spend additional time processing the target because they notice (though not consciously) the incorrect confusable phoneme that causes the stimulus to be a nonce word.

The outcome of this task illustrated that RT measures can give an insight into the stages of phonological development that accuracy measures fail to provide, and are able to deliver the granularity of information that can lead to a more accurate proficiency assessment.

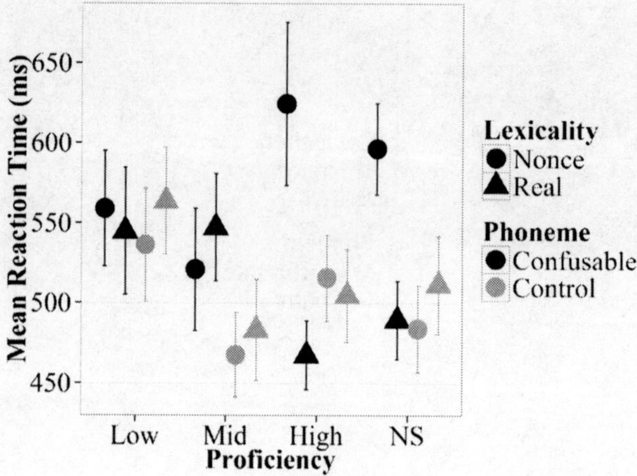

◆ **Figure 6.5.** Arabic LDT mean RT. Errors bars represent +/− 1 SE

LCP Future Directions

The current conceptual framework provides an important foundation for future research to evaluate the interpretation of test results and their utility for diagnostic applications. The original purpose of the LCP project was to investigate how linguistic knowledge aligned with functional proficiency levels as measured by global assessments such as the DLPT (Long, Gor and Jackson 2012). Current research, as the name suggests, is merely correlative: we expect that higher performance on the LCP tests will generally correlate with higher levels of functional proficiency. Correlation, however, does not imply causation; it is an empirical question whether or not a learner would achieve a higher proficiency score if they were to focus on specifically improving performance on those features relevant to the KSAs targeted by the LCP battery. Investigating this would be a worthwhile pursuit as we seek to build an evidence-based argument for improving LCTL language instruction.

Unlike commonly used standardized tests of language proficiency, each LCP is designed to measure the *developing* command of the linguistic features in the language. This is distinct from *functional* proficiency, which depends on other skills such as reading comprehension or reasoning ability. Functional proficiency is an ability to comprehend a sample of language by using various cognitive mechanisms, with some of them unrelated to linguistic knowledge, such as inference, correct interpretation of questions (which are in English for the DLPT), test-taking strategies, or reliance on background knowledge. As an example, most items included in the DLPT measure the ability of the learners to comprehend extended discourse, which typically spans several sentences or even multiple paragraphs. As many readers vary in the degree of their comprehension of what they read in their native language, so too do nonnative readers, irrespective of their level of proficiency in that language. In contrast, the LCP batteries assess linguistic features of the language and minimize the role of more general comprehension or test-taking strategies. The resulting measurement of performance is a more direct assessment of the learners' linguistic knowledge of the foreign language. Future integration of cognitive performance measures, such as RT, will further contribute to this goal.

The LCP is not intended as a replacement for functional proficiency tests, but taken together, global proficiency assessments and LCPs reveal a more complete picture of learners' foreign language ability. Crucially, learners' control of features is tightly aligned with functional proficiency levels, which makes it possible to use the results of LCP testing to aid in curriculum development and also to facilitate teachers' efforts to support advanced learners' continued progress. Specific sets of tasks target language-specific features in order to assess learners' phonological, morphological, syntactic, and lexical abilities. The particular tasks included in each LCP battery address a sample of those linguistic features that a learner should master when approaching higher levels of proficiency. It is also important to note that the specific features being tested are not exhaustive, but rather a representative sample of the language-specific features that measure proficiency within particular domains and subdomains of knowledge that are relevant to learners across languages. The developmental trajectory established for each feature in the LCP battery is an indication of the level of difficulty and the slope of the learning curve for this particular feature.

From the current framework there are other possible directions for future research that are worth mentioning, one of which is the expansion of the domains being assessed by the LCP batteries. One knowledge domain that is not currently a part of the structure described in this report is that of pragmalingusitic knowledge. That is, languages employ a range of different linguistic devices in order to capture nonliteral meanings such as implicature and attitude. Given the importance of pragmatic competence (e.g., reading between the lines) at higher proficiency levels and pedagogical demands for teaching pragmatics in the classroom, it is reasonable to expect that such features may be very valuable additions to the LCP batteries, especially given the stated research goals of measuring and describing the progress of learners at higher proficiency levels. Challenges inherent in this work include task development; assessment of features within this domain is still relatively novel, and much less established than the assessment of the types of features currently in the LCP batteries (see Roever 2011 for a review). Additional challenges in development include refinement of existing tasks. Testing times for the current LCP batteries range from two to three hours, and decisions to add features need to be balanced with testing considerations; replacement of features also requires additional validation work.

The research to date has demonstrated that the LCP batteries now in development provide a unique and potentially illuminating window into understanding the linguistic knowledge, skills, and abilities of advanced second language learners. Our results suggest that the descriptive profiles of learners generated using LCP methodology can complement and enrich the picture obtained by considering functional proficiency alone and can further assist instructors in identifying specific learning challenges for each individual learner. Empirical results from this research suggest that the breadth, depth, and specificity of information provided by these test batteries is not only promising for but potentially critical to informing and properly evaluating new methods in language learning and instruction for LCTLs. Future research directions promise to further explore the utility of the LCP batteries in practice.

Notes

1. The emphasis here is on listening and reading because these are the skills tested by the DLPT, the test of record throughout the US Department of Defense, and because LCPs currently only evaluate receptive modes of language use.
2. The ACTFL Proficiency Guidelines is the most widely used foreign language proficiency scale in education and academia.
3. For the purpose of this discussion we present results from a set of reduced models that provide adequate model-data fit to support interpretation of parameters and also allow us to answer the questions we are currently asking of task construction (e.g., are native speakers close to ceiling, and does the feature seem to track with proficiency).
4. For the linear MLM to analyze reaction times, we consider $|t| > 1.65$ as marginal ($p < .10$) and $|t| > 2.00$ as significant ($p < .05$) due to ongoing debate in calculating p-values for linear MLMs and the recommendation of Gelman and Hill (2007).
5. Note that the t-value is trending while the likelihood ratio test deems the term as a significant improvement to model fit.
6. Descriptive results of RT as a function of proficiency displayed in figure 6.5 are grouped into low, mid, and high proficiency according to cloze score for ease of interpretation, but cloze scores were entered continuously into the MLM.

References

Baayen, Harald, Douglas Davidson, and Douglas Bates. 2008. "Mixed-Effects Modeling with Crossed Random Effects for Subjects and Items." *Journal of Memory and Language* 59 (4): 390–412. doi:10.1016/j.jml.2007.12.005.

Bates, Douglas, Martin Maechler, Ben Bolker, and Steven Walker. 2015. "lme4: Linear Mixed-Effects Models Using 'Eigen' and S4." R Package Version 1.1–9. https://CRAN.R-project.org/package=lme4.

Brysbaert, Marc, Matthias Buchmeier, Markus Conrad, Arthur M. Jacobs, Jens Bölte, and Andrea Böhl. 2011. "The Word Frequency Effect." *Experimental Psychology* 58:412–24. doi:10.1027/1618-3169/a000123.

Buckwalter, Tim, and Dilworth Parkinson. 2011. *A Frequency Dictionary of Arabic: Core Vocabulary for Learners*. New York: Routledge.

Cook, Svetlana V., Nick B. Pandža, Alia K. Lancaster, and Kira Gor. 2016. "Fuzzy Nonnative Phonolexical Representations Lead to Fuzzy Form-to-Meaning Mappings." *Frontiers in Psychology* 7 (1449). doi:10.3389/fpsyg.2016.01345.

Darcy, Isabelle, Danielle Daidone, and Chisato Kojima. 2013. "Asymmetric Lexical Access and Fuzzy Lexical Representations in Second Language Learners." *Mental Lexicon* 8 (3): 372–420. doi:10.1075/ml.8.3.06dar.

DeKeyser, Robert. 2007. "Skill Acquisition Theory." In *Theories in Second Language Acquisition: An Introduction*, edited by Bill VanPatten and Jessica Williams, 97–113. Mahwah, NJ: Lawrence Erbaum.

Dulay, Heidi C., and Marina K. Burt. 1974. "Natural Sequences in Child Second Language Acquisition." *Language Learning* 24 (1): 37–53. doi:10.1111/j.1467-1770.1974.tb00234.x.

Ellis, Nick. C. 2002. "Frequency Effects in Language Processing." *Studies in Second Language Acquisition* 24 (2): 143–88. http://dx.doi.org/10.1017/S0272263102002024.

Favreau, Micheline, and Norman S. Segalowitz. 1983. "Automatic and Controlled Processes in the First- and Second-Language Reading of Fluent Bilinguals." *Memory & Cognition* 11 (6): 565–74. doi:10.3758/BF03198281.

Forster, Kenneth I., and Jonathan C. Forster. 2003. "DMDX: A Windows Display Program with Millisecond Accuracy." *Behavior Research Methods, Instruments, & Computers* 35 (1): 116–24. doi:10.3758/BF03195503.

Gelman, Andrew, and Jennifer Hill. 2007. *Data Analysis Using Regression and Multilevel/Hierarchical Models*. New York: Cambridge University Press.

Interagency Language Roundtable. 2011. "Interagency Language Roundtable Language Skill Level Descriptions – Speaking." ILR Speaking Skill Scale. http://www.govtilr.org/Skills/ILRscale2.htm.

Jiang, Nan. 2004. "Morphological Insensitivity in Second Language Processing." *Applied Psycholinguistics* 25 (4): 603–34. http://dx.doi.org/10.1017/S0142716404001298.

Keating, Gregory D., and Jill Jegerski. 2015. "Experimental Designs in Sentence Processing Research." *Studies in Second Language Acquisition* 37 (1): 1–32. http://dx.doi.org/10.1017/S0272263114000187.

Larsen-Freeman, Diane. 1995. "On the Teaching and Learning of Grammar: Challenging the Myths." In *Second Language Acquisition: Theory and Pedagogy*, edited by Fred Eckman, Diane Highland, Peter Lee, and Rita Rutkowski Weber, 131–50. Mahwah, NJ: L. Erlbaum.

Linck, Jared A., and Ian Cunnings. 2015. "The Utility and Application of Mixed-Effects Models in Second Language Research." *Language Learning* 65 (S1): 185–207. doi:10.1111/lang.12117.

Long, Michael H., Kira Gor, and Scott Jackson. 2012. "Linguistic Correlates of Second Language Proficiency." *Studies in Second Language Acquisition* 34 (1): 99–126. http://dx.doi.org/10.1017/S0272263111000519.

Phillips, Natalie A., Norman Segalowitz, Irena O'Brien, and Naomi Yamasaki. 2004. "Semantic Priming in a First and Second Language: Evidence from Reaction Time Variability and Event-Related Brain Potentials." *Journal of Neurolinguistics* 17 (2): 237–62. doi:10.1016/S0911-6044(03)00055-1.

Pienemann, Manfred. 1998. *Language Processing and Second Language Development: Processability Theory*. Studies in Bilingualism vol. 15. Amsterdam: John Benjamins Publishing.

Posner, Michael I. 1978. *Chronometric Explorations of Mind*. Oxford: L. Erlbaum.

R Core Team. 2015. "The R Project for Statistical Computing." R Foundation for Statistical Computing. http://www.R-project.org/.

Roever, Carsten. 2011. "Testing of Second Language Pragmatics: Past and Future." *Language Testing* 28 (4): 463–81. doi:10.1177/0265532210394633.

Segalowitz, Sidney J., Norman S. Segalowitz, and Anthony G. Wood. 1998. "Assessing the Development of Automaticity in Second Language Word Recognition." *Applied Psycholinguistics* 19 (1): 53–67. http://dx.doi.org/10.1017/S0142716400010572.

Chapter 7

Face-to-Face Speaking Assessment in the Digital Age

Interactive Speaking Tasks Online

LARRY DAVIS, VERONIKA TIMPE-LAUGHLIN, and LIN GU
Educational Testing Service

GARY OCKEY
Iowa State University

IN BUSINESS CONTEXTS, THE degree to which someone can interact smoothly and appropriately in spoken communication may have important consequences for establishing relationships with clients and collaborating with colleagues; accordingly, this ability is of interest for decisions such as hiring, promotion, or training. Making inferences regarding interactional ability requires evaluation of the resources that speakers bring to a given situation including the ability to smoothly execute turn-taking, collaborate in the development of topics, reproduce expected participation patterns, and generally establish a shared understanding of what is being communicated (Kramsch 1986; Young 2011). Unfortunately, current computer-based tests of speaking generally elicit monologic speech and so do not provide direct evidence of these resources. In contrast, face-to-face assessments have the potential to elicit direct evidence of interactional resources, but they are logistically complex to administer and consistency in administration and scoring can be challenging to achieve. However, with the increasingly widespread use of video-mediated communication tools such as Skype, it has become possible to assess spoken interaction using online video. This has the potential to combine the convenience and consistency associated with computer-based assessment with the ability to elicit samples of interactive language. Studies have investigated the possibility of using video-conferencing technology to deliver the International English Language Testing System (IELTS), a speaking test used for university admissions and other high-stakes purposes (Berry, Nakatsuhara, and Inoue 2016; Nakatsuhara et al. 2015), and in addition, a variety of vendors now offer online video interviews for high-stakes uses, such as hiring or university admission, which in at least one case includes an assessment of speaking ability (Vericant, n.d.). With these developments, it seems highly likely that video-mediated interview assessments will be used more commonly in the future.

Beyond more efficient delivery of existing assessment formats, the use of video-mediated communication also opens possibilities for a variety of innovations in speaking assessment. First, incorporation of "face-to-face" interaction in a computer-based platform potentially facilitates the implementation of diverse and innovative task types. For example, computer-based tasks could be devised that require test-takers to collaborate in ways that are more immersive or engaging, or that better simulate discursive practices of interest to assessment users. Video-mediated communication also facilitates automated scoring of spoken responses, and as technology continues to develop, may allow the automated evaluation of facial expressions or gestures (e.g., Chen et al. 2014). Despite the considerable potential for video-mediated communication to enable innovation in speaking assessment, basic questions remain unanswered regarding its feasibility. Specifically, little information is available regarding the reliability of video-mediated technology or its usefulness for eliciting evidence of interactional competence. The purpose of this study was therefore to conduct an initial evaluation of the feasibility and usability of speaking assessment tasks where an examiner and one or more test-takers interacted through online video.

Background

Influential frameworks describing communicative competence include the ability to use language appropriately in particular situations (Bachman 1990; Canale and Swain 1980), and it has been argued for some time now that the concept of communicative competence should explicitly incorporate interaction (He and Young 1998; Kramsch 1986). Beyond applied linguistics, researchers in cognitive science have argued for the centrality of interaction in human spoken communication, hypothesizing that conversation takes advantage of processing mechanisms that link perception and behavior, even asserting that "humans are 'designed' for dialogue rather than monologue" (Garrod and Pickering 2004, 8).

The ability to interact with other speakers has often been framed in terms of interactional competence, which Kramsch (1986) defines as the ability for two or more speakers to create a shared understanding or intersubjectivity. This definition has more recently been extended in the work of Richard Young (2008). While Young considers interactional competence to be something jointly constructed by speakers in an interaction, he identifies a number of resources that are employed by a speaker to interact appropriately and effectively. These resources include the knowledge of the roles of individuals within an interaction (identity resources), as well as the knowledge of specific linguistic features that characterize a certain context (register) or that are used to communicate particular types of meanings (verbal resources). Of particular interest for the current study are interactional resources, which include the appropriate use of speech acts, the ability to manage turn-taking, the ability to repair breakdowns in interaction, and the knowledge of conversational boundaries, such as openings and closings. Finally, Young also includes the ability to effectively employ visual behaviors, such as facial expression and posture.

Features of interactional competence have traditionally been elicited in face-to-face tests of speaking by using dialogic tasks wherein the test-taker speaks with an examiner and/or one or more other test-takers. A challenge inherent in this approach is that test-takers and the examiner must be in the same place, with the various logistical requirements this entails. An appropriate space must be made available and all involved must travel to this location; this requirement inconveniences the participants, limits the availability of test administrations, and may prevent administration of the test altogether in remote or hazardous locations. In contrast, computer-based tests require fewer resources and are easier to administer at large scale (Chapelle and Douglas 2006), but current computer-based speaking tests employ monologic tasks and so do not elicit direct evidence of interactional competence. With advancements in technology, delivery of speaking assessment using video-mediated communication has the potential to combine the advantages of both face-to-face and computer-based approaches. Like face-to-face tests, a video-mediated assessment allows for synchronous spoken interaction with simultaneous visual input and so has the potential to produce evidence of interactional resources. Like computer-based tests, examiner and test-takers need not be colocated, simplifying the logistics of test administration. Compared to a face-to-face format, video-mediated assessment might also facilitate consistency in test administration and scoring through standardization of materials and procedures within a common assessment delivery platform or by allowing use of a centralized group of full-time expert examiners or raters.

However, many questions remain regarding the usefulness of video-mediated communication for assessment purposes. One question is whether video communication technology is reliable enough to support interaction between speakers. Disruptions in the audio or video stream have obvious potential to interfere with communication, and while such disruptions may elicit evidence of the ability to carry out conversational repair, they are problematic for eliciting evidence of other aspects of interactional competence such as smooth turn-taking. A second question concerns the adequacy of video input for supporting naturalistic interaction. Studies of video-mediated communication have noted that language elicited in both video and audio-only conditions differed from face-to-face speech in terms of turn-taking behaviors, such as pausing and backchanneling (Sellen 1995). More broadly, it has also been argued that the visual input provided by single-camera video, as is typical of most current video-mediated communication platforms, is insufficient to support the full range of features found in interactive communication (Groen et al. 2012). In a speaking assessment, diminished visual input could impact the perceptions of test-takers in a variety of ways. For example, negative impact could occur if communication is perceived as hampered by an inability to see another speaker's body language, or conversely, there could be a positive impact if a test-taker feels less exposed or nervous because they are not fully visible to the examiner or other test-takers.

The current study is an attempt to investigate the use of video-mediated communication in speaking assessment. In this exploratory study it was not possible to address all of the questions raised above; rather, the study was limited to a more modest goal of collecting initial evidence regarding the feasibility and usability of video-mediated communication technology to assess speaking ability. Specifically, we were interested in evaluating the delivery of business-related tasks using a simple type of video-conferencing technology, where several speakers could see and hear each other from their computers. The video-conferencing service used for the study (Skype) represents a platform commonly used for the purpose of business communication. Although more elaborate systems are available, our goal was to start with a simpler and more secure approach where Skype was used solely for video, and accessory context was delivered through a separate secure platform similar to those we have previously used to research speaking assessment in international contexts.

Specifically, the study addressed three questions:

1. Is it feasible to deliver interactive speaking assessment tasks using current video-conferencing technology?
2. What are participants' perceptions of video-mediated speaking tasks delivered online?
3. To what extent can evidence of language ability be elicited and scored under such circumstances?

Methods

In the first phase of the study, video-mediated group speaking tasks were developed, along with a platform for task delivery. The materials and platform were then piloted with participants in the United States and China to investigate the feasibility of delivering interactive speaking tasks online, and to collect participant perceptions. Finally, spoken responses to the tasks were used to develop scoring rubrics, and then responses collected in the United States were scored. This process is described in detail below.

Prototype Tasks and Technology

Prototype speaking tasks and a delivery platform were developed for the study. The tasks were designed to be delivered in a session including a moderator and two or three participants, and they incorporated different combinations of speakers as well as monologic and dialogic response formats. A variety of tasks were tried because it was hypothesized that different response formats would be differently vulnerable to technology disruptions and elicit different language features. Specifically, it was expected that time delay in transmitting audio or video would have less impact on responses to monologic tasks, where it is not necessary to coordinate turns with another speaker. In addition, the tasks incorporated different speaker combinations, which provided a variety of interlocutors for each test-taker. This was considered to be useful for evaluating the impact of interlocutor effect on participants' language production.

Four tasks were developed for the study wherein participants spoke on various workplace- or business-related topics. In task 1, each participant spoke with the moderator, introducing themselves and answering two opinion questions, such as "Do you think social media is important for businesses? Why or why not?" Participants were allowed thirty seconds to answer each of the two questions. The purpose of this task was to assess the test-taker's ability to express their opinion in a relatively controlled context. In task 2, a business challenge was briefly introduced by the moderator, and then three videos were shown in which a speaker proposed a solution to the problem (about 60 seconds each). After the group viewed each video, one participant was given forty-five seconds to summarize the content. This task was intended to provide an indication of the participant's ability to understand and summarize information with minimal potential for impact from an interlocutor. After all three videos had been shown and summarized, the participants then discussed the proposals in task 3. Individuals were asked to argue for the proposal they had summarized in task 2 and were allowed five to six minutes for discussion. Task 3 was intended to elicit evidence of the participant's interactional competence, as well as the capability of the technology to support video-mediated interaction between several individuals in different locations. Finally, in task 4 each participant delivered a two-minute presentation on a business-related topic of their choice, speaking from a single slide they prepared before the session. After this, they then had two minutes to answer questions from the other participants. A brief preparation guide was provided to each participant before the session, which contained instructions regarding topic choice and preparation of the presentation slide. This task was intended to elicit evidence of the ability to speak on a prepared topic and answer questions. (More information on the tasks can be found in Ockey et al., forthcoming.)

Speaking tasks were delivered using a platform developed by Educational Testing Service, with Skype used as the video communication tool (figure 7.1). Skype was used as is, and performance of the video-communication system was based on Skype technology and infrastructure at the time of data collection (late 2014 and early 2015). The delivery platform was installed on each speaker's local computer and included basic tools for administering speaking tasks, including a list of participants, a whiteboard for presenting task materials, and a timer. The moderator platform included a "continue" button for manually advancing through the tasks, as well as the ability to select names from the list of participants to indicate who should be speaking. During sessions, video frames in Skype were highlighted with a thin blue boundary to show the person(s) currently speaking; in figure 7.1, participant 1 (middle) is the active speaker, and the moderator is shown at the bottom. The appearance of the participant platform was identical except that (1) there was no "continue" button, and (2) the participant would appear at the bottom while the moderator would appear in one of the large frames above.

Investigating the Usability and Reliability of Tasks and Platform

The platform and tasks were piloted in two separate trials, first with participants located in the United States and then with participants located in China. In the US

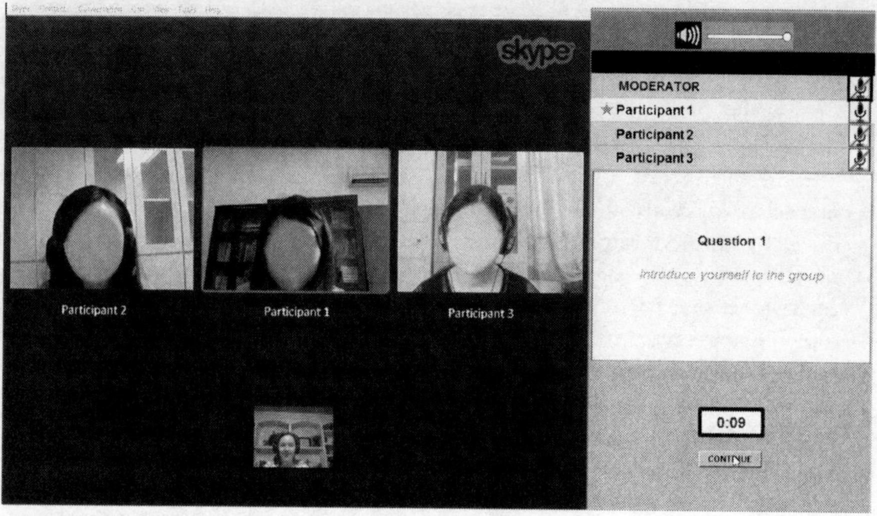

◆ **Figure 7.1.** Delivery platform for interactive speaking tasks, moderator version (*Note*: Black and white reproduction of color interface)

trial, participants were located in three geographically separated US states (New York, Iowa, and Utah), with the moderator located in New Jersey. This arrangement of multiple speakers in distant locations was used to provide a challenging test of the reliability of the platform and video communication technology. A local coordinator was available in each location to set up sessions and assist participants with any problems, and identical laptop computers and headsets were sent to each location to standardize the equipment used. A total of twenty-eight sessions was conducted from November 2014 through February 2015, with two or three participants in each session. Each session was roughly forty-five minutes long, not including time used for setup and a postsession survey.

A second trial was conducted with participants in China to provide a stronger test of the technology and collect user perceptions in an EFL context where familiarity with video communication technology might be different. Participants were located in three major Chinese cities (Shanghai, Nanjing, and Guangzhou) with the moderator once again located in New Jersey. Unlike the US trial, it was not feasible to standardize the equipment used, and sessions were conducted with the computers and headsets available in each location. As before, local coordinators set up sessions and managed participants, and sessions were roughly forty-five minutes long. Twenty-five sessions were carried out in June of 2015, with all but one session including three participants.

In both the US and China trials, the sessions were video recorded by the moderator using Camtasia screen-recording software, which recorded the moderator's computer screen and system audio. This captured video was subsequently used for scoring and for analysis of technical difficulties, except one session in the China trial where the video was lost due to technical problems.

Participants

A total of seventy-two adult English language learners participated in the US trial, and seventy-four adult learners participated in the China trial. Most participants were recruited from language schools or universities. Local coordinators were instructed to recruit participants of intermediate proficiency or higher and the majority of participants reported having studied English for six years or more. Participants in the US trial were more diverse in both the amount of time they had studied English and their self-assessment of their language ability; these differences reflected the diversity of the study locations. In one location all participants were community college students, in a second location many participants were graduate students, and in the third location participants were a mix of students and community members. Individuals in the US trial reported a total of fourteen first languages, with the most common being Chinese (29%), Japanese (18%), South Asian languages (14%), Korean (12%), Arabic (7%), and Spanish (6%). In the China trial, all but one participant (98%) reported Chinese as their L1. Most of the US participants (90%) reported using video chat to communicate at least once a month; many were international students and may have been using video technology to communicate with friends and family in their home countries. A smaller majority of Chinese participants (66%) also reported using video communication.

Collection of Participant Perceptions

Following the speaking tasks, each participant completed a background questionnaire as well as a survey that collected their perceptions of the tasks and technology used in the session. The survey consisted of Likert-scale questions where participants responded to a series of statements by choosing "strongly agree," "agree," "neutral," "disagree," and "strongly disagree." Separate sections of several questions each were used to collect reactions toward each task, with an additional section used to collect general perceptions regarding usability of the technology, and a final section to compare the experience to face-to-face communication. For the purposes of this paper, only participant perceptions of the impact of the technology on their communication are reported (full results can be found in Ockey et al., forthcoming).

Additionally, in the China trial a ten-minute focus group was held in Chinese immediately following each session, where participants were asked to discuss various aspects of tasks and technology. Given that preferences for face-to-face versus online communication were not directly addressed in the written survey, of particular interest was one question that stated, "These tasks were done online. How does this compare to speaking in person? Which do you like better?" Participant responses to this question were paraphrased by a Chinese L1 researcher and then common themes were identified and summarized by the authors.

Rubric Development and Scoring

The primary focus of the study was to evaluate the technical feasibility of an online-mediated interactive speaking test and to collect user perceptions; however, it was felt useful to also score the responses as a first step in evaluating the quality and range of language performance elicited. Analytic scoring rubrics were developed for each task to better capture task-related differences in performance across different aspects of language. Three analytic categories were used: linguistic control, topic management, and interaction. Linguistic control included foundational aspects of language performance such as fluency, rhythm, pronunciation, and the range and accuracy of grammatical structures and vocabulary. Topic management included features of organizational structure, elaboration, and content, with the latter conceptualized as either content accuracy or relevance depending on the task. The scale for interaction was intended to capture aspects of interactional competence, including turn-taking (e.g., taking the floor smoothly at appropriate times), collaboration (e.g., sharing the floor), engagement (e.g., contributing to elaboration of topics), and appropriateness (e.g., communicating in a pragmatically appropriate way). The descriptors for collaboration and engagement were intended to capture features of conversational dominance (Itakura 2001) and mutuality (Damon and Phelps 1989; Storch 2002).

Analytic rubrics were independently developed for each task except for the rubric for linguistic control, which was developed using responses to task 2 (retell) and then used to score all tasks based on the assumption that performance features in this category would be similar. Scoring was done from video captured from the moderator's screen, with each response edited into a separate clip for ease of handling. All tasks were scored for linguistic control and topic management, while interaction was scored only for tasks 3 and 4, which were expected to elicit evidence of interactional resources. In addition, for task 4 (presentation) the topic management score was based on the presentation while the interaction score was based on the question and answer section. This approach reflected the differing emphases in these sections on delivering information versus interacting with others.

Results
Technical Feasibility

The reliability of the platform and Skype video-conferencing technology was evaluated in twenty-eight sessions in the US trial and twenty-four sessions in the China trial, with each session lasting roughly forty-five minutes. The frequency of technology problems varied widely across the two trials, with technical disruptions being relatively few in the United States and very common in China (table 7.1). In the US trial, eighteen sessions (64%) were carried out with no substantive disruptions, while in another two sessions (7%) minor problems were observed while setting up, but did not impact the rest of the session. In the remaining eight sessions (29%), there were problems with delivery of content within the assessment platform. The most common issue was a participant's slide not being visible in task 4 (presentation); all but one instance was associated with a single location, where the slide uploaded from that location was not visible by one or more other participants. During task 2 there was a delay in the replay of stimulus video materials in three sessions, and the video could not be viewed by a participant in one additional session. In three sessions, the Skype video connection was dropped one or more times but audio communication continued, and, more seriously, the Skype connection was lost completely in three sessions. In one of these three cases the connection was reestablished after about a minute, but in the other two cases the connection was lost late in the session (task 4) and not reestablished. In these latter two cases human error may have been a contributing factor: the connection was lost while the participant was sitting down or standing up to deliver their presentation and the laptop computer may have been jostled. Other generally minor problems included brief interruptions to audio and upload of an incorrect slide at the start of a session.

In the China trial, technology problems were more common and of greater impact (table 7.1). Every session encountered difficulty of some kind, typically with instances of several different kinds of problems. Dropped Skype video occurred in most sessions (92%) and affected all three sites in China, but one location was most problematic with dropped video in twenty of twenty-five sessions. Problems in this location seem to be associated with the speed of the internet connection. Compared to the US trial, there were also more dropped Skype calls, although this occurred in only about a fifth of the sessions (21%). In another nine sessions (38%), the moderator recalled a participant to establish a better connection, but this typically did little to improve the quality of the audio or video. Difficulties in content delivery via the assessment platform were also common, particularly lags in replay of video stimulus material in task 2, where video was transmitted from a server in the United States. Early in the China trial it became clear that such lags were ubiquitous and varied in duration across locations, so after the first few sessions the moderator would confirm with participants that they had all finished watching the video before continuing. There were also problems in displaying participant presentation slides (task 4), partly due to operator error in uploading slides at the beginning of the session, and in some cases, apparently due to connectivity problems at the local site. We also note that the analysis was based on a recording of the moderator's computer screen, and problems visible only to participants may not have been captured. A number of

Table 7.1. Reliability of the technology

	Number of sessions	
	US (**N** = 28 sessions)	**China** (**N** = 24 sessions)
No problems	18 (64%)	0 (0%)
Minor problem at start	3 (11%)	*common*
Video replay lag (Task 2)	4 (14%)	*common*
Slide not visible (Task 4)	5 (18%)	12 (50%)
Skype video (only) dropped	3 (11%)	22 (92%)
Skype call dropped (video + audio)	3 (11%)	5 (21%)
Moderator re-call to improve connection	0 (0%)	9 (38%)
Other	6 (21%)	5 (21%)

Note: "*Common*" means that the problem was observed in most sessions based on comments from participants, but the exact frequency was difficult to establish because participant screens were not recorded.

other issues were observed, including lag in the start of the countdown timer, echo in the audio feed, and the local coordinator restarting the assessment platform in an attempt to establish a better connection.

Participant Perceptions

Positive perceptions of online speaking tasks were observed in both the US and China trials. In both instances, 80% or more of participants indicated that they "agreed" or "strongly agreed" with statements that video input made the tasks engaging and facilitated their understanding of how other speakers were reacting (table 7.2). Large majorities also agreed with the statement that it was possible to interact successfully in the video-mediated tasks, although fewer participants in the China trial agreed (74% versus 87% in the US trial). Somewhat smaller majorities also agreed with the statement that video allowed them to express themselves.

Perceptions of the reliability of the technology differed dramatically between the United States and China. A large majority of Chinese participants (82%) indicated that technology problems had interrupted the session in some way, and a smaller majority (66%) agreed with the statement that technology issues had actually interrupted the flow of conversation. In contrast, only 13% of participants in the US trial felt that the technology had interrupted the session, and only 8% reported that

◆ **Table 7.2.** Responses to postsession survey questions

Question	US trial				China trial			
	N	**Agr.**	**Neut.**	**Disgr.**	**N**	**Agr.**	**Neut.**	**Disgr.**
Seeing other people made the activity engaging/interesting.	72	89	8	3	74	89	11	0
Seeing other people made it easy to understand their reactions.	72	85	14	1	74	81	14	5
Video allowed us to interact well.	70	87	12	1	74	74	20	6
Video made it easy to express myself.	72	65	29	6	74	62	35	3
There were interruptions because of the technology.	72	13	19	68	74	82	7	11
There were unnatural pauses because of the technology.	72	8	24	68	74	66	19	15
I felt I was interacting like the way I do in real life.	70	81	13	6	74	58	27	15
There is a difference communicating through technology and face-to-face.	69	48	20	32	73	88	7	5

Note: "Agr." is the percentage of participants selecting "agree" or "strongly agree," "Neut." is the percentage choosing "neutral," and "Disgr." is the percentage answering "disagree" or "strongly disagree."

interaction had been impacted. Similar though less extreme differences were seen in responses to two statements comparing the online tasks to participants' real-life, face-to-face spoken communication. A small majority of Chinese participants indicated that they responded to the tasks as they would in real life, while a large majority (86%) felt that video-mediated communication was different from face-to-face communication. The opposite pattern was seen in the US trial, where a large majority (81%) agreed that the tasks reflected their real-life speaking and 48% felt there was a difference between online and face-to-face communication.

The focus groups in the China trial were also asked about their preference for face-to-face versus online communication. Despite the frequent technology problems in the China trial, a majority of focus group participants (69%) indicated that they would prefer online speaking assessment, while only 18% indicated that they would prefer a face-to-face format (table 7.3). Participants most commonly said they preferred the online format because it was viewed as less stressful than meeting an examiner or other test-takers face-to-face, but the convenience of not having to go to a test center was also mentioned. A few individuals also commented that they felt the online environment would be more controlled and thus fairer to test-takers. But many of those preferring online tasks also brought up the issue of technical problems and qualified their support by saying that online assessment was preferable *if* technical issues could be solved. A few participants also noted that, in an online format, it would be easy to cheat by using notes outside the view of the camera.

Reasons for preferring a face-to-face format included the ability to see the full range of other speakers' gestures and body language, while a few individuals simply stated they preferred face-to-face interaction or were concerned about technical problems. Several participants noted that, while they preferred face-to-face interaction, they thought doing the tasks online would be more convenient.

Feasibility of Eliciting and Scoring Evidence of Language Ability

Participants were able to interact with each other successfully using the video-conferencing technology when technology issues did not interrupt. In the US trial, there were few if any disruptions that had any noticeable impact on the language produced by participants. In the China trial, poor internet connectivity meant that tasks could not be completed in some cases, and at times there were noticeable breakdowns in communication. The lack of video signal from one or more participants may have also impacted communication in unknown ways. Nonetheless, in the China trial there were instances where the technology worked without interruption. Eliciting language performance was therefore possible but could not be done reliably.

As described in the methods section, responses from the US trial were used to develop analytic scoring rubrics for each task, and then the remaining US responses were triple-scored by three researchers. Average scores were similar across tasks and subscales and close to the center point of the scale (table 7.4). This is unsurprising given that scoring rubrics were constructed using responses taken from the same data collection, which means the rubrics should have covered a range of performances similar to the sample that was scored.

◆ **Table 7.3.** Participant preferences from the China focus groups

Participant opinion	Participants (*N* = 62)
Prefer face-to-face	11 (18%)
Major themes (number commenting)	
Can see gestures/expressions (5)	
Prefer human interaction (3)	
Avoid technical problems (2)	
But online is more convenient (3)	
Prefer online	43 (69%)
Major themes (number commenting)	
Less stressful (20)	
Convenient (8)	
More fair/consistent (5)	
But technology is a problem (15)	
But cheating is possible (2)	
Both formats have strengths/weaknesses	5 (8%)
No opinion expressed	3 (5%)

Average correlations between rater pairs varied with tasks and analytic scale and ranged from .59 to .83 (table 7.5). Instances of exact agreement between two raters accounted for 48%–64% of the total, with disagreement by one score band accounting for most of the remainder. Rater agreement was relatively low for the interaction subscale (tasks 3 and 4) and for topic management in the presentation task (task 4). This would suggest that raters found it more challenging to consistently judge interaction and that the presentation task was particularly demanding. In addition, the scoring of topic management in the presentation was complicated by variability in the effectiveness of the slides and the organization of the presentation, as in some cases when participants ran out of time before covering substantial parts of their presentation content. The question and answer session following the presentation was used for scoring interaction, but this turned out to be problematic due to the wide variation in the quality and length of questions asked of the presenter by the other participants. While offering participants the opportunity to present on a topic of their choice and to ask and answer meaningful questions may encourage test-taker agency and is consistent with real-world contexts, it was apparent that the question and answer session, as formulated, would need revision to elicit more consistent evidence of ability.

Discussion

We investigated the use of online, video-mediated communication technology to collect samples of spoken interaction for assessment of language ability. In the

◆ **Table 7.4.** Distribution of average scores (US trial)

		n	$\bar{X}$	SD	Score distribution 1	2	3	4
Task 1								
	Control	56	2.4	0.87	9	21	17	9
	Topic mgmt.	56	2.4	0.94	14	22	11	9
	Interaction	...	...	...	...	...	...	...
Task 2								
	Control	53	2.5	0.86	6	24	15	8
	Topic mgmt.	53	2.4	1.00	9	19	17	8
	Interaction	...	...	...	...	...	...	...
Task 3								
	Control	56	2.4	0.88	9	22	15	10
	Topic mgmt.	56	2.6	0.89	5	18	22	11
	Interaction	56	2.6	0.92	6	16	24	10
Task 4								
	Control	52	2.5	0.82	7	24	14	7
	Topic mgmt.	52	2.6	0.77	5	18	21	8
	Interaction	52	2.6	0.82	4	20	17	11

Note: Average scores are all on a 1–4 scale, averaged across three raters. For score distributions, counts are based on the average score from three raters rounded to the nearest whole number.

US trial, the technology generally worked as expected, and it was possible to elicit scorable samples of speech. Conditions in the China trial were more challenging, with frequent technological problems that in some cases prevented individuals from fully participating. Nonetheless, there were instances in the China trial where the technology worked without major problem, and in the great majority of cases language samples were obtained. We were able to score speech samples collected in the US trial with some degree of reliability given the relative lack of established scoring materials and raters, although rater agreement tended to be higher for linguistic features than interaction. These findings suggest that while video-mediated assessment of speaking is possible, development of such an assessment may require that considerable resources be put into the development of appropriate tasks, a reliable infrastructure for administering the test, and materials to support scoring.

Participants generally reacted positively toward the online format, with large majorities agreeing that the video input supported their interactions with others. Smaller majorities indicated that video made it easier to express themselves, and opinions differed across trials regarding whether communicating through video was similar to real-life spoken communication. While majorities of participants in

◆ **Table 7.5.** Rater agreement

	Total agreement instances	Agreement				Average interrater correlation
		Exact	1	2	3	
Task 1: Q&A						
Control	168	110 (65%)	56 (33%)	2 (1%)	0 (0%)	.79
Topic mgmt.	168	96 (57%)	68 (40%)	4 (2%)	0 (0%)	.80
Interaction	...	...	...	...	...	...
Task 2: Retell						
Control	159	76 (48%)	77 (48%)	5 (3%)	1 (1%)	.71
Topic mgmt.	159	82 (52%)	64 (40%)	13 (8%)	0 (0%)	.77
Interaction	...	...	...	...	...	...
Task 3: Discussion						
Control	168	103 (61%)	64 (38%)	1 (1%)	0 (0%)	.83
Topic mgmt.	168	106 (63%)	54 (32%)	6 (4%)	2 (1%)	.74
Interaction	168	87 (52%)	74 (44%)	7 (4%)	0 (0%)	.71
Task 4: Presentation						
Control	156	91 (58%)	62 (40%)	3 (2%)	0 (0%)	.74
Topic mgmt.	156	78 (50%)	66 (42%)	10 (6%)	2 (1%)	.59
Interaction	156	79 (51%)	64 (41%)	13 (8%)	0 (0%)	.66

both trials indicated that their video-mediated interactions were similar to spoken interactions in real life, the percentage of US participants agreeing with this position was considerably higher than for China (81% versus 58%). Similarly, only 48% of participants in the US trial felt that communicating through the technology was different from face-to-face interaction, compared to 88% of individuals in China. These differences likely reflect the higher reliability of the technology in the US trial, but participants in the US trial may have also been more comfortable using video-communication technology to communicate with friends or relatives in their home countries.

While online video technology has promise for assessing spoken interaction, our experiences highlight a number of challenges for implementation. First, an obvious issue is the reliability of the technology for delivering video and administering the assessment, although the importance of this issue will likely diminish as communication technology and internet connectivity continues to improve. In the meantime it may be possible to design assessments that work within current technology limits by minimizing the number of participants or their geographic separation. We note that our approach of including up to four speakers in widely separated locations was an intentionally challenging test of the technology, and certainly systems could be devised that make fewer demands on internet bandwidth and other infrastructure.

Beyond technological reliability, another implementation challenge is test-takers' familiarity with and access to the technology used, and it is possible that those who do not use this technology in their daily life may feel less at ease communicating through this mode. In addition, for high-stakes uses, test security may be an issue if using a nonsecure communication tool, such as Skype, or if test-takers participate from their own locations without adequate supervision.

We also note that the current study represents only an initial exploration of video-mediated assessment of spoken interaction; major limitations of the study are that a face-to-face condition was not included for comparison and that there was no systematic analysis of the language features elicited by the tasks. Researchers in computer-mediated communication have long noted that video does not provide the full range of visual input available in a face-to-face conversation, which may impact the features of spoken language produced (Groen et al. 2012; Sellen 1995). The potential significance of this impact for speaking assessment remains unclear, however. In a recent comparison of face-to-face and video-mediated versions of the IELTS speaking test, Nakatsuhara et al. (2015) reported that while scores and speaking behavior were largely equivalent in face-to-face and online versions, there were subtle differences in the language functions observed in each mode. Further investigation of the characteristics of speech produced in video-mediated tasks is needed to both document the comparability of performances elicited by video and face-to-face modes of communication and to inform a better understanding of the speaking construct actually measured in video-mediated environments.

To close, video-mediated online communication is becoming an increasingly common channel for spoken interaction, and it seems natural that speaking assessment will evolve to make use of this mode. Aside from reflecting the reality of twenty-first-century language use, such assessments also have the potential to provide a platform for the introduction of a variety of innovations, such as new kinds of collaborative tasks and new technologies for evaluating performance. Such innovation both opens new ways of assessing speaking and provides opportunities for studying spoken interaction in a new domain.

References

Bachman, Lyle F. 1990. *Fundamental Considerations in Language Testing*. Oxford: Oxford University Press.

Berry, Vivien, Fumiyo Nakatsuhara, and Chihiro Inoue. 2016. "Face-to-Face and Video-Conferencing Technology Delivered Speaking Tests: Comparing Constructs." Paper presented at the 2016 Language Testing Research Colloquium, Palermo, Italy, June.

Canale, Michael, and Merrill Swain. 1980. "Theoretical Bases of Communicative Approaches to Second Language Teaching and Testing." *Applied Linguistics* 1:1–47. doi:10.1093/applin/I.1.1.

Chapelle, Carol, and Dan Douglas. 2006. *Assessing Language through Computer Technology*. Cambridge: Cambridge University Press.

Chen, Lei, Chee Wee Leong, Gary Feng, and Chong Min Lee. 2014. "Using Multimodal Cues to Analyze MLA'14 Oral Presentation Quality Corpus: Presentation Delivery and Slides Quality." In *Proceedings of the 2014 ACM Workshop on Multimodal Learning Analytics Workshop and Grand Challenge*, 45–52. New York: Association for Computing Machinery. doi:10.1145/2666633.2666640.

Damon, William, and Erin Phelps. 1989. "Critical Distinctions among Three Approaches to Peer Education." *International Journal of Educational Research* 58:9–19. doi:10.1016/0883-0355(89)90013-X.

Garrod, Simon, and Martin J. Pickering. 2004. "Why Is Conversation So Easy?" *Trends in Cognitive Sciences* 1:8–11. doi:10.1016/j.tics.2003.10.016.

Groen, Martin, Marian Ursu, Spiros Michalakopoulos, Manolis Falelakis, and Epameinondas Gasparis. 2012. "Improving Video-mediated Communication with Orchestration." *Computers in Human Behavior* 28:1575–79. http://dx.doi.org/10.1016/j.chb.2012.03.019.

He, Agnes W., and Richard Young. 1998. "Language Proficiency Interviews: A Discourse Approach." In *Talking and Testing: Discourse Approaches to the Assessment of Oral Proficiency*, edited by Richard Young and Agnes W. He, 1–24. Philadelphia: John Benjamins.

Itakura, Hiroko. 2001. "Describing Conversational Dominance." *Journal of Pragmatics* 33:1859–80. doi:10.1016/S0378-2166(00)00082-5.

Kramsch, Claire. 1986. "From Language Proficiency to Interactional Competence." *Modern Language Journal* 70:366–72. doi:10.1111/j.1540-4781.1986.tb05291.x.

Nakatsuhara, Fumiyo, Chihiro Inoue, Vivien Berry, and Evelina Galaczi. 2015. "Exploring Performance across Two Delivery Modes for the Same L2 Speaking Test: Face-to-Face and Video-Conferencing Delivery." *IELTS Partnership Research Papers* 1. https://www.ielts.org/teaching-and-research/research-reports/ielts-partnership-research-paper-1.ashx.

Ockey, Gary, Veronika Timpe-Laughlin, Larry Davis, and Lin Gu. Forthcoming. *Exploring the Potential of a Video-Mediated Interactive Speaking Assessment*. Educational Testing Service Research Report. Princeton: Educational Testing Service.

Sellen, Abigail J. 1995. "Remote Conversations: The Effects of Mediating Talk with Technology." *Human-Computer Interaction* 10:401–44. doi:10.1207/s15327051hci1004_2.

Storch, Neomy. 2002. "Patterns of Interaction in ESL Pair Work." *Language Learning* 52:119–58.

Vericant. n.d. "Spoken English Evaluation (SEE)." https://www.vericant.com/see/.

Young, Richard F. 2008. *Language and Interaction: An Advanced Resource Book*. London: Routledge.

———. 2011. "Interactional Competence in Language Learning, Teaching, and Testing." In *Handbook of Research in Second Language Teaching and Learning*, vol. 2, edited by Eli Hinkel, 426–43. New York: Routledge.

Chapter 8

◆ Task-Based Language Assessment for L1 and L2 Speakers in Primary Education

Designing a Useful Task-Specification Framework

KOEN VAN GORP
Michigan State University

CLASSROOM-BASED LANGUAGE ASSESSMENT CAN take many forms and serve many purposes. Traditionally, summative assessment or assessment *of* learning (for grading purposes) is distinguished from formative assessment or assessment *for* learning (for diagnostic purposes or to support students' ongoing learning processes). Additionally, assessment is also about teaching; it is about teachers questioning the impact of their teaching on the basis of their students' assessment results (Hattie and Yates 2014; Rea-Dickins 2001). Hattie and Yates (2014, 118) note that "when teachers ask about who has been impacted, what they have been impacted by, and what the magnitude of impact is, then they are more likely to adapt their instructional methods and attend carefully to their students' learning progress."

In task-based language teaching (TBLT), students acquire language by performing authentic, meaning-oriented language tasks that have a clear and motivating goal (Van den Branden 2006). Tasks are both targeted learning outcomes and essential pedagogic constructs that "drive" classroom activity (Samuda and Bygate 2008). As a critical component of TBLT, task-based language assessment (TBLA) subscribes to a "can-do" approach to language testing by assessing, as directly as possible, whether test-takers can perform specific language tasks in particular, meaningful communicative settings (Van Gorp and Deygers 2014). TBLA aims to raise awareness in learners, teachers, and other stakeholders about what language learning is all about by emphasizing valued and authentic language performance and target-task learning throughout the program (i.e., washback; Norris 2009).

Currently, TBLA has a considerable range of uses or practices (Norris 2016), ranging from defining standards of ability to proficiency assessment to employment certification. In language education, tasks are used for both summative and formative assessment purposes. For educational uses, TBLA faces the challenge of assessing whether the pedagogical tasks that drive the classroom activity help students to become more proficient users of the target language and, more specifically, help them to successfully complete the target tasks of a given task-based curriculum. However, TBLA should enable teachers to do more than acknowledge whether students have performed a specific task successfully. To reach its full didactic potential, TBLA should help teachers to provide their students with diagnostic feedback. Norris (2009, 587) states that TBLA has to provide "frameworks for tracking and interpreting important aspects of learner development over time." For Norris, this means that teachers should be made aware of task specifications, of expected task performance, and of task performance strategies so they can help learners improve their performance. This links up with Harding, Alderson, and Brunfaut's (2015, 333) recent observation that "task-based language teaching pedagogy will need to identify a way to merge discrete diagnostic information with a holistic, task-outcome-focused approach."

The potential strength of a theoretically sound, interpretive framework based on task specifications is that it underscores the interdependent and symbiotic relationship between learning, teaching, and assessment. It seems evident that, in a task-based approach, the processes of teaching and assessment are informed by one and the same model of learning; assessment must be aligned with learning goals, and this alignment is better accomplished if teaching and assessment are actually conducted in the same way (National Research Council 2001). Seeing that "ultimately, language learning does not depend on a few super moments, but on thousands of interactional moments" (Van den Branden 2010, 296), assessment can and should also not be limited to a handful of "super moments." Assessment tasks should be considered as much as possible to be learning tasks (Carless 2007) and, likewise, learning tasks should be considered as assessment tasks (Colpin and Van Gorp 2007; Van Gorp and Deygers 2014).

Developing a Task-Based Language Assessment Framework

In order for TBLA to reach its full didactic potential, it must rely on an assessment framework that generates useful information about in-class learning and teaching processes. This section describes the development of such a task-based language assessment framework for primary education in Flanders, Belgium.

A Task-Based Language Syllabus for Primary Schools

The assessment framework that was developed for the task-based syllabus, TotemTaal, is an example of how a task-specification framework can guide syllabus design and inform both teaching and assessment. TotemTaal is a task-based, Dutch-language syllabus for Dutch-medium primary schools in Belgium (Berben et al. 2007b). It is a Dutch-language curriculum that encompasses listening, speaking, reading, writing, spelling, and language awareness tasks for both L1 and L2 speakers from grades two to six.

The syllabus was developed from 2005 to 2008 by a team of task-based syllabus designers at the Centre for Language and Education (KU Leuven/University of Leuven). The syllabus was commissioned by a commercial publisher and Priority Policy Brussels (PPB), a nonprofit educational network of school advisors responsible for the support of Dutch-medium primary schools in Brussels since 2000. Both primary-school teachers and school advisors from PPB were involved from the start in the development of TotemTaal as members of a feedback and pilot group.

The curriculum of TotemTaal focused on acquiring the language of schooling or the academic register as stated in the official attainment targets by the Flemish Department of Education. The attainment targets for Dutch within the language arts program in the curriculum consist of language proficiency and language awareness goals. All goals have to be mastered by all students including L2 learners.

In Flemish primary education, L1 Dutch speakers and L2 Dutch learners (i.e., students who mainly speak a language other than the language of instruction at home) share a classroom and are taught the same curriculum. The number of L2 speakers in the Flemish educational system varies according to region (Flemish Region versus Brussels-Capital Region) and areas (rural versus urban). In the Flemish Region, on average 15.3% of the students in primary education are L2 learners; in the Brussels-Capital Region the average is 71.8% (Departement Kanselarij & Bestuur 2016). In the Flanders Region, L2 Dutch learners are predominantly found in the cities. For example, the average percentage of L2 learners in Antwerp (the largest city in Flanders) is 41.7% and in Ghent (the second largest city in Flanders) it is 30.5% (Departement Kanselarij & Bestuur 2016). In these cities most L2 learners are located in a small number of schools with large populations of L2 speakers, from 50% to more than 90%.

Whereas L2 and L1 speakers attend the same classrooms, newcomers receive additional instruction outside of the classroom for a couple of hours per week in the first year of their arrival in Flanders. Newcomers receive special tutoring focused on language and other skills necessary for integration into the regular classroom.

Despite the heterogeneity of the classes, the attainment targets and the curriculum are the same for L1 and L2 speakers. Therefore, the task-based syllabus focused on the commonalities all types of learners have when learning the academic register of a language. However, the syllabus created opportunities for differentiation and remediation for struggling L1 and L2 speakers based on the task-specification and assessment framework.

Task-Specification Framework

The starting point of the task-based syllabus was the set of official attainment goals (Departement Onderwijs 1998) and the curricula and timetables developed by the three major "educational networks" in Flanders (community education; subsidized, publicly run schools; and subsidized, privately run schools). These curricula are the main instructional directives that schools must follow, while the attainment goals are the official standards that every pupil has to reach at the end of primary education (see example 8.1).

◆ **Example 8.1.** Extract from the Flemish attainment goals for reading proficiency (Departement Onderwijs 1998)

> Information level = structuring (i.e., being able to order the information in a text in a personal and clear way)
>
> The students can order information in level- and age-appropriate (a) school and study texts and activity instructions, and (b) stories, novels, dialogues, poems, journals, and encyclopedias.

On the basis of the attainment goals and the curricula of the Flemish educational networks, target tasks were identified. For example, a target task capturing the above learning goal would be reading a magazine article with the aim to select and order information according to a personal or a given criterion. Once identified, target tasks were then operationalized in specific pedagogical tasks. For example, students could be given illustrated identity cards of different animals and be asked to identify which animal they would like for a pet and why. A more complex pedagogical task would be reading a longer informational text on different dog species in order to identify which dog species would provide a suitable pet, taking into account certain criteria for a house pet. For students to learn to perform the target tasks linked to the standards, several encounters with relevant types of pedagogical tasks varying in degrees of complexity are necessary in order to build up the linguistic abilities required for more difficult target task performances.

To enable task sequencing, monitor task complexity, and track learning opportunities, a task-specification framework was developed. This framework built on the Centre for Language and Education's research into task complexity and difficulty (Duran and Ramaut 2006) and defined task characteristics by means of six parameters closely related to the attainment targets (and thereby reflecting the constructs intended in the official standards). Each task challenged students to practice one or more of the four *language skills* while processing or producing a *text type* for a certain *audience*, about a specific topic, representing or revealing a *world*, with a certain *function* or *purpose*. In addition, dealing with the information in the text demanded a certain *level of processing*. Furthermore, the text could be linguistically easy or difficult depending on vocabulary, syntax, structure, code, conventions, and so on. Table 8.1 (from Berben et al. 2007b) illustrates these parameters for a reading task.

The task-specification framework provided the syllabus designers with all the information they needed to incrementally build a task-based curriculum for primary education. In this process a team of six persons worked collaboratively; each team member designing tasks for almost all aspects of the curriculum. Additionally, a pair of experts was responsible for keeping track of the overall development of a language skill or particular domain (e.g., language awareness or cooperative learning) within a grade and across grades. The experts checked which pedagogical tasks were linked to the intended language goals and task types. They monitored the gradual increase in complexity along the lines laid out in the task-specification framework. For example, they asked themselves the question: Do students over time have to process information in comparable, age-appropriate magazine articles in more and more complex ways? In other words, does the syllabus create opportunities for students to move

Table 8.1. Task-specification framework for the reading task "Family looking for a robot" (fourth grade) in TotemTaal

Goals	
Parameters	**Settings**
Skill	Reading
Level of processing	Evaluating
Text type	Advertisements
Audience	Peers
World	Recognizable fantasy world: Robots
Function	Selecting information
Attainment goals	The students can order information in level- and age-appropriate stories. (Dutch Language Standard 3.5)
	The students can evaluate information in advertisements. (Dutch Language Standard 3.7)

Source: Berben et al. 2007b, 42.

from understanding literal information over finding implicit information in a text to comparing or evaluating information from different sources? Spreadsheets describing all pedagogical tasks according to the different parameters of the task-specification framework allowed the experts to oversee how the curriculum was shaped (e.g., the diversity and complexity of pedagogical tasks) and to notice underserved or missing areas (e.g., a certain text type, audience, or level of processing). For all skills and areas, a similar approach was adopted.

Assessment Framework

The assessment framework of TotemTaal consists of four components. Table 8.2 (from Berben et al. 2007a) provides an overview of the four components.

This multicomponential, interpretive framework provides varied opportunities to gather information about the students' developing language skills. The four components have partly overlapping intended purposes:

1. Observation of task performance in order to provide teacher support to the student if necessary and to form a first opinion on what a student can and cannot do with the language

2. Observation and analysis of task performance and task outcome of individual students to get a more detailed and substantiated picture of what students can and cannot do with language

3. Learner reflection and portfolio for self-assessment of task performance and language proficiency level to provide an extra layer of planned formative information to the previous component

4. Task-based tests for summative use

The key element linking the four components is an analysis diagram for each of the four language skills. The skill-specific analysis diagram links all assessment tasks with the task-specification framework on the one hand and key processes related to listening, speaking, reading, and writing on the other hand. It guides the teacher in

◆ **Table 8.2.** Assessment framework in TotemTaal

Function	Format	Who	Focus	Pedagogic tools	Documentation
Incidental formative assessment	Observation and support	Teacher	Students' task performance (process)	Guidelines for teacher support of four language skills	Not applicable (mental notes)
Planned formative assessment	Observation and analysis	Teacher	Students' task performance (process) and outcome (product)	Analysis diagram for the observation and analysis of four language skills	Systematized notes
	Reflection	Student and teacher	Own task performance (process) and outcome (product)	Teacher guidelines for reflective talks; Portfolio guidelines for students	Worksheets; Portfolio
Summative assessment	Tests	Student and teacher	Students' outcomes of task-based tests (product)	Task-based tests for listening, reading, writing, spelling and language awareness	Rating rubrics; Test score

Source: Berben et al. 2007a, 156.

the observation and analysis of a student's task performances and helps the teacher decide whether the student can perform the task independently or needs the help and support of the teacher or other students.

The analysis diagram for reading tasks provides the teachers with information about which aspects are essential to the performance of reading tasks in general and allows them to systematically track this information for individual students in an observation and analysis worksheet. The aspects that were identified as relevant, based on meta-analyses of effective reading programs, are reading goals, level of information processing, topic familiarity, reading strategies, self-reliance, attitudes, and reflection (National Reading Panel 2000; Slavin 2013; Slavin et al. 2009). Other aspects are technical reading skills (e.g., fluency and accuracy), conventions of the text type, relations in the text (e.g., function words expressing grammatical relations), vocabulary, and visual aspects (e.g., illustrations, layout). These aspects, specifically the focus on functional goal, levels of processing, and strategies, are largely similar for all language skills in TotemTaal's assessment framework. For the other skills, and especially for writing, the analysis diagrams were also based on meta-analyses or reviews of effective listening, speaking, and writing instruction. For example, for writing the analysis diagram was based (among others) on the different meta-analyses by Graham and Perin (2007a, b, c).

The analysis diagrams for the four language skills and all the other documentation needed to realize the four assessment components of the TBLA framework were made available to the teacher in the form of a binder. In this teacher manual, the guidelines for teacher assistance, observation, and analysis and student reflection specify how these aspects of the reading process can be realized in a specific pedagogical task and what realistic expectations are for students of a certain grade. This close connection between all the pedagogic tools in the syllabus should enable teachers to combine analysis and support, to integrate instruction and assessment. It provides teachers with an interpretive framework, or a "lens," to look at students' task performances, draw inferences about a student's current proficiency level, and engage in contingent pedagogy to advance the student's language development (Heritage, Walqui, and Linquanti 2013).

A Small-Scale Implementation Study

To investigate how the assessment framework was adopted by teachers seven years after the introduction of Totem Taal in schools, a small-scale survey was conducted. The aims were to find out to what extent the intended uses of the assessment framework were realized, and to gain insight in the strengths and weaknesses of the framework as perceived by teachers and pedagogic advisors.

Context

Totem Taal, the teaching materials and the underlying TBLT approach, was introduced to the schools in Brussels by lectures and workshops given by the publisher and PPB. In these sessions assessment was one of the topics that was addressed. Teachers were introduced to the variety of assessment materials and opportunities that the syllabus presented. However, during the first two years, as schools started to implement the syllabus, the PPB organized in-service training and workshops for all schools mainly on aspects of TBLT: goal setting, powerful tasks for the four language skills, and differentiation. Only in the third year workshops were offered on the assessment framework of Totem Taal, which all schools were encouraged to attend. From that moment onward, schools could also receive in-service training and coaching on language assessment.

Assessment and instructional support was provided by school advisors. Traditionally, one becomes a school advisor after at least ten years of experience in a regular classroom. School advisors work very closely with the schools they provide support for. They have meetings with headmasters, school teams, and individual teachers about specific language teaching topics that the school wants to focus on. They give workshops to school teams and provide more personalized coaching opportunities. They engage in conversations with the teacher about language education and the use of the syllabus on a regular basis. They observe teacher classroom behavior if the teacher allows it, and discuss their observations with the teacher. Each PPB school advisor supports six to seven schools.

To study the use of the assessment framework and its perceived strengths and weaknesses, we turned to the Brussels-Capital Region, knowing that these schools received support in the implementation of the syllabus and its assessment framework. In addition to PPB, another educational network of school advisors has been active in the Brussels-Capital Region since 2008: Brussels Education Center (BEC). PPB and BEC work together and, although there are differences in vision and mission as well as the number of schools a school advisor coaches (most BEC advisors coach one or two schools and three schools at the most), both have been active supporters of task-based classroom practices. We therefore decided to submit a short questionnaire to the school advisors of both PPB and BEC about the use of the assessment framework. We felt that school advisors working with just a few schools knew their schools thoroughly and would be able to provide us with a professional, detached, and objective perspective on the use of the assessment framework in schools that have been using the task-based syllabus from the beginning. Because of the limited scope and resources of this study, a survey of the teachers was not possible. We believed a survey of the school advisors would provide us with close enough first-hand information and a more bird's-eye view of teacher practices to get a good overall impression on how the assessment framework was being used in the schools.

Purpose, Participants, and Method

A short pen-and-paper questionnaire of seven questions was distributed to all eighty-four school advisors from PPB and BEC in March 2015. They filled out the questionnaire anonymously. The results were scanned and mailed to the researcher by the directors of the educational networks. No background information about the respondents was gathered, seeing that they all had more or less the same profile and were working with primary schools in similar contexts. The purpose of the questionnaire (and the study) was to get an overall idea of the implementation and the perceived usefulness of the (different parts of the) assessment framework by identifying the strengths and weaknesses of the framework, as perceived by teachers but reported by the school advisors of those teachers. The questionnaire was comprised of six open-ended response items and five rating-scale items (question seven). Open-ended items asked about topics, such as the number of schools the respondent supervises that use TotemTaal's assessment framework (questions one and two); the perceived strengths and weaknesses of the framework from the teachers' (questions three and four) and from the advisors' (question six) points of view; and reasons why certain schools do not use the assessment framework (question five). Rating items asked respondents to rate how consistently different parts of the assessment framework (i.e., observation of tasks, analysis diagrams, tests, portfolios, reflection) are used on a five-point, Likert-type scale ($1 = $ never; 2, 3, 4, $5 = $ consistently).

The questionnaire was sent to eighty-four school advisors; twenty-nine school advisors responded—a response rate of 34.5%. The twenty-nine school advisors advised thirty-six primary schools working with TotemTaal. Out of a total of 123 Dutch-medium primary schools in Brussels, this represents 29% of the schools in Brussels.

Questionnaire Data Analysis

Questions one, two, and seven were analyzed quantitatively in SPSS. The answers to questions three to six (addressing strengths and weakness and why schools do not use the framework) were analyzed both quantitatively and qualitatively in Excel. First, all the answers of the respondents were coded as representing the teachers' voices (corresponding with questions three and four) versus representing the school advisors' voices (corresponding with questions five and six). Although the answers to a particular question were not always delivered in the space provided for that question, it was clear whether a school advisor was speaking on his or her own behalf or on behalf of the teachers. Second, all comments were coded as indicating a strength or a weakness. Third, the positive and negative comments were grouped in categories allowing the data to shape emergent categories (Dörnyei 2007). Two overall categories emerged: comments that referred to the assessment framework in general (labeled "overall comments") versus comments that referred to specific parts of the assessment framework (labeled "specific comments"). The specific comments were subdivided and labeled according to the specific components of the assessment framework that emerged from the data: "analysis diagrams," "observations," "tests," "portfolio," and "reflection." Fourth, the comments within these subcategories were grouped based on a content analysis.

Results

The responses to the survey will be discussed in relation to the weaknesses and strengths of implementing an integrated TBLT-TBLA approach as perceived by teachers and school advisors, as well as how a TBLA framework can contribute to understanding and improving language learning and teaching.

Perspective of the Teachers as Reported by the School Advisors

The twenty-nine school advisors, supporting thirty-six schools in Brussels that work with Totem Taal, claimed that all schools use the assessment framework. However, the schools did so to a different extent. In fact, seven school advisors (SAs 5, 7, 11, 19, 20, 27, 31) added the following nuances to question two ("How many of these schools [working with Totem Taal] use the assessment framework?"): "a little" (SA5); "the tests and portfolio for writing" (SA7); "not the analysis diagrams or portfolios" (SA11); "[only the] analysis diagrams for reading and spelling (adapted)" (SA19); "sometimes under my guidance; some teachers do, some don't" (SA20); "both [schools] but only the tests, and analysis diagrams depending on their focus (speaking and reading)" (SA27); and "two schools work intensively with the analysis diagrams for both observing and testing reading; a third school in assessing spelling" (SA31). These spontaneous notes immediately make clear that the implementation of the assessment framework is quite diverse and fragmented.

The answers to question seven about the systematic use (from "never" to "consistently" on a five-point, Likert-type scale) of the different components of the assessment framework also underscored the disparate usage of the assessment framework (see table 8.3).

Looking at the cumulative percentage of the two ratings indicating high consistency (ratings of 4 or 5), we can conclude that tests are by far the most consistently used component of the framework (97.5%), followed by the analysis diagrams (27.8%), reflection activities (16.7%), observation of tasks (13.9%), and finally portfolios (8.4%).

Regarding the strengths and weaknesses of the assessment framework, the answers to the questionnaire revealed more weaknesses than strengths. All twenty-nine school advisors mentioned weaknesses perceived by their teachers. A total of seventy-two

◆ **Table 8.3.** Number (*N* = 36) and percentage of schools that use the different components of the assessment framework according to their school advisors

| | Never | | | | | | | | Consistently | |
| | 1 | | 2 | | 3 | | 4 | | 5 | |
Components	*n*	%	*n*	%	*n*	%	*n*	%	*n*	%
Observation	5	13.9	10	27.8	**16**	**44.4**	5	13.9	...	...
Analysis diagram	3	8.3	11	30.6	**12**	**33.3**	8	22.2	2	5.6
Tests	...	...	1	2.8	...	...	2	5.6	**33**	**91.7**
Portfolio	**24**	**66.7**	9	25.0	2	5.6	1	2.8	...	...
Reflection	...	...	11	30.6	**19**	**52.8**	4	11.1	2	5.6

negative comments were recorded. These were grouped into five categories of overall comments and twelve categories of specific comments (see table 8.4). In contrast, twenty-three school advisors mentioned strengths that their teachers perceive in the assessment framework; six school advisors provided no positive comments whatsoever. A total of thirty-nine positive comments were recorded; these were grouped into three overall comments and eight specific comments (see table 8.5).

Overall, the assessment framework seemed to be too time consuming for the teachers. They seemed overwhelmed because it was new and unfamiliar. It was just too much, too elaborate, and too complex. The idea that it was too difficult and often also too vague related to all components of the framework but especially to the analysis diagrams, the observation component, and the use of portfolios in the classroom. The following school advisors' comments in the questionnaire illustrate these findings:

> *It is very difficult to implement all components. The tests are fine. The alternative assessments are more difficult. (SA1)*
>
> *Too difficult to track the progress of all students using the analysis diagrams. (SA11)*
>
> *Portfolios are unknown and teachers are fearful of all the work involved. (SA27)*

Negative comments about the tests were about their difficulty level for the students, some inconsistent results that appeared to be the outcome of different tests, and the fact that the results were not norm-referenced, which meant the teachers could not really compare their students' performances to the performances of students in the Flemish educational system. Interestingly, some teachers wanted to see more tests, probably because they were something they are familiar with, and the scores could go on the report cards of the students as SA13 notes in the questionnaire: "They [teachers] use the tests especially because they need points for their report cards." The outcomes of the alternative assessments they found more difficult to report to parents.

One school advisor pointed out that, for some teachers, the language of the assessment framework was too difficult; this unexpected finding might indicate that

Table 8.4. Assessment framework weaknesses reported by school advisors overall and by specific components

Comments	School advisors (*n*)
Overall	
1. Too time consuming	18
2. Too complex	13
3. Unfamiliar	3
4. No points for students' report cards	2
5. Language is too difficult	1
Specific	
Tests	
6. Not enough	5
7. Too difficult (for students)	3
8. Not norm-referenced	2
9. Sometimes inconsistent results	2
Analysis diagrams	
10. Too difficult	5
11. Too vague	4
12. Too much work	3
Observation	
13. Too extensive (time-consuming)	5
14. Too vague	1
Portfolio	
15. Unfamiliar	3
16. Too vague	1
17. Unwieldy	1
Total	72 comments

the instructions in the syllabus were too theoretical for the taste of the teacher or that the teacher was just unfamiliar with some of its core concepts, suggesting a need for the development of teachers' assessment literacy.

Most positive comments (see table 8.5) focused on the tests in Totem Taal; tests were definitely the component of the assessment framework that teachers liked the most. As SA8 mentions concisely: "The tests are good."

According to one teacher, tests did provide points for students' report cards, but the most important strengths of the tests were the clear rating rubrics and the fact that these provided teachers with a comprehensive overview of the language proficiency level of the class group (see table 8.5). The rating rubrics are based on the same task specifications and key processes as the analysis diagrams. So, both

◆ **Table 8.5.** Assessment framework strengths reported by school advisors overall and by specific components

Comments	School advisors (*n*)
Overall	
1. Broad, diverse evaluation opportunities	5
2. Links assessment with follow-up actions	5
3. A clear curricular design	2
Specific	
Tests	
4. Provide classroom performance level	6
5. Tests in general	5
6. Rating rubrics	4
7. Provide points for students' report cards	1
Analysis diagrams	
8. Diagnostic nature	6
9. Support spelling skills	3
Observation	
10. Provide opportunities	1
11. Reflection	
12. Provide opportunities	1
Total	39 comments

provided teachers with diagnostic information about students' performances and supported the development of skills (e.g., spelling skill).

> *They [teachers] analyze every test the students take. They make an overview of how the class scores and discuss this with the support teacher. Based on these results, they take action. (SA28)*

A teacher liked the opportunities the syllabus created for observation of student behavior. Another teacher liked the moments students reflected on their own performances. There were some teachers, as mentioned by SA14, who liked the broad and alternative perspective on assessment:

> *Allows for a broader evaluation of students' language proficiency, especially oral skills. (SA14)*

Teachers liked the fact that the assessment framework embeds all assessment components in a clear curricular design that allows them to act on the assessment results by providing follow-up actions for the whole-class group and for individual students.

> *The interpretation of the class scores form the basis of differentiated support in the classroom. (SA29)*

Perspective of the School Advisors

So, what did the school advisors themselves think of the assessment framework? Analyzing their answers to question six (about strengths and weaknesses of the assessment framework), a clear narrative appeared—a narrative supported by more than two-thirds of the school advisors (twenty-one out of twenty-nine). The school advisors liked that the syllabus had a clear vision on assessment and that it propagated a broad, alternative assessment perspective (SAs 1, 8, 11, 24, 27, and 29). However, they acknowledged that for teachers to act on it they would need a deep understanding of alternative assessment and would also need to evolve their own ideas on assessment and classroom practice in the direction of alternative assessment (SAs 6, 7, 9, 10, and 26). In addition, they thought some teachers should be made more aware of the big questions of why, who, what, and when to assess (SAs 10 and 14):

It helps teachers to think about what you assess at what time and why. (SA10)

The advisors found especially the reflective component of the assessment framework very powerful (SAs 13, 17, 18, and 21). One advisor liked the targeted observations (SA7) and another one the self-evaluation of the students (SA24). However, this was not always easy to implement for many teachers (SAs 7 and 26):

Reflection is the Achilles heel of the framework. Although most teachers acknowledge its importance, they drop it because of time constraints. It happens but not systematically. Especially individual reflection by students happens not often enough. (SA26)

According to respondent SA18, the strength of the framework was that the assessment not only provided an analysis of the students' products but also of the underlying processes. Furthermore, the outcome of the assessment provided teachers with information that they could use to shape their subsequent teaching activities, both for the whole-class groups and for individual students (SAs 11, 15, and 17). The assessment underpinned a more differentiated approach to teachers' teaching practices and students' learning opportunities (SA21). Again, this is not evident for all teachers, especially if they were teaching a large group of children by themselves, as respondent SA5 pointed out. Another school advisor (SA3) would like to see the syllabus provide more support for such a differentiated approach. Three advisors acknowledged that a syllabus could only provide such support to a certain extent (SAs 1, 15, and 26). Indeed, the advisors found it to be their job to coach teachers and provided them with tips and support to better adapt their teaching to students' individual needs (SAs 6, 14, 15, 20, and 26).

The analysis of reading comprehension tasks helps the teachers to gain more insight into the different information-processing levels and item difficulty in the reading tests. Taking the analysis diagram as our starting point, we look at what items the students had difficulty with. This helps us to obtain a clear picture of the reading performance of each individual child as well as the whole class. (SA26)

The biggest problem for the implementation of the assessment framework was that, unlike most school advisors, most school teams did not agree on adopting such a broad assessment perspective and that the framework was not supported by the whole school team (SAs 4, 8, 9, and 29).

It has a lot to offer, but it has to be part of a view on broad assessment, and this is often a problem in the school. (SA9)

Teachers are still developing a view on broad assessment, so they do not exploit all the opportunities offered by the curriculum. It often depends on the assessment policy of the school. Assessing students in a different way also implies a different way of reporting results or progress. However, many teachers are attached to a report card using "points." (SA29)

One school advisor (SA22) points out that such a perspective on assessment relates to a more functional and proficiency-related—and less formal view—on language acquisition and that such a view was not yet acknowledged by all the teachers in a school. One advisor (SA28) nicely explained that the implementation of the assessment framework was directly connected to the teaching skills of the teacher, linking up with the need for further professional development of primary school teachers.

Everything stands and falls with the teacher's professional skills. That is both strength and weakness. (SA28)

However, it seemed that a new syllabus could act as an impetus for the professional development of teachers and could even inspire teachers or school teams to go beyond the actual framework:

In the school, we now try to adapt the analysis diagrams to observe specific reading tasks. (SA26)

The analysis diagrams are often too general. Teachers create task-specific diagrams by using the suggestions for task support in the teacher manual. In this way, the task-specific diagram underpins the actual observation in the classroom. (SA29)

Discussion and conclusions

Developing a new, task-based language syllabus for Dutch-medium primary schools in Belgium was the ideal moment to think about classroom-based language assessment from a task-based perspective. The curriculum and syllabus designers opted for a task-based assessment framework, integrating "classical" assessments like tests with alternative assessments like observation, portfolios, self-reflection, and so on. Such an integration allowed teachers to develop a broader, more comprehensive picture of the language development of the class group as well as individual language learners. It also encouraged teachers to strive toward a better integration of instruction and assessment, using pedagogical tasks to inform assessment and assessment tasks to inform teaching. To link instruction and assessment, a clear framework of task specifications was developed, providing teachers with a lens to look at tasks and task performances. The task-specification framework and analysis diagrams focused teachers' attention on aspects essential to the performance of tasks (e.g., language goal, audience, level of information processing, strategies, and so on) and provided them with a systematic way of tracking these task-essential aspects in students' performances. The assessment framework in TotemTaal encouraged teachers to look at students' performances for both product-evaluation (i.e., the actual product or outcome of the task) and process-evaluation (i.e., the process of the actual task performance) purposes and provided them with a shared language to talk about students' results and progress. This kind of assessment is an indispensable part of a responsive, task-based pedagogy and is an inextricable part of good teaching (Rea-Dickins 2001).

Presenting such a framework to teachers was not self-evident. It was introduced as part of a task-based language syllabus. And while schools chose willingly a syllabus focusing on challenging and motivating listening, speaking, reading, and writing tasks, they might have been overwhelmed by the complex assessment framework of the syllabus. Seven years after the initial implementation of the assessment framework, we were positively surprised about the extent to which the assessment model was implemented in Brussels. School advisors were more convinced of the value and potential of the framework than teachers, who sometimes found it too much, too elaborate, and too complicated, but all schools were using the assessment framework in one way or another.

In some schools the framework had an impact on important discussions within school teams: the scope of assessment (narrow or broad, classical test versus alternative forms), the link between instruction and assessment (how can assessment inform classroom practice and actions), and the schools' assessment policies (vision, mission, report cards, etc.). However, the fact that the number of negative comments was greater than the number of positive comments and the fact that six school advisors reported nothing positive about the TBLA framework is a reason for concern.

On the one hand, some of the comments of the school advisors pointed to a clear need of professional development for teachers, especially with respect to language assessment literacy. Although formats of broad and alternative assessment have been advocated for some time now, teachers still tend to stick to old, familiar formats of assessment; that is, tests and quizzes for reasons of summative assessment (Struyf, Vandenberghe, and Lens 2001). Some of the assessment formats and purposes offered in TotemTaal seemed too unfamiliar to some of the teachers. Adopting new formats and especially integrating a comprehensive, innovative task-based assessment approach in their teaching might still be one step too far for most teachers.

On the other hand, the respondents pointed to a lack of a clear language assessment policy at the school level. Such an overall assessment policy is needed to answer some of the big questions driving language teaching: What are the language goals? Do the students meet these goals? How can teachers help students to meet these goals? What is the role of each school team member and the school team as a whole? How does the school team evaluate the impact of its teaching? However, we know that implementing a language-in-education policy or a school language policy is a long and winding road (Van den Branden 2010). It takes time and challenges all school team members to develop a coherent and supported vision and mission and to act upon that vision (Berben 2012). The merit of the TBLA framework is that it got at least some school teams discussing some of these big questions, helping teachers overcome the existing tension between assessment for and of learning (East 2016).

Overall, the practicality of the assessment framework remains a concern. If, after seven years, teachers still focus mainly on the test component and believe it is too difficult to put into practice, we might have to look for ways to reduce its complexity without diminishing its value and potential. TBLT is an ongoing innovation. Nevertheless, we may conclude that a multicomponent framework based on language tasks provided the teachers with a rich and balanced assessment repertoire allowing at least some of the teachers to integrate instruction and assessment more closely. It allows for multiple sources of assessment evidence (Shohamy 1996) and the collection of multiple performances over time to provide evidence of growth and learning. Such a repertoire enables teachers to make a variety of inferences about the capacities for language use that students have, or about what they can or cannot yet do. Again, according to the respondents, some teachers were able to use the instruments provided in the syllabus to do precisely this: Describe students' language development in a more detailed and precise manner and adapt their teaching accordingly.

Finally, we have to conclude that this small-scale survey was exploratory in nature and that its findings were based on the experiences and perceptions of school advisors. The school advisors work intensively in the schools that they are reporting on. They have a bird's-eye view and reported objectively about what is happening in the schools. However, they are important stakeholders themselves and in most cases they are fervent petitioners of alternative assessment methods. So, these findings might be biased and not entirely representative of the teachers' own voices. In a follow-up study, teachers should be addressed directly and, what's more, students should also be heard about how they experience and perceive the impact of the assessment framework. The voices of these important stakeholders are needed to make more informed decisions about the future directions of TBLA in classroom settings.

Acknowledgements

This chapter would not have been possible without the work and dedication of everyone involved in designing the task-based syllabus for primary education, TotemTaal: Martien Berben, Ine Callebaut, Marleen Colpin, Sigrid François, Martien Geerts, Marjon Goethals, Sara Jonkers, Katelijn Vander Meeren, Goedele Vandommele, and Silvie Vanoosthuyze. A special thanks to Kris Van den Branden who provided me with the opportunity to provide leadership to this wonderful group of people.

I would also like to thank all the school advisors from Priority Policy Brussels and Brussels Education Center for filling out the questionnaire and the directors Magda Deckers, Marc Reynders, and Marie-Paule Quix (PPB), and Piet Vervaecke (BEC) for their support. And finally, thanks to the editors of this volume for their suggestions that helped to improve this chapter and to Bart Deygers for providing feedback on the paper presentation that got this implementation study started.

References

Berben, Martien. 2012. "Hoe een taalbeleid het beleidsvoerend vermogen van je school kan verhogen." *Impuls* 43:88–98.
Berben, Martien, Ine Callebaut, Marleen Colpin, Sigrid François, Martien Geerts, Marjon Goethals, Katelijn Vander Meeren, Goedele Vandommele, and Koen Van Gorp. 2007a. *TotemTaal. Inleiding en evaluatie 4*. Mechelen, Bel.: Wolters Plantyn.

———. 2007b. *TotemTaal. Themahandleiding en kopieerbladen 4A*. Mechelen, Bel.: Wolters Plantyn.

Carless, David. 2007. "Learning-Oriented Assessment: Conceptual Basis and Practical Implications." *Innovations in Education and Teaching International* 44:57–66. doi:10.1080/14703290601081332.

Colpin, Marleen, and Koen Van Gorp. 2007. "Task-Based Writing in Primary Education: The Development and Evaluation of Writing Skills through Writing Tasks, Learner and Teacher Support." In *Tasks in Action: Task-Based Language Education from a Classroom-Based Perspective*, edited by Kris Van den Branden, Koen Van Gorp, and Machteld Verhelst, 194–234. Newcastle: Cambridge Scholars Publishing.

Departement Kanselarij & Bestuur. 2016. "Lokale inburgerings- en integratiemonitor." http://regionalestatistieken.vlaanderen.be/monitor-lokale-inburgering-en-integratie.

Departement Onderwijs. 1998. *Ontwikkelingsdoelen en eindtermen. Informatiemap voor de onderwijspraktijk: gewoon basisonderwijs*. Brussels: Afdeling Informatie en Documentatie.

Dörnyei, Zoltan. 2007. *Research Methods in Applied Linguistics: Quantitative, Qualitative and Mixed Methodologies*. Oxford: Oxford University Press.

Duran, Goedele, and Griet Ramaut. 2006. "Tasks for Absolute Beginners and Beyond: Developing and Sequencing Tasks at Basic Proficiency Levels." In *Task-Based Language Education: From Theory to Practice*, edited by Kris Van den Branden, 47–75. Cambridge: Cambridge University Press.

East, Martin. 2016. *Assessing Foreign Language Students' Spoken Proficiency*. Singapore: Springer.

Graham, Steve, and Dolores Perin. 2007a. "A Meta-analysis of Writing Instruction for Adolescent Students." *Journal of Educational Psychology* 99: 445–76. doi:10.1037/0022-0663.99.3.445.

———. 2007b. "What We Know, What We Still Need to Know: Teaching Adolescents to Write." *Scientific Studies in Reading* 11:313–36. doi: 10.1080/10888430701530664.

———. 2007c. *Writing Next: Effective Strategies to Improve Writing of Adolescent Middle and High School*. Washington, DC: Alliance for Excellence in Education.

Harding, Luke, J. Charles Alderson, and Tineke Brunfaut. 2015. "Diagnostic Assessment of Reading and Listening in a Second or Foreign Language: Elaborating on Diagnostic Principles." *Language Testing* 32: 317–36. doi: 10.1177/0265532214564505.

Hattie, John, and Gregory C. R. Yates. 2014. *Visible Learning and the Science of How We Learn*. New York: Routledge.

Heritage, Margaret, Aida Walqui, and Robert Linquanti. 2013. "Formative Assessment as Contingent Communication: Perspectives on Assessment as and for Language Learning in the Content Areas." Paper presented at the annual meeting of the American Educational Research Association, San Francisco, CA. http://ell.stanford.edu/sites/default/files/Assessment%20as%20contingent%20learning%20for%20AERA%202013%20FINAL.pdf.

National Research Council. 2001. *Knowing What Students Know: The Science and Design of Educational Assessment*. Washington, DC: National Academies Press.

National Reading Panel. 2000. *Reports of the National Reading Panel: Teaching Children to Read; An Evidence-Based Assessment of the Scientific Research Literature on Reading and Its Implications for Reading Instruction: Reports of the Subgroups*. Rockville, MD: NICHD Clearinghouse.

Norris, John M. 2009. "Task-Based Teaching and Testing." In *The Handbook of Language Teaching*, edited by Michael H. Long and Catherine J. Doughty, 578–94. Malden, MA: Wiley-Blackwell.

———. 2016. "Current Uses of Task-Based Language Assessment." *Annual Review of Applied Linguistics* 36: 230–44. doi:10.1017/S0267190516000027.

Rea-Dickins, Pauline. 2001. "Mirror, Mirror on the Wall: Identifying Processes of Classroom Assessment." *Language Testing* 18:429–62. doi:10.1177/026553220101800407.

Samuda, Virginia, and Martin Bygate. 2008. *Tasks in Second Language Learning*. London: Palgrave Macmillan.

Shohamy, Elana. 1996. "Language Testing: Matching Assessment Procedures with Language Knowledge." In *Alternatives in Assessment of Achievements, Learning Processes and Prior Knowledge*, edited by Menucha Birenbaum and Filip Dochy, 143–59. Boston: Kluwer Academic Publishers.

Slavin, Robert E. 2013. "Effective Programmes in Reading and Mathematics: Lessons from the Best Evidence Encyclopaedia." *School Effectiveness and School Improvement: An International Journal of Research, Policy and Practice* 24:383–91. doi:10.1080/09243453.2013.797913.

Slavin, Robert E., Cynthia Lake, Bette Chambers, Alan Cheung, and Susan Davis. 2009. "Effective Reading Programs for the Elementary Grades: A Best-Evidence Synthesis." *Review of Educational Research* 79:1391–466. doi:10.3102/0034654309341374.

Struyf, Elke, Roland Vandenberghe, and Willy Lens. 2001. "The Evaluation Practice of Teacher as a Learning Opportunity for Students." *Studies in Educational Evaluation* 27:215–38. doi:10.1016/S0191-491X(01)00027-X.

Van den Branden, Kris. 2006. "Introduction: Task-Based Language Teaching in a Nutshell." In *Task-Based Language Education: From Theory to Practice*, edited by Kris Van den Branden, 1–16. Cambridge: Cambridge University Press.

——. 2010. *Handboek Taalbeleid Basisonderwijs*. Leuven, Bel.: ACCO.

Van Gorp, Koen, and Bart Deygers. 2014. "Task-Based Language Assessment." In *The Companion to Language Assessment*, vol. 2, *Approaches and Development*, edited by Antony John Kunnan, 578–93. Malden, MA: Wiley Blackwell.

Chapter 9

◆ Predicting Placement Accuracy and
Language Outcomes in Immigrants'
L2 Finnish Education

TAINA TAMMELIN-LAINE, ARI HUHTA, REETA NEITTAANMÄKI, TUIJA HIRVELÄ, and
SARI OHRANEN
Centre for Applied Language Studies, University of Jyväskylä, Finland

ELINA STORDELL
Testipiste, Helsinki, Finland

ASSESSMENTS USED IN INTEGRATION training can be divided into three types or purposes: placement, formative, and summative (see, e.g., Brown 2012). The current study focuses on placement assessment although data from the final summative assessments also contribute to the investigation.

The purpose of the placement assessment described in this study is to guide immigrants to the most suitable training track with respect to their readiness for studies and the most suitable language module according to their Finnish language proficiency (Finnish National Board of Education 2012a). Correct placement is important in terms of time and other resources, but it also saves both immigrants and their teachers from frustration resulting from placement in an inappropriate level or type of course, even if it is possible for learners to change courses or tracks if need be.

Placement of immigrants in training tracks is not standardized. A national curriculum (Finnish National Board of Education 2012a) provides only very broad guidelines for integration training. Decisions about placement and other types of assessment (such as formative and summative), as well as about instruction, are made locally at the level of regional employment areas and individual institutions. The national curriculum, however, defines the target level for second language (L2; Finnish or Swedish) studies at the end of integration training. Placement is typically based on combining several sources of information, including immigrants' initial

Finnish language proficiency and information considered to indicate their readiness for formal language studies, such as their previous educational level and whether they have studied languages before.

Recently, a particular approach to placement was promoted in a project at the Centre for Applied Language Studies (CALS) at the University of Jyväskylä with funding from the Ministry of Economic Affairs and Employment, which is responsible for immigrants' integration training. The ministry cannot dictate that a specific placement procedure be used across the country because the administrators of both placement assessment and integration training are selected on the basis of competitive tendering in different regions. The ministry was, however, concerned about the comparability of placement procedures and was, therefore, funding a project that aimed to create and maintain a network of institutions that will commit to using the same procedure. The placement procedure designed by Testipiste, an organization specializing in immigrants' placement assessment, was selected by the ministry as the system to be advanced at the national level.

Starting systematic research on the validity of the Testipiste placement system was one of the aims of the project. Informal feedback gathered from the users of the Testipiste placement system has been quite positive. However, more empirical evidence about the procedure is needed.

Two issues have been addressed in our research so far and are reported here. The first concerns the lack of precise guidelines for assessors to combine different kinds of information collected during placement; recommendations about the most suitable track are based on assessors' subjective judgment about the importance of different pieces of information but also on feedback received from the teachers. To begin to formulate guidelines for combining and possibly weighing different kinds of information in placement recommendations, thus improving their comparability across assessors and institutions, we examined which information contributed to assessors' decisions.

The second issue we investigated was the extent to which the placement procedures predict immigrants' attainment of L2 proficiency, which is the main target in integration training. Effective placement assessment "should reflect the features of the teaching context" (Davies et al. 1999, 145). At this stage of research, the only information available to us about the teaching context was the track in which the learners had participated; therefore, we began our research by investigating the relationship between placement assessments and the (language) outcomes of teaching. In the future, we plan to examine the predictive validity of placements by gathering detailed information about the characteristics and activities in the different training tracks, as will be discussed at the end of this chapter.

There is no previous research on how placement assessments relate to outcomes in the context of training of immigrants in Finland; such studies also appear rarely internationally (however, see Gonzalves 2016). However, understanding how placement procedures relate to success, or lack thereof, in training is potentially useful information both for improving placement procedures and for increasing the use of placement information by the teachers (e.g., for identifying learners who might struggle if left without additional support).

Our results indicate that only certain types of information collected during placement are used by assessors for making placement recommendations and that only some of that information predicts L2 learning outcomes. Besides improving our understanding of the placement procedure, such findings can be used to shorten the procedure by removing uninformative parts from it, thus making it more practical. This research can also help us improve current placement tasks and develop new procedures.

Immigration and Language Learning in Finland

In 2015, approximately 6% of the population of Finland spoke other native languages in addition to Finnish, Swedish, or Sami, which are the traditionally spoken languages of the country (Statistics Finland 2016). The largest language groups were Russian (22% of all with a foreign background), Estonian (14.6%), Somali (5.4%), English (5.4%), and Arabic (5.1%; Statistics Finland 2016). Because of the growing number of immigrants, the Act on the Promotion of Immigrant Integration (1386/2010) came into effect in 2011 to (1) support immigrant integration; (2) make it easier for immigrants to play an active role in Finnish society; and (3) promote gender equality, nondiscrimination, and positive interaction between different population groups. Integration training is considered key to becoming a member of Finnish society since it includes learning the Finnish or Swedish language and communication skills, learning civic and working-life skills, and participating in guidance counseling (Finnish National Board of Education 2012a).

Integration training in Finland is divided into two separate types of courses: one for adults who are literate in any language and another for nonliterate adults. Both are implemented to enhance professional, job-related adult education. Instruction is full time, based on the national curriculum, and led by professional teachers. The training is cost free, and learners receive integration assistance and compensation for expenses for the course days. The length of education depends on immigrants' previous skills and needs, which are evaluated during an interview as part of the placement assessment. The number of students in integration training in 2015 was 14,742 (Työministeriö 2016).

For literate adults, the maximum length for integration training is sixty credit units (two thousand one hundred lesson hours during approximately one year), and the goal of language training is level B1.1 (i.e., low B1 on the Common European Framework of Reference [CEFR]; Finnish National Board of Education 2012a). This level is a threshold for applying for many benefits, including Finnish citizenship or entering many vocational training programs. The types of available integration-training courses are divided into different tracks that differ by speed or pace of instruction: slow, intermediate, and fast.

Nonliterate adults first participate in literacy training (a maximum of forty credit units). The objective is to learn basic oral and written Finnish or Swedish skills and to attain, on average, A1.2; that is, mid-A1 on the CEFR (Finnish National Board of Education 2012b). However, according to Tammelin-Laine (2014), many adults with no previous education do not achieve the targeted Finnish skills during literacy training in order to continue on to integration training. The acquisition of literacy skills is particularly challenging for them.

Placement Assessment as a Decision-Making Instrument

Placement assessment is widely used at colleges and universities, for example, to divide students into homogeneous groups based on their language abilities (Green and Weir 2004). Plakans and Burke (2013) argue that the potentially high stakes of placing students into different program levels calls for a careful understanding of test use, decision-making, and the impact of test results on test-takers' lives. Therefore, the use of standardized proficiency tests for placement purposes, while quite common in some contexts, can be problematic (see Kokhan 2013) since, for instance, such tests might not be able to address the needs of the particular context. Placement of immigrants into language training is probably a context in which language proficiency test scores alone are not sufficient, as other types of information about immigrants' backgrounds are likely needed for appropriate placement decisions, particularly if training courses differ not only in terms of their language requirement but also, for example, in their pace of progress.

We are not aware of any international surveys of placement assessment of immigrants, but it is likely that most countries with language programs for immigrants use procedures that are designed, or adapted, for the specific context. Such procedures probably vary considerably according to country. Canada, for example, uses the Canadian Language Benchmarks Placement Test (CLBPT), referenced to the Canadian Language Benchmarks (Hajer and Kaskens 2012). CLBPT is a task- and competency-based standardized assessment tool testing L2 English skills for communicating in the real world. In contrast, the German placement-assessment system monitors learners' motivation and other indicators of learning progression alongside language skills (Perlmann-Balme and Dengler 2007).

Testipiste: Finnish Placement Assessment for Immigrant Adults

The current study relates to a project titled "Finnish Placement Assessment for Immigrant Adults" (2015–16), coordinated by CALS at the University of Jyväskylä and funded by the Ministry of Economic Affairs and Employment. The project focused on a placement-assessment system for L2 Finnish developed in 2010–13 by Testipiste, an assessment center for adult migrants, originally funded by the European Social Fund. The project aimed to improve placement assessment in Finland, to standardize it by encouraging a wider use of the Testipiste system, and to develop the system further. Research reported here contributes to the further development of the system.

Testipiste placement test procedures start with an interview (thirty minutes), which includes word dictation and mechanical reading. If the interview reveals participants have low literacy skills, they continue with more detailed literacy tests. If they have some oral skills in Finnish, they will continue with the speaking test (fifteen minutes long). Next, most participants will take tests on morphological reasoning and basic mathematics (fifteen minutes each). If they have some oral and written Finnish ability, examinees proceed to the reading (one hour), listening (one hour), and writing tasks (forty minutes).

The recommendations given by the assessor(s) are used at employment services for placing the migrants into integration training. All the tracks except the literacy track are divided into four modules according to the starting level of language proficiency (see table 9.1). For the literacy track, the starting level of language modules is based on literacy skills. The tracks differ slightly in terms of their goals and L2 proficiency starting levels; the main difference between the tracks is the pace of study.

Placement tests cannot fully predict learners' course performance because of the effect of many contextual variables (Green and Weir 2004, 474). However, placement assessment gives information that is useful for teachers by showing, for example, what kind of tasks the participants are used to working with, and whether, as is the case in the partly computerized Testipiste system, they are familiar with using a computer.

Table 9.1. Language module CEFR levels available in capital region in each integration-training track

Language module/ Starting level	Literacy track	Slow track	Intermediate track	Fast track
1	Below 0	0	0	0
2	...	A1.3	A1.3+	A2.1
3	...	A2.1	A2.1+	A2.2
4	...	A2.2	A2.2+	B1.1
Goal	A1.2	A2.2–B1.1	B1.1	B1.1–B1.2

Methods

The objective of the study was to improve our understanding of the placement procedure developed at Testipiste by (1) investigating how different types of information contributed to assessors' recommendations about placement of immigrants in training tracks, and by (2) examining to what extent placement could predict L2 learning outcomes at the end of integration training. While the placement of immigrants into appropriate levels of language modules within each training track is a key aspect of the placement process as a whole and was also examined in the current study, we do not cover that in detail here. The main reason for this is the fact that the use of L2 test results in the placement of immigrants into language modules is very straightforward; almost everybody was placed into the level indicated by their lowest result across speaking, listening, reading, and writing. In contrast, placement into training tracks and prediction of L2 learning outcomes is much more complex and therefore deserves to be analyzed in more detail.

Given these concerns, the current study had the following two research questions:

RQ1.   What information determines the subjective placement of the learners into the training track (literacy, slow, intermediate, or fast)?

RQ2.   Do the different parts of the placement assessments explain the L2 proficiency achieved by the immigrants at the end of the integration training?

Participants

Two hundred eighty-six immigrants participated in the study. They came from (a) five institutes of adult education and (b) one private company providing integration training in the capital region. Altogether, seventy-one nationalities with sixty native languages were represented among the participants, including Russian (21.7%) and Arabic (11.5%), which are also among the five biggest language groups in Finland (Statistics Finland 2016). Most participants were female (69.6%; male: 30.4%). Participants' mean age was 33 years (SD = 8; under 30: 41.6%; 30–39 years: 39.2%; over 40: 19.2%). The mean length of residence in Finland before the placement assessment was twenty-two months (SD = 31.7). However, 50% of the participants had taken the placement assessment within seven months after their arrival to Finland. Participants' educational background varied considerably; 23.4% had a maximum of nine years of previous formal education; 4.2% reported having no education at all; 33.9% had graduated from vocational education or an upper-secondary school; and 42.7% had a bachelor's degree, polytechnic diploma, or a master's degree. The participants had studied 1.1 languages on average (excluding Finnish; SD = .8), but they reported knowing 1.4 languages on average (SD = .8).

All four tracks were included in the recommendations for the immigrants in our study (literacy track: 11.2%; slow track: 15.0%; intermediate track: 69.6%; fast track: 4.2%), but in practice, they studied only in the intermediate or slow track, apparently because integration training in the fast track program was not available for them in the particular institutions. Those who received a literacy track recommendation attended literacy training first and then continued to integration training on the slow track. It is important to note that track recommendations in the current sample differ notably from recommendations for all immigrant learners in the capital region as whole. In 2015, based on a total of 3,868 examinees, the percentages of the track recommendations were as follows: literacy 19.2%, slow 24.9%, intermediate 44.8%, and fast 8.8%.

Data Collection and Analysis

Data were collected from 286 immigrants who (a) participated in the placement assessments at Testipiste, (b) completed integration training, and (c) received final, summative grades in L2 Finnish in 2015–16.

A variety of assessment data-collection tools were used both in the placement assessment and the final, summative assessment to investigate the learners' language and other skills, as well as background information. All the language test tasks used in the placement assessment were carefully developed and piloted with over a thousand learners, and cut scores for proficiency levels have been defined via standard-setting procedures.

Placement Assessments

In the Testipiste model, oral language skills are assessed during the placement assessment interview and in a separate speaking-test task integrated in the interview. In the interview, the participants are asked about the following background information topics in Finnish: name, address, phone number, country of origin, native language, age, time of arrival to Finland, previous Finnish or Swedish courses, known and studied languages, impression of themselves as language learners, length of education in home country, occupation and work experience, IT skills, motivation and capability to study Finnish or Swedish at school and at home, and plans and wishes for the future.

Participants with no or very little command of Finnish are interviewed primarily in a shared language or in their first language with the help of an interpreter. In the speaking-test task, the participants are first asked to describe a picture; the theme expressed in the picture is then discussed more widely and at a more general level, if possible. Both the interview and the speaking-test task are used for assessing the participants' speaking skills, and the need to take additional language tests is determined by that assessment.

The placement assessments were comprised of different components capturing four different sets of skills: (1) readiness, (2) writing, (3) reading, and (4) listening comprehension. The "readiness skills" tests aim to help estimate if the learner is ready to fully participate in formal education and possesses some of the basic study skills needed in integration training. These skills are assessed with the following four tests: word dictation, mechanical reading, morphological reasoning, and basic mathematics. Word dictation and mechanical reading are included in the interview part of the placement-assessment procedure. Word dictation includes ten words. The first five are shared with all the participants. Then the last five words are selected either from the lower or higher level based on participants' performance in the first part. This task is used for assessing phonological working memory, knowledge of the Roman alphabet, understanding of grapheme-phoneme correspondences, and discrimination of Finnish phonemes. The mechanical reading (reading aloud) test is used for investigating participants' accuracy, fluency, and speed of reading a Finnish text—or their ability to read a text written in the Roman alphabet in the first place. It is not used for assessing reading comprehension or pronunciation. The test on morphological reasoning tests accuracy and fluency of reading, detection of similarities and differences in the elements of an artificial language, and making analogous conclusions based on the models resembling linguistic structures. The basic mathematics test includes such fundamental mathematical operations as addition, subtraction, multiplication, and division with whole numbers and decimals; percentage calculation; time transformations; and simple equations.

For assessing immigrants' writing skills in Finnish, there are tests at two level ranges. The lower level covers CEFR levels A1.3–A2.2, and the higher one covers levels A2.1–B1.1. The decision on the appropriate level for the participant is made during the interview part. At both levels, tasks include writing about personal life and responding to an e-mail message. Additional tasks include picture-based writing (lower level) and expressing an opinion (higher level).

The reading and listening comprehension subtests include six to eight tasks with thirty to thirty-five multiple-choice or true/false items. The tests are administered at two difficulty levels in the same way as the writing tests. The texts are short messages and narratives, and the audio recordings are announcements, discussions, and interviews.

Final Summative Assessment at the End of Integration Training

In the institutions from which the current data come, the final assessment of learners' Finnish language skills at the end of integration training was conducted by the teachers with the help of an end-of-program test designed at Testipiste. However, the teachers combine the test results with the information they gather during the training by using a range of approaches, which varies among teachers. The final summative grades are, thus, not arrived at in a standardized way and obviously vary in terms of their reliability. Final language grades are expressed as CEFR levels (using the more fine-grade Finnish version of the CEFR scale) and reported separately for speaking, listening, reading, and writing.

Analyses

The contribution of different types of placement information to the recommendation of the training track (RQ 1) was investigated with an ordered probit regression analysis (in Mplus 7.4; Muthén and Muthén 2015) with the track as the dependent variable and age, number of studied languages, mechanical reading, word dictation, basic mathematics, morphological reasoning, length of residence in Finland, level of education, and gender as independent variables. The model was estimated by using a robust weighted least squares estimator. Ordered probit regression was used because the dependent variable (track recommendation) was an ordinal-scale variable. The 264 participants were analyzed in ordinal probit regression analysis. Of the 264, 5% ($n = 13$) were recommended for track 1 (literacy track); 16% ($n = 42$) for track 2 (slow track); 75% ($n = 198$) for track 3 (intermediate track); and 4% ($n = 11$) for track 4 (fast track). Some of the participants recommended for the literacy track could not be included in the analysis because they were not given all the "readiness" tests.

The assessors do not use a fixed formula for weighing specified factors for track recommendations. They are instructed to use the results of skills other than L2 Finnish (because L2 results are used for determining the starting level of the language course [module], not the track) and all relevant background information about the learner gathered during the placement interview. However, how the assessor balances all those factors is left to their judgment. Therefore, the current study was a post hoc analysis to discover which factors the trained and highly experienced assessors at Testipiste took into account when making training-track recommendations.

The relationship between placement assessment and final, summative language assessment (RQ 2) was investigated with a linear regression analysis with Mplus, using MLR estimation (maximum likelihood parameter estimation, which is robust to nonnormality in the data). The assumptions underlying the use of linear regression (e.g., collinearity and distribution of residuals) were checked with IBM SPSS Statistics 22. The four language grades (speaking, listening, reading, and writing) were used as dependent variables and the same potentially predictive factors that were used in the analysis of the training-track recommendations were used as independent variables. In addition, some further variables were used as independent variables: those that turned out not to explain training-track recommendation (e.g., length of residence in the country) or that are not used in the placement for the track but rather in decisions about the L2 starting level (in this case, the level of speaking skills in Finnish that is assessed for all test-takers). The reason for including initial L2 speaking skills as one of the predictors was the possibility that differences in initial L2 proficiency persist till the end of training, despite teachers' efforts to bring immigrants' language skills to the same level.

Results
Results of Placement and Final Summative Assessments
Table 9.2 shows participants' performance on the four tests of "readiness" skills. Participants received the highest mean scores on word dictation and mechanical reading (83% and 88% of the maximum, respectively). The average results for basic mathematics and morphological reasoning were somewhat lower (65% and 72% of the maximum, respectively).

Table 9.3 presents learners' mean writing, listening, reading, and speaking scores from the placement assessments. Most (about 75%–80%) had such low Finnish skills that they participated in the speaking test only. Their mean speaking level was only slightly higher than A1.2, while the highest level achieved was B1.2. About one fourth

◆ **Table 9.2.** Results of the tests of readiness skills (placement assessment)

Placement assessment	N	$\overline{X}$	SD	Med.	Min.	Max.
Word dictation	285	2.54	0.65	3	0	3
Basic mathematics	265	13.15	5.17	14	0	20
Morphological reasoning	267	21.64	7.93	24	0	30
Mechanical reading	286	2.63	0.68	3	0	3

◆ **Table 9.3.** Proficiency in language skills (placement assessment)

Placement assessment	N	$\overline{X}$	SD	Med.	Min.	Max.
Speaking	286	2.25	2.85	0	0	12
Writing	71	5.24	1.76	5	2	10
Reading comp.	58	6.45	1.76	7	3	11
Listening comp.	56	6.68	1.98	7	3	11

Note: The results refer to CEFR levels; 0 = below A1.1 and 12 = B1.2.

of the test-takers participated in the writing test and one fifth in reading and listening assessments. In those tests, the mean level was A1.3–A2.1, and the highest level was above B1.1.

As table 9.4 shows, the speaking results were the highest and writing and reading comprehension had the lowest mean scores on the final, summative assessment after integration training. The lowest CEFR level attained was A1.2 and the highest was B2.1. The median level was A2.2.

◆ **Table 9.4.** Proficiency in language skills (final, summative assessment), *N* = 286

Final grade	$\bar{X}$	SD	Med.	Min.	Max.
Speaking	5.44	0.94	5	2	8
Writing	5.09	0.98	5	2	8
Reading comp.	5.09	0.88	5	3	8
Listening comp.	5.16	0.86	5	3	8

Note: The results refer to CEFR levels; 2 = A1.2 and 8 = B2.1.

Understanding Decisions on Placement to Training Tracks

Recommendations based on placement assessment in fact concern two aspects of integration training: estimation of Finnish language proficiency (language level) and the pace at which the learner is expected to make progress in their studies (track). As mentioned earlier, we focus on the training track placements (RQ 1), as the way the assessors weigh different kinds of information from the background interview and readiness tests is unknown and likely to be much less straightforward than the placement into the appropriate L2 level module (which is based on the weakest score across the four language skills).

Table 9.5 summarizes the results of the regression analysis with the training-track recommendation (four tracks) as the dependent variable and the most likely predictors that the assessors were using for their recommendations as the independent variables. It should be noted that none of the nonsignificant variables were removed from the model because, at this stage, we wanted to investigate the contribution of all potentially useful variables. A very high proportion of the decisions (91.2%) could be explained with the following factors: readiness skills (mechanical reading, word dictation, and morphological reasoning) and certain background information, such as number of studied languages (excluding Finnish) and educational background. Learners' age, gender, or length of residence in the country did not explain track recommendations significantly.

Because all the statistically significant regression coefficients are positive, an increase in the test scores, number of languages studied, level of previous education, and so on relates to a higher (i.e., faster) track recommendation and vice versa.

Finally, a comparison of the adjacent threshold estimates in table 9.5 supports the assumption that the assessors could distinguish between four different tracks with the help of placement information. This is indicated by the fact that the estimates for the thresholds between the different tracks (i.e., between tracks 1 and 2,

◆ **Table 9.5.** Ordered probit regression model for predicting training-track recommendation (standardized model results), $N = 264$

Variables	Est. B	SE	*p*-value
Age (in years)	0.057	0.059	0.334
Number of studied languages	0.153	0.051	0.003
Mechanical reading	0.303	0.067	0.001
Word dictation	0.295	0.076	0.001
Basic mathematics	0.163	0.093	0.081
Morphological reasoning	0.251	0.080	0.002
Length of residence in Finland	−0.040	0.059	0.497
Level of education	0.159	0.069	0.022
Gender	0.064	0.047	0.174
Thresholds			
Track 1	3.356	0.423	0.001
Track 2	4.588	0.451	0.001
Track 3	6.573	0.475	0.001
R 2	0.912	0.026	0.001

tracks 2 and 3, and tracks 3 and 4) differed significantly from each other (at the .001 level).

In a separate analysis with only the readiness tests as predictors of track recommendations, they jointly explained 85% of the variance, from which we can deduce that background information plays a smaller role in the placement than readiness test results.

Relationship between Placement Assessment and Final Summative Assessment

As the first step in trying to understand to what extent it might be possible to predict ultimate (language) achievement in integration training, we examined the relationship between placement assessment and the final language grades given by the teachers at the end of the typically close-to-one-year courses. These final, summative assessments are a combination of an external, final test designed by Testipiste and the teachers' own continuous assessment. Final language grades are reported separately for the four skills on the Finnish version of the CEFR scale. We used the four final language grades as dependent variables in linear regression analyses. As independent variables, we used the four tests of "readiness" skills and certain background variables (age, gender, educational level, length of residence, and number of languages studied), as they are generally considered potentially important factors in language learning or they had been found statistically significant in our analyses of the track placements reported for RQ 1 above. We also used the actual track the learners had been through (only two tracks were in fact available to them) and the speaking-test grade from the placement test as further independent variables. The other language tests could not be used, as only speaking was assessed for practically all learners during placement; the other skills were not assessed for learners who did not know any Finnish in the placement stage.

Table 9.6 shows the results for predicting the final reading and writing grade (these models include also the nonsignificant variables). A total of 36% of the variance in the final reading grades and 38% in the writing grades were explainable on the basis of the information gathered about learners' during placement procedures. Exactly the same variables turned out to be significant predictors for both skills. The findings indicate that women and younger learners achieved higher levels of reading and writing than men and older learners. Furthermore, higher scores in the basic mathematics test and higher initial speaking skills were related to better performance in reading and writing at the end of the integration training.

The findings concerning speaking and listening are somewhat different although there were some similarities with written skills. As table 9.7 demonstrates, the amount of explained variance was lower for the final oral skills—about 29% for speaking and 25% for listening—than for the written skills. Only three statistically significant predictors of listening comprehension could be identified; namely, age, the score on the basic mathematics test, and the initial speaking proficiency in Finnish. We note here that these same variables also predicted writing skills, as reported above, and that they were also statistically significant predictors of the final speaking grades (see table 9.7). However, two further variables were found to

◆ **Table 9.6.** Linear regression model for predicting the final grade in writing and reading skills (standardized model results), $N = 264$

Variables	Writing final grade			Reading comp. final grade		
	Est. B	SE	*p*-value	Est. B	SE	*p*-value
Age (in years)	−0.219	0.067	0.001	−0.212	0.063	0.001
Number of studied languages	0.082	0.057	0.148	0.093	0.063	0.143
Mechanical reading	0.072	0.052	0.169	0.028	0.051	0.577
Word dictation	0.008	0.049	0.871	0.075	0.051	0.139
Basic mathematics	0.358	0.081	0.001	0.363	0.083	0.001
Morphological reasoning	0.004	0.100	0.966	−0.009	0.102	0.933
Length of residence in Finland	−0.076	0.052	0.144	−0.061	0.059	0.302
Level of education	0.028	0.061	0.646	−0.019	0.058	0.738
Gender	−0.162	0.047	0.001	−0.143	0.045	0.002
Placement assessment speaking	0.145	0.051	0.004	0.163	0.056	0.004
Actual training track	0.093	0.077	0.226	0.112	0.079	0.156
Intercept	4.666	0.471	0.001	5.221	0.467	0.001
R^2	0.378	0.047	0.001	0.364	0.048	0.001

account for variance in the final speaking grades: number of languages studied (the more the better) and gender (women did better).

Discussion and Conclusion
Summary of the Findings
The first part of the study aimed at understanding the decision-making of the assessors at Testipiste in terms of the factors they consider when recommending a particular pace of learning (i.e., track; RQ 1). Results showed that the tests of readiness skills (mechanical reading, in particular) were the key determiners of the recommendation although specific background variables (number of previously studied languages and educational background) also contributed to the decision. Fewer than 10% of the track recommendations could not be explained from the variables identified in this study; this result suggests that the assessors at Testipiste work systematically. Although their interrater reliability could not be estimated from the available data, the fact that the track recommendations were separable from each other suggests they assess fairly consistently.

In the second part of the study, we investigated whether different parts of the placement assessment predict the final language grades (RQ 2). As could perhaps be expected, most of the variance in the final language grades could not be explained

◆ **Table 9.7.** Linear regression model for predicting the final grade in oral skills (standardized model results), *N* = 264

Variables	Speaking final grade			Listening comp. final grade		
	Est. B	SE	*p*-value	Est. B	SE	*p*-value
Age (in years)	−0.285	0.066	0.001	−0.279	0.066	0.001
Number of studied languages	0.161	0.067	0.016	0.095	0.068	0.162
Mechanical reading	−0.009	0.059	0.878	0.008	0.065	0.900
Word dictation	0.072	0.055	0.188	0.047	0.054	0.389
Basic mathematics	0.180	0.083	0.029	0.306	0.088	0.001
Morphological reasoning	0.027	0.101	0.789	0.002	0.107	0.986
Length of residence in Finland	−0.009	0.061	0.879	−0.060	0.062	0.334
Level of education	−0.084	0.062	0.174	−0.055	0.065	0.393
Gender	−0.111	0.051	0.030	−0.088	0.051	0.082
Placement assessment speaking	0.226	0.052	0.001	0.196	0.063	0.002
Actual training track	0.131	0.090	0.145	0.044	0.077	0.568
Intercept	5.648	0.481	0.001	6.045	0.492	0.001
R^2	0.286	0.046	0.001	0.252	0.048	0.001

on the basis of placement assessments. However, for reading and writing, about one third of the variance could be predicted from previous performance on the tests of mathematics and speaking (Finnish), age, and gender. Prediction of listening and speaking was more modest, which suggests that progress in these may be more variable across individuals; it is probably affected also by the amount and nature of training at workplaces that immigrants have during integration training. Interestingly, initial differences in L2 speaking skills before starting the training seemed to persist to some degree up to the end of the program since command of spoken L2 predicted higher achievement in all four language domains. Perhaps even a small initial advantage in, for example, being able to follow instructions right from the start helps such learners to make more rapid progress compared with those with no or very little command of the L2.

Issues to Be Studied in the Future and Lessons Learned

The current study was a starting point for more extensive and longer-term research into the validity of the placement assessments used for immigrants' integration training in Finland, and more generally, into the effectiveness of the integration training system, particularly as regards immigrants' L2 learning. In the future, a network of institutions will use the Testipiste placement system and will engage in systematic study of the factors affecting learning outcomes. In the remainder of the chapter, we review the main issues with placement and final assessments, as well as integration training more generally, that we identified during the current study. We also discuss the types of data that will be needed in the future to study placement assessments as well as the effectiveness of integration training more thoroughly.

Current Placement Assessment System

Although we could explain over 90% of the variance in the track recommendations in an exploratory analysis of a number of variables, we still need to do further analyses (series of model fitting) to find out the most optimal combination of variables that explain placement recommendations. Determining if all the collected background information is relevant for track recommendations is rather straightforward and can be addressed, at least partly, with our current data. We know now which of the readiness tests and background information items are likely to contribute most to the recommendations, which paves the way for a construction of a formula for weighing the different factors that all assessors could use. This would increase the reliability of decisions, especially when new assessors are recruited. However, we would need a more comprehensive data set to validate the present findings because the literacy and fast track recommendations were clearly underrepresented in the data.

In the future, one of the foci will be research-based development of the readiness tests in cooperation with experts on special education in order to increase the validity of the tests. The measurement properties of some of these tests (word dictation and mechanical reading) might also be improved by lengthening their currently very short scoring scale.

In addition, more detailed information about the placement assessments and assessment processes than was available in the current study would also be useful in future studies. We did not know which assessments were provided by which rater, nor was there detailed background information available about the raters. In addition, in some cases, two different versions of the tests were used, but information about a given version was not available; therefore, we could only assume that the scores provided from different test versions were comparable.

Final Summative Assessment

Although the same final language test was used in all the institutions from which data was gathered, the final language grades were affected by all the other information that the teacher had collected during the course. To enable a more precise evaluation of learners' L2 proficiency at the end of the training program, we need to know both the final test results and teachers' own evaluations based on continuous assessment of the learners. Currently, final assessment varies across institutions in the country, and only some use the tests designed at Testipiste. In future studies, we obviously need to make sure that data on learners' language achievement is gathered with the same, validated measures across the institutions involved in the research.

Effectiveness of Instruction in the Training Tracks

Placement assessment is an important part of immigrants' integration training system in Finland but only one part of the entire system. The current study was the first step in a larger-scale and longer-term investigation of the effectiveness of the integration training and, particularly, whether the division into four tracks functions as intended. Therefore, we conclude the discussion by outlining what future studies of the whole training system should consider.

Investigating the usefulness of track recommendations is a far more complex issue than can be captured by predicting those recommendations from information from the placement procedure. To study properly the meaningfulness of organizing training in terms of tracks requires that we know much more about how the tracks differ from each other in terms of teaching activities, materials, and methods used, as well as approaches to formative assessment and feedback. We know that slower tracks are typically longer in terms of duration and number of contact hours, which is one obvious way to try to ensure that both kinds of tracks reach the same goals. However, besides that, we know very little about how the tracks differ. Are the differences between different educational institutions and teachers salient enough that one can really identify a track? That is, are the between-track differences clearly bigger and more important than within-track differences? Therefore, one of the key requirements in the longer-term investigation of integration training is that we gather more comprehensive information about the training period itself.

More detailed information will be needed on both learners and teachers. We need, for example, to know the actual length of study for each learner, as well as information about their on-the-job training and L2 learning during that training. Furthermore, we should know about learners' motivation and attitudes, particularly toward using and learning the L2. As for teachers, information will be needed about their characteristics, such as teaching experience, preferred teaching and assessment methods, and strategies for providing learners feedback.

Conclusion

Increasing immigration to Finland poses challenges to L2 education, and one solution has been the creation of integration training programs with different tracks and language modules for different kinds of learners. We know, however, rather little about the effectiveness of integration training and how the different kinds of assessment (placement, formative, summative, etc.) function as part of the training system. To begin to address these gaps in our knowledge, the University of Jyväskylä and the Testipiste assessment center carried out a study, investigating the underlying characteristics of the track recommendations made in the placement process and the relationship between placement and final assessments. The study paves the way to more systematic and longer-term research on integration training in the future.

Note

1.   According to the constitution of Finland, Finnish and Swedish are the two official languages of the country.

References

Brown, Annie. 2012. "Uses of Language Assessments." In *The Encyclopedia of Applied Linguistics*, edited by Carol Chapelle. Chichester, Eng.: Wiley-Blackwell. doi:10.1002/9781405198431.wbeal1237.

Davies, Alan, Annie Brown, Cathie Elder, Kathryn Hill, Tom Lumley, and Tim McNamara. 1999. *Dictionary of Language Testing*. Studies in Language Testing 7. Cambridge: Cambridge University Press.

Finnish National Board of Education. 2012a. *National Core Curriculum for Integration Training for Adult Migrants 2012*. Helsinki: Finnish National Board of Education.

——. 2012b. *National Core Curriculum for Literacy Training for Adult Migrants 2012*. Helsinki: Finnish National Board of Education.

Gonzalves, Lisa. 2016. "When Standardized Tests Fail: Informal Assessment of LESLLA Learners in California Adult Schools." Paper presented at the Low Educated Second Language and Literacy Acquisition (LESLLA) symposium, Granada, Spain, September 8–10, 2016. http://wdb.ugr.es/~leslla2016/wp-content/uploads/other-areas_otras-areas.pdf.

Green, Anthony B., and Cyril J. Weir. 2004. "Can Placement Tests Inform Instructional Decisions?" *Language Testing* 21:467–94. doi:10.1191/0265532204lt2930a.

Hajer, Anne, and Anne-Marie Kaskens. 2012. *Canadian Language Benchmarks: English as a Second Language for Adults*. Ottawa: Citizenship and Immigration.

Kokhan, Kateryna. 2013. "An Argument against Using Standardized Test Scores for Placement of International Undergraduate Students in English as a Second Language (ESL) Courses." *Language Testing* 30:467–489. doi:10.1177/0265532213475782.

Ministry of Employment and the Economy, Finland. 2011. Act on the Promotion of Immigrant Integration 1386/2010. Unofficial translation. www.finlex.fi/en/laki/kaannokset/2010/en20101386.pdf.

Muthén, Linda K., and Bengt O. Muthén. 2015. *Mplus User's Guide*. 7th ed. Los Angeles: Muthén & Muthén. https://www.statmodel.com/download/usersguide/MplusUserGuideVer_7.pdf.

Perlmann-Balme, Michaela, and Stefanie Dengler. 2007. *Einstufungssystem für die Integrationskurse in Deutschland. Handreichungen für Einstufende* [Placement assessment system for integration courses in Germany. Guidelines for placement]. Munich: Goethe-Institut.

Plakans, Lia, and Maureen Burke. 2013. "The Decision-Making Process in Language Program Placement: Test and Nontest Factors Interacting in Context." *Language Assessment Quarterly* 10:115–134. doi:10.1080/15434303.2011.627598.

Statistics Finland. 2016. "Population 31.12.2015 by Year, Language, Sex and Age." http://pxnet2.
    stat.fi/PXWeb/pxweb/en/Maahanmuuttajat_ja_kotoutuminen/Maahanmuuttajat_
    ja_kotoutuminen__Maahanmuuttajat_ja_kotoutuminen/030_kieli.px/table/
    tableViewLayout1/?rxid = b81a4bf1-f54b-4969-a1ec-bd265db9d7bb.
Tammelin-Laine, Taina. 2014. *Aletaan alusta. Luku- ja kirjoitustaidottomat aikuiset uutta kieltä oppimassa* [Let's
    start from the beginning. Non-literate adults learning a new language]. PhD diss., University of
    Jyväskylä. Jyväskylä Studies in Humanities.
Työministeriö. 2016. *Työnvälitystilasto* [Statistics on employment services]. Helsinki, Fin.: The Ministry of
    Economic Affairs and Employment.

Part Three

Validity Evaluation

Chapter 10

◆ University Entrance Language Tests

Examining Assumed Equivalence

BART DEYGERS
University of Leuven

IN FLANDERS—THE DUTCH-SPEAKING, NORTHERN part of Belgium—international students with a mother tongue (L1) different from Dutch have to pass a university entrance language test before they can register for university. Currently, all Flemish universities accept both STRT (Ready-to-Start Higher Education) and Interuniversitaire Taaltest Nederlands Voor Anderstaligen (ITNA; inter-university test of L2 Dutch) as equivalent measures of Dutch language proficiency, and international students who pass either of these tests can register for university. STRT explicitly positions itself as a test designed for people who intend to pursue higher education at a Dutch-medium institution (Certificaat Nederlands als Vreemde Taal [CNaVT] 2016), but ITNA's intended use is more ambivalent (ITNA 2016). It is used as an achievement test at the end of a second language (L2) learning trajectory, but around 70% of the ITNA candidates take the test for university admission purposes (Inter-University Test Consortium [IUTC] 2015).

As part of a larger research project that investigates the policy that regulates international L2 students' access to Flemish universities from different perspectives, the current study examines a claim made explicitly or implicitly in the admission policies of the largest universities in Flanders (Ghent University 2016; KU Leuven 2016; Universiteit Antwerpen 2016). This claim says that ITNA and STRT are equivalent measures of language proficiency. The purpose of the current paper is to investigate the equivalence claim, which has remained unsubstantiated to date. If the claim is true, or largely true, accepting either STRT or ITNA poses no immediate problem. But, if it is false it could lead to an unjust entrance policy, and the appropriateness of the equivalence claim could be questioned. The current study, then, fundamentally investigates the impact of unfounded test equivalence claims made by university admission boards, using the Flemish context as a case in point. In investigating whether the target level and the constructs of STRT and ITNA are comparable, this study draws on Kane's (2013) Interpretation/Use Argument and on Phillips's (2007) ideas on policy effectiveness. The implications of the findings are discussed with regard to justice (McNamara and Ryan 2011; Rawls 2001; Sen 2010).

Examining Equivalence

Universities often require prospective international students to pass a language test as a precondition for admission. The rationale behind distinguishing among foreign students on the basis of language test results is to ensure that all incoming students will have the same required minimum level, allowing them to participate linguistically at university (Fulcher 1997; McNamara and Ryan 2011). In Europe, the most commonly required language level for this purpose is the B2 proficiency level on the Common European Framework of Reference for Languages, or CEFR (Council of Europe 2001; Deygers et al. 2017).

The B2 level is the fourth of six consecutive language proficiency levels on the CEFR, which starts at A1 and goes up to the very advanced C2 level. A B2 language learner is described as somebody who can understand the main ideas of complex texts, can interact fluently and spontaneously with native speakers, can produce clear and detailed oral and written texts, and can develop a sustained line of reasoning (Council of Europe 2001). The CEFR has been widely adopted by educational policymakers, and its levels are used to determine entrance requirements in a wide variety of contexts (Figueras 2012). Unfortunately, however, the CEFR bands are rather broad (Fulcher 2004), and two tests that link to the same level are not necessarily equally difficult, even though policy may assume that they are (Green, forthcoming).

The validation framework adopted in this study is Kane's (2013) Interpretation/ Use Argument. Kane's central tenet is that validating a test score interpretation holds little meaning without considering the way in which a score is used. Consequently, what requires validation is not the score itself but the interpretation or the use of that test score (Messick 1989 first emphasized this as the focus of validation). The implication of Kane's approach is that when scores of two different tests carry equal weight in a university entrance policy, this claim requires specific validation, since the way in which universities use scores has important social consequences for the candidates.

In Kane's (2013, 62) logic, the test developer is not held unaccountable, however. Test developers are responsible for developing adequate measurement tools in contexts they recommended, promote, or should be able to foresee. Consequently, since STRT and ITNA are explicitly marketed as university entrance tests, developing tests that are fit for purpose in this context is their responsibility. Importantly, however, the claim of level equivalence between STRT and ITNA is only made by university admission boards, who have not provided any evidence in this respect.

Level Equivalence

When a university claims that the certificates of two different tests are equivalent measures of a certain level of language proficiency and this claim is wrong or unsubstantiated, it may have rather serious consequences for the educational standards of a university and on the lives of test-takers. The way in which university admission boards use language tests is a rare topic of research, but it is of considerable importance none-theless. First, when a university entrance language policy wrongfully assumes language tests measure an equivalent level of language proficiency, this policy may cause unac-ceptable variation in the language abilities of the admitted student population, thereby defeating its main purpose. Second, when two tests are assumed to be equivalent, test takers should have a comparable chance of passing either test. When test-takers need to make a choice between two tests on the basis of unreliable information, the justice of the university entrance policy can be questioned.

A number of studies have examined the relationship between scores on two uni-versity entrance tests by calculating correlations. The Educational Testing Service (ETS 2010) reported a .73 correlation between the Test of English as a Foreign Language Internet-Based Test (TOEFL iBT) and the International English Language Testing System (IELTS), and correlations between .44 (writing) and .68 (speaking) for the subskills. The ETS researchers further investigated the relationship between the tests using regression-based prediction, equipercentile linking, and conditional probability. Zheng and De Jong (2011) compared the Pearson Test of English (PTE) Academic test to English language tests that are used for university admission purposes, such as the Test of English for International Communication (TOEIC); ($r = .76$) and TOEFL iBT ($r = .75$), and used regression analysis to map PTE Academic scores onto the CEFR ($r^2 = .5$). Lastly, Riazi (2013), building on the aforementioned study, found an overall correlation of $r = .82$ between IELTS and PTE Academic scores, and correlations between $r = .66$ (listening) and $r = .72$ (speaking) for the four skills. Riazi reported medium effect sizes for the productive skills (speaking $\eta^2 = .50$; writing $\eta^2 = .50$), and close to medium effect sizes for the receptive skills and the overall score (listening $\eta^2 = .38$; reading $\eta^2 = .44$; overall $\eta^2 = .45$).

Construct Equivalence

Another important aspect of assessment equivalency is the extent to which two tests used for the same purpose in the same context measure similar constructs. In lan-guage testing, little quantitative research has been conducted to examine construct equivalence, even though it may contribute to a deeper understanding of the outcomes of level equivalence research. For score users, such as admission boards, students, or teachers, it could be quite informative to know why test results differ and where tests that serve the same purpose are actually dissimilar. Universities offering post-entry language courses for international L2 students could use this information for instruc-tional purposes, for example. Or, programs with strict writing requirements could be interested in learning how ratings on equivalent tests relate to each other.

Policy Effectiveness and Justice

Investigating level and construct equivalence is of primary importance when dis-cussing the use of language test scores as equivalent measures of B2 proficiency. Test scores are not used in a contextual vacuum, however; they are part of a policy that determines who is allowed in and who is not. If the claim of equivalence is mis-guided, it could have a substantial impact on people's lives.

In this study, the impact of the assumptions in the university entrance policy is investigated using Phillips's (2007) decision rule and Rawlsian (Rawls 1971; Sen 2010) principles of justice. Phillips (2007), observing that policy measures are not always founded on empirical data, recommends critically examining policy claims by identifying the problem that the policy was intended to solve, and by evaluating the effectiveness of the proposed solution on the basis of evidence. The decision rule (Kane 2013; Phillips 2007) quite simply states that a policy measure cannot be upheld if it does not solve the problem it was meant to address. Translated to the context of this study, the decision rule implies that, if the use or interpretation of a test score within a university entrance policy is unsupported by empirical data, there may be reason to doubt its effectiveness.

Kane, referring to Phillips (2007), requires that the evidence used to validate a policy claim be proportionate to the social consequences of that claim. And, when the stakes are high, all the evidence should support the claims made by score users (Kane 2013). If empirical evidence does not support the way in which policy uses test scores (in this case, as equivalent), the policy would not achieve its main goal of maintaining a minimal language level within the international student population. Consequently, the policy would not meet the basic demand of the decision rule. The policy would therefore be ineffective, but it might also be unjust.

Justice, in this case, is concerned with the effect of the introduction of one or more language tests on a larger population. In line with Rawlsian logic, the prerequisite for justice is fairness; that is, freedom from bias (Rawls 2001; Sen 2010). But, even if all tests accepted in a university admission policy are equally fair, the admission policy can be unjust when it causes an indefensible disequilibrium in a population (McNamara and Ryan 2011). Two fair tests can thus be part of an unjust policy when they are treated as equivalent but actually discriminate on a different basis. When a candidate is more likely to get into university simply because they picked test A rather than test B, without being aware of a possible difference in pass probability, the university entrance policy may be unjust.

Research Questions

This paper investigates a claim about the relationship between the scores on STRT and ITNA made by the admission boards of the three largest Flemish universities (Ghent, Leuven, and Antwerp). In the entry requirements of these universities, STRT and ITNA are referred to as equivalent measures of B2 proficiency. To the best of my knowledge, this is the first study that employs Kane's (2013) validation principles to investigate level-equivalence claims made in a university entrance policy, by posing the following research questions:

RQI.   Is there empirical evidence to support the claim that STRT and ITNA certificates are equivalent measures of Dutch language proficiency in the Flemish university entrance policy?

RQ2.   What is the nature of the relationship between comparable ITNA and STRT tasks, constructs, and criteria?

Material and Methods: STRT and ITNA

STRT and ITNA are comparable on a number of parameters. Both tests have undergone a successful audit by the Association of Language Testers in Europe (ALTE), offering an independent assessment of their stability, reliability, and consistency, which are prerequisites for a comparative study of this kind. They also share the same primary purpose (i.e., testing nonnative speakers of Dutch for university admission) and refer to communicatively oriented conceptualizations of language proficiency as primary sources of their construct. Finally, both ITNA and STRT have been formally linked to the B2 level, and since both tests are pass/fail, candidates either attain B2 or they do not.

The oral STRT and ITNA components are highly comparable in terms of task types and rating criteria. Both tests consist of an argumentation task, which requires candidates to weigh two alternatives, and a presentation task, in which candidates use tabular or graphic input to discuss research findings.

ITNA and STRT differ most in the written components. STRT is a paper-based test that includes four productive, integrated-skill tasks: two argumentation tasks (one based on a reading prompt and the other on a listening prompt) and two summarization tasks (one based on listening to a scripted lecture, and one based on a popularizing article). In contrast, the written component of ITNA is a computer-based test that does not require test-takers to produce extended texts but consists of cloze tasks and selected-response tasks. Candidates drag jumbled paragraphs to order them correctly, fill out missing words in a text, and answer multiple-choice questions about reading or listening prompts. Even though the operationalizations differ, ITNA and STRT both include reading, listening, vocabulary, grammar, and cohesion.

The ITNA oral component is scored immediately after the test by two trained examiners who reach a consensus score for five linguistic criteria based on the candidate's performance on both tasks. STRT is centrally scored by two trained raters who score content criteria in a binary way (i.e., whether the candidate mentions all the required aspects) and linguistic criteria on a four-point scale. The linguistic criteria in both tests are based on the same CEFR descriptors (vocabulary, grammar, cohesion, fluency, and pronunciation), but the STRT rating scale includes two additional criteria (register and initiative). Scoring on the ITNA computer test is binary and automated. As in the oral component, the written part of STRT is scored for content criteria and formal linguistic criteria by two independent, trained raters.

STRT candidates do not typically receive a detailed score report that lists scores on task or criterion levels. Instead, it provides a certificate for candidates who achieved an overall Rasch measure at or above 1.42 (Certificaat Nederlands als Vreemde Taal [CNaVT] 2014). ITNA informs candidates whether or not they passed the computer test via e-mail on the same day as the administration. Candidates get their results on each section of the computer test, and those who reached the cut score of 54% are invited to take the oral exam. After the oral component, the overall cut score required to get ITNA certification is 52.5% (private communication).

Data Collection

In order to determine whether the same candidates received comparable scores on STRT and ITNA, and, if not, why, test performance data of the same candidates on both tests were collected for the purpose of this study. From May 2014 through September 2014, all ITNA candidates ($N = 802$) were invited to take STRT free of charge. Since ITNA scores are communicated to the candidate within two days of taking the test (but it may take up to a month before STRT results are known), it was assumed that successful ITNA candidates would be disinclined to still take STRT. Thus, to avoid attrition, all 138 participants who took part in the study first took STRT no more than one week prior to taking ITNA.

All written STRT tests were administered under the conditions prescribed in the examination manual and in the presence of the researcher. Trained examiners conducted the oral examinations, the procedure for which is highly comparable in STRT and ITNA. The candidate receives the speaking tasks, gets preparation time (typically ten minutes), and returns to perform the task in front of the examiner. All participants also took the ITNA computer test under prescribed examination conditions. Trained ITNA examiners administered the oral ITNA tasks. All performances were scored by trained STRT and ITNA raters.

After omitting incomplete performances (some participants gave up during one or both tests), 118 participants remained in the dataset that was used to compare the results of $STRT_{written}$ and $ITNA_{computer}$. Since ITNA candidates who score below 54% on the computer test cannot take part in the oral component, the number of participants that could be meaningfully compared for the oral tests was reduced to 82.

Participants

The participant population was representative for the population of both tests in terms of age (sample $\overline{X} = 27$, SD $= 7$; ITNA $\overline{X} = 28$, SD $= 8$; STRT $\overline{X} = 26$, SD $= 7$), gender (sample 70% female; ITNA 67% female; STRT 65% female), L1 (predominantly French), and nationality (approximately half of the sample and the ITNA and STRT populations had European backgrounds). Results reported in Deygers, Van Gorp, and Demeester (forthcoming) indicate that no statistically significant differences were found between scores of the sample population and the available scores of STRT and ITNA candidates.

Data Analysis
Level Equivalence

In order to facilitate the interpretation of the descriptive statistics, the total raw scores of STRT and ITNA (172 and 125) were recalculated into a percentile scale. The significance of the difference between overall, written, and oral test results was determined using t-tests (Riazi 2013). Cohen's d was used to calculate the effect size for the difference between test results for the full population ($N = 118$). Since it was assumed that both tests were likely to agree on the best and the worst performances, the scores within the interquartile range (i.e., the range excluding the 25% highest and 25% lowest performances) were examined as well. Wilcoxon's rank-sum test, a nonparametric test, was used to determine the significance of the differences within the interquartile range, and Cohen's d was used to estimate their magnitude.

Both parametric (r) and nonparametric (τ) correlations were used to describe the strength of the relationship between the overall scores, the written scores, and the oral scores. Interquartile correlations were used to measure the strength of the agreement around the cut-off point.

For university admission, only one thing really counts, and that is getting the B2 certificate. In order to get a clear idea of the disagreement in terms of pass/ fail judgments, a crosstab was constructed on the basis of binary overall STRT and ITNA outcomes. Furthermore, the probability of passing either test was computed. McNemar's binomial sign test served to determine whether the difference in pass/ fail judgments between the two tests was significant.

Furthermore, in order to gauge the strength of the relationship between overall test scores and scores on the written and the oral components, parametric and non-parametric correlation coefficients were computed for the full population and for the interquartile population. The Pearson correlation coefficient was used to assess the strength of the relationship between the total scores and between the scores on the written components. Because of the sample size (Howell 1997) and because of considerations regarding restriction of range (Field, Miles, and Field 2012), Kendall's Tau (τ) was chosen to correlate the oral and the interquartile data.

Construct Equivalence

The ITNA and STRT speaking components contain the same task types and many corresponding rating criteria. Both scales are based on the same four CEFR levels, but for certain skills (e.g., grammar), the ITNA scale differentiates between basic proficiency levels and plus levels, where STRT only has one level. When the ITNA rating scale included a plus level, but the STRT scale did not, both ITNA levels were merged (i.e., ITNA's B1 and B1+ both became B1, and ITNA's B2 and B2+ both became B2). All scores were recoded in collaboration with the coordinators of both tests to ensure that no interpretative errors were made. Any recoding was done after the performances were rated, so all raters used their own scales in the way they were trained to use them.

Since the rating criteria were known to be correlated, oblique promax rotation was used to run a principal component analysis (PCA) on the standardized z-scores of the oral component. Since ITNA only offers scores on both tasks combined, the PCA was run using the STRT scores for both tasks combined. After having determined that the preconditions for a PCA were met (Bartlett's test of sphericity: $X^2 [4] = 358, p < .000, KMO = .82$), the initial analysis showed that three factors had eigenvalues at or above 1, explaining 70% of the score variance. The scree plot was used for confirmatory purposes, and showed that a three-factor solution was warranted.

Linear regression was used on the written and the oral datasets to determine how well STRT ratings predicted ITNA scores (Zheng and De Jong 2011). In both datasets, the number of cases with large residuals (written, 4%; oral, 4% after removal of two outliers) was within limits, Cook's distance was never >1, no individual cases were more than three times the average leverage, the covariance ratio was satisfactory, and the assumptions of independence and multicollinearity were not violated (Norris 2015). A multiple linear regression analysis was conducted to determine how much score variance in $ITNA_{computer}$ was predicted by $STRT_{written}$ scores. For the oral test component, a regression model was constructed with the overall oral ITNA scores as a function of the STRT criteria scores. Given the limited sample size, we could not reliably assess the contribution of the predictors in the oral model, but we were able to generalize from the overall model fit (Field, Miles, and Field 2012).

A Multi Faceted Rasch Analysis (MFRA) was used in this study to compare the relative difficulty of $ITNA_{computer}$ and $STRT_{written}$ ($N = 118$) and to rank the tasks of both tests in terms of relative difficulty. For this purpose, all tasks were weighted equally in the Rasch model. A second Rasch model was constructed using equally weighed oral criteria ($N = 82$) in order to determine how the criteria on both tests ranked in terms of difficulty. Lastly, a third MFRA used the real weights of the oral criteria to compare the actual difficulty of both oral tests relative to each other.

The analyses described above were conducted using the R packages *psych* (descriptive statistics, examining normality), *ggplot2* (plotting the data), *prob* (pass probability), *exacti* (McNemar's test), *MASS* (principal component analysis), *Hmisc* (correlations), *car* (regression), and *QuantPsyc* (regression). FACETS (Linacre 2015) was the software used for MFRA.

Results
Level Equivalence
The overall STRT-ITNA correlation is strong ($r = .767^{**}$), as is the relationship between $STRT_{written}$ and $ITNA_{computer}$ ($r = .694^{**}$). Other correlations result in much lower coefficients, and considering the similarity of the oral components, the low correlation there ($\tau = .387^{**}$) is striking. Low interquartile correlations (total $\tau = .19^{*}$; written $\tau = .06$; oral $\tau = .09$) indicate a lack of agreement between the two assessments around the cut-off point.

The overall correlation could be taken as support for the assumption of level equivalence, but all other analyses point toward a different conclusion. For a start, the descriptive statistics (table 10.1) indicate that the ITNA mean scores (standardized to a percentile scale for the purpose of comparison) are lower than those on STRT,

◆ **Table 10.1.** Descriptive statistics (percentile scale)

	ITNA			STRT		
	Computer	Oral	Total	Written	Oral	Total
N	118	82	118	118	82	118
X̄	59.31	50.97	48.06	66.76	73.16	67.68
SD	15.54	19.69	20.09	12.63	10.33	11.72
Med	58.42	48.75	51.63	67.33	72.54	69.19
SE	1.42	2.17	1.84	1.16	1.14	1.07

both overall and for the separate components. T-tests confirmed that the differences between STRT and ITNA are significant (total: t [236] = −9.20, p < 0.001; written: t [236] = −4.061, p < 0.001; oral: t [162] = −9.036, p < 0.001), with medium (written: d = −0.53) to large (total: d = −1.19; oral d = −1.41) effect sizes. The differences between the two tests remain significant within the interquartile range, with large effect sizes (total: W = 135, p < .000, d = −2.14; written: W = 775, p < .000, d = −1.04; oral: W = 190, p < .000, d = −1.16).

In order to determine whether the difference in mean scores meant that fewer candidates passed ITNA, a crosstab of STRT and ITNA pass/fail judgments was constructed. Table 10.2 confirms that more participants failed ITNA than STRT and that 24% of the population received a different pass/fail judgment. McNemar's binomial sign test shows that this difference is significant at p < .001. Additionally, the pass probability is significantly (W = 6,010, p = .02) lower for ITNA (P_{ITNA}^{pass} = .35) than for STRT (P_{STRT}^{pass} = .50).

◈ Table 10.2. Pass/Fail crosstab

		STRT		
		Fail	Pass	Total
ITNA	**Fail**	53	23	76
	Pass	5	37	42
	Total	58	60	108

Construct Equivalence

In order to explain why more candidates failed ITNA than STRT, the written and the oral test components were examined.

Writing Component

The first step in explaining the nature of the relationship between the written components was constructing a multiple linear regression model (table 10.3) to determine to what extent STRT task scores predicted the total ITNA score. The model explains 48% of the ITNA score variance. The strongest predictors are the writing-from-listening summarization task and the writing-from-reading argumentation task.

If all tasks are weighted equally, the MFRA reliably (.90) shows that ITNA$_{computer}$ is more difficult than STRT$_{written}$, mainly due to the relative difficulty of ITNA's vocabulary and grammar items as well as the relative facility of the argumentative STRT tasks. The MFRA model reliably (.93) identified three distinct levels of difficulty in the tasks, the borders between which are indicated with a dashed line in table 10.4. The most difficult tasks are the ITNA vocabulary and grammar tasks, and the least challenging ones are the STRT argumentative tasks. The dictation task in ITNA misfits the model constructed and STRT's writing-from-reading argumentation task (STRT) is redundant.

◆ **Table 10.3.** ITNA computer scores as a function of STRT written scores

	STRT				
	ArgAudio	**SummAudio**	**ArgRead**	**SummRead**	**Constant**
B	.373	2.514	3.784	1.845	2.996
SE B	1.034	.781	1.155	.828	7.491
β	.031	.322	.280	.206	
p-value	*ns*	<.01	<.001	<.05	*ns*

Note: Total R^2 adjusted is .482 ($p < .001$).

◆ **Table 10.4.** MFRA written tasks (equal weights)

Task	Test	Measure	SE	Infit MnSq
Language-in-use: Vocabulary (cloze)	ITNA	.43	.10	1.42
Language-in-use: Cloze (small)	ITNA	.40	.07	.71
Language-in-use: Vocabulary (MC)	ITNA	.38	.07	1.22
Language-in-use: Grammar (gaps)	ITNA	.33	.07	.72
Language-in-use: cloze (big)	ITNA	.10	.07	.97
Note-taking (listening)	STRT	−.01	.08	.88
Written summary (reading)	STRT	−.04	.08	.95
Structuring (drag-drop)	ITNA	−.07	.08	1.06
Multiple choice reading	ITNA	−.08	.09	1.40
Multiple choice listening	ITNA	−.15	.08	1.01
Dictation (fill in the gaps)	ITNA	−.18	.09	1.71
Argumentative writing-from-reading	STRT	−.51	.10	.42
Argumentative writing-from-listening	STRT	−.59	.11	.83

Summary statistics:

Candidate: Model, Random (normal): $X^2 = 98.4$; $df = 115$; $p = .87$

Task: Model, Fixed (all same): $X^2 = 164.5$; $df = 12$; $p = .00$

Speaking Component

In order to investigate the similarities and differences between STRT and ITNA, a multiple linear regression analysis was run in which the STRT criteria were regressed onto the ITNA scores. The regression model explains 28% of the ITNA score variance ($p < .001$) and retains only *grammar* ($\beta = .38$, $p < .05$) as predictor.

The regression hints at a possible discrepancy in the rating of STRT and ITNA. When highly similar tasks and criteria are used to score the same pool of candidates, one would expect the regression model to retain more predictors than it did. Consequently, in order to determine to what extent corresponding criteria fit the same underlying constructs, a PCA (table 10.5) was conducted on the standardized z-scores of the oral test components. The PCA confirmed that the ratings of corresponding criteria do not match; corresponding criteria in STRT and ITNA do not load onto the same factors, which one would expect if they measured the same underlying constructs. Instead, all STRT criteria cluster together, as do all ITNA criteria, except for *pronunciation*.

Finally, the first Rasch model—in which the criteria were weighted equally in order to allow for a clear comparison—reliably (.98) identifies seven distinct difficulty levels in the STRT and ITNA criteria. In this model, the oral components of both tests cannot be reliably separated in terms of difficulty (reliability .00; X^2 [1] = .2, *ns*), but the measures of the criteria reveal some telling mismatches. Table 10.6 shows that *pronunciation* in ITNA ranks as markedly difficult, and content in STRT's argumentation task is disproportionately easy. The MFRA further shows that, except for *vocabulary*, corresponding STRT and ITNA criteria invariably belong to a different difficulty band. This would most likely not be the case if both tests interpreted corresponding criteria in the same way. As such, the first MFRA confirms the PCA and adds an extra layer of information to it; corresponding criteria probably measure different constructs, and—except for *vocabulary*—do so at distinctly different difficulty levels.

The MFRA, with equally weighted criteria, offers a clear picture of the relative difficulty of the criteria, but in reality, not all criteria are weighted equally. STRT weighs linguistic criteria double to compensate for the amount of content criteria, and ITNA—having no content criteria—assigns a weight of 2 and 1.6 to *grammar* and *vocabulary*. A Rasch model that uses the actual weights of the criteria reliably

◆ Table 10.5. Promax-rotated factor loadings

	TC 1	TC 2	TC 3
STRT			
Vocabulary	.92		
Cohesion	.85		
Grammar	.80		
Fluency	.70		
Pronunciation	.68		
ITNA			
Vocabulary		.97	
Fluency		.81	
Grammar		.75	
Cohesion		.58	
Pronunciation			.96
Eigenvalue	3.32	2.54	1.16
Proportion explained	.47	.36	.17

Note: Factor loadings ≤ .3 were omitted.

◆ **Table 10.6.** MFRA oral criteria (equal weights)

Task	Test	Measure	SE	Infit MnSq
Pronunciation	ITNA	1.34	0.20	1.49
Fluency	STRT	1.09	0.20	1.06
Coherence	STRT	0.65	0.20	1.13
Grammar	STRT	0.57	0.20	0.92
Content presentation	STRT	0.40	0.21	1.02
Pronunciation	STRT	0.23	0.21	0.97
Vocabulary	ITNA	−0.35	0.22	0.91
Vocabulary	STRT	−0.35	0.22	0.97
Initiative	STRT	−0.40	0.22	0.70
Coherence	ITNA	−0.89	0.23	0.80
Fluency	ITNA	−0.94	0.23	1.04
Grammar	ITNA	−1.37	0.23	0.45
Register	STRT	−1.69	0.24	0.80
Content argumentation	STRT	−5.52	0.39	1.85

Summary statistics:

Candidate: Model, Random (normal): $X^2 = 63.6$; $df = 71$; $p = .72$

Task: Model, Fixed (all same): $X^2 = 419.1$; $df = 13$; $p = .00$

(.88) identifies ITNA as the most difficult by half a logit. Applying actual weights instead of equal ones also changes the relative order of the criteria (table 10.7). All corresponding criteria now appear in distinctly different difficulty bands; *grammar* in ITNA becomes the most difficult criterion by nearly two logits, and *content* in the STRT argumentation task is roughly four logits easier than the second easiest criterion, misfitting the Rasch model, as does *pronunciation* in ITNA.

Discussion

This study showed the correlation ($r = .77^{**}$) between overall STRT and ITNA scores to be rather strong and comparable to coefficients reported in previous research (e.g., ETS 2010 [$r = .73$]; Zheng and De Jong 2011 [$r = .75$]). However, since overall correlations can be misleading, supplementary analyses were conducted, all of which revealed that STRT and ITNA do not map onto each other quite as seamlessly.

When considering only the interquartile range, the correlation between STRT and ITNA scores becomes virtually zero, indicating that test-takers without a distinctly strong or weak profile were assessed differently by STRT and ITNA. This hypothesis is confirmed by an analysis of the descriptive data, which shows significantly lower mean scores on ITNA than on STRT. Perhaps the most telling piece

◆ Table 10.7. MFRA oral criteria (actual weights)

Task	Test	Measure	SE	Infit MnSq
Grammar	ITNA	2.89	0.33	1.11
Fluency	STRT	0.90	0.14	1.01
Vocabulary	ITNA	0.79	0.21	1.25
Pronunciation	ITNA	0.65	0.15	1.64
Coherence	STRT	0.47	0.14	1.04
Grammar	STRT	0.43	0.14	0.79
Pronunciation	STRT	0.02	0.15	0.88
Content (presentation task)	STRT	−0.13	0.21	1.06
Vocabulary	STRT	−0.46	0.15	0.81
Initiative	STRT	−0.55	0.15	0.76
Coherence	ITNA	−1.69	0.16	0.75
Fluency	ITNA	−1.74	0.16	1.01
Register	STRT	−1.76	0.16	0.79
Content (argumentation task)	STRT	−5.71	0.44	1.64

Summary statistics:

Candidate: Model, Random (normal): $X^2 = 66.1$; $df = 70$; $p = .61$

Task: Model, Fixed (all same): $X^2 = 679.3$; $df = 13$; $p = .00$

of evidence to discount the claim of level equivalence is the significant difference in pass-fail judgments; 24% of the participants received a different outcome on STRT and ITNA. In most cases of disagreement, candidates failed ITNA but passed STRT. Accordingly, the probability of passing STRT is significantly higher than the probability of passing ITNA.

The evidence presented in this study casts doubt on any claim of level equivalence. The overall correlation aside, none of the analyses offered evidence in support of the policy claim, which, as a result, cannot be considered valid (Kane 2013). Moreover, following Phillips's decision rule (Kane 2013; Phillips 2007), the university entrance policy is unlikely to solve the problem it was intended to fix—that is, assuring a consistent minimum language level among the international student population.

These results have implications beyond the immediate research context. First, they reaffirm the danger of assuming that tests that share a CEFR level are equally difficult (Green, forthcoming). Policymakers often rely on CEFR levels when determining language requirements, but since CEFR levels are wide and leave room for interpretation (Fulcher 2004), direct cross-test comparison of the kind presented in this study might be a safer, more robust option. Even tests that have been linked to the same CEFR level may differ substantially in pass/fail judgments. Secondly, this study confirms existing criticism toward using correlational data in validation research (Norris 2016) and underscores the importance of supplementing purely correlational results with impact data (i.e., pass/fail decisions) and with information concerning the nature of a relationship between two variables (i.e., construct equivalence).

The construct equivalence analyses indicate substantial differences between comparable STRT and ITNA tasks. STRT task scores explain 48% of the score variance on ITNA's written component, and STRT's argumentative tasks contribute less to the regression model than the summarization tasks. This is not entirely surprising, since argumentative tasks require knowledge transformation, whereas summarization tasks rely on repetition and are more in line with the multiple-choice items found in ITNA. The MFRA identifies the argumentative STRT tasks as the easiest tasks in both tests, which could explain why they contribute little to the regression. This observation, combined with the fact that ITNA's vocabulary and grammar tasks are nearly half a logit more difficult than the most difficult STRT task, explains why ITNA's written component is the most difficult.

Even though the oral components of STRT and ITNA are highly similar in terms of task types and rating criteria, the evidence in favor of construct equivalence is weak. In the multiple linear regression analysis, STRT criteria explained 28% of the ITNA score variance, the PCA showed that corresponding criteria from both tests do not load onto the same factor, and the MFRA with equally weighed criteria mapped most of the corresponding criteria into different difficulty bands. The analyses all indicate that corresponding criteria likely measure different constructs. Moreover, an MFRA, using the actual weights of the criteria, reliably shows that the oral component of ITNA is the hardest because it assigns the greatest weight to comparatively difficult criteria (*grammar* and *vocabulary*), and because a large proportion of the STRT scores is derived from relatively easy content criteria. Importantly, the difference between STRT and ITNA only becomes substantial when the actual weights are operationalized in the Rasch model. A Rasch model with equal weights for every criterion did not reliably differentiate between the difficulty levels of the two tests.

It is important to note that ITNA's greater level of difficulty does not automatically imply that it is a better university entrance language test. Answering that question requires a different set of data. These data do provide substantial evidence to argue that STRT and ITNA measure different constructs, even when the tasks and the criteria are highly similar. Additionally, these analyses show that the relative importance assigned to content, grammar, and vocabulary in STRT and ITNA is the most likely cause of the differing difficulty levels in the oral and the written components.

Conclusion: A Just Policy?

Sen (2010) proposes that justice be considered as the absence of injustice, which can be defined as the restriction of freedom without a rationally sound explanation. Since it is not unlikely that one and the same candidate would fail ITNA but would pass STRT—yielding very different outcomes regarding university admission—there are no guarantees that international students' freedom is restricted on rationally defensible grounds. As such, the university entrance policy cannot be considered entirely just. Quite likely, this situation occurs at a large number of universities, but since no other studies have yet considered the level equivalence of university entrance language tests from the perspective of justice, the scale of the problem is uncertain (McNamara and Ryan 2011). What is certain, however, is that the situation in Flanders can be improved, perhaps even without invoking drastic measures. Providing candidates with accurate information about the construct and the way in which that construct is measured might suffice (see International Language Testing Association [ILTA] 2007, 3). It would benefit the justice of testing policies if test-takers received accurate information about the actual differences and similarities between tests that are presented as equivalent options.

For a large part, the problem related to the matter of test equivalence in university entrance policies seems to stem from the use of the CEFR in that context, especially in Europe (Deygers et al. 2017; Fulcher 2004). The B2 level covers quite a range of performances, and it is hardly precise enough to act as a measurement scale. One way to surpass the problems this could entail is to conduct test-equivalence studies as presented here or conducted earlier (e.g., ETS 2010; Zheng and De Jong 2011). Another approach, which does not necessarily reduce the need for equivalence studies, is to select or construct tests that meet the specific language needs and requirements of a program.

References

Certificaat Nederlands als Vreemde Taal. 2014. "STRT Validity Argument." Unpublished policy document.
———. 2016. "Educatief Startbekwaam (STRT) – B2." Last modified October 25, 2016. http://cnavt.org/examen/examenprofiel/educatief-startbekwaam-strt---b2.
Council of Europe. 2001. *Common European Framework of Reference for Languages: Learning, Teaching, Assessment.* Strasbourg, Fra.: Council of Europe.
Deygers, Bart, Koen Van Gorp, and Thomas Demeester. Forthcoming. "The B2 Level and the Dream of a Common Standard." *Language Assessment Quarterly.*
Deygers, Bart, Beate Zeidler, Dina Vilcu, and Cecilie Hamnes Carlsen. 2017. "One Framework to Unite Them All? The Use of the CEFR in European University Entrance Policies." *Language Assessment Quarterly.*
Educational Testing Service. 2010. *Linking TOEFL iBT™ Scores to IELTS® Scores—A Research Report.* Princeton: Educational Testing Service. https://www.ets.org/s/toefl/pdf/linking_toefl_ibt_scores_to_ielts_scores.pdf.
Field, Andy, Jeremy Miles, and Zoe Field. 2012. *Discovering Statistics Using R.* London: Sage.
Figueras, Neus. 2012. "The Impact of the CEFR." *ELT Journal* 66:477–85. doi:10.1093/elt/ccs037.
Fulcher, Glenn. 1997. "An English Language Placement Test: Issues in Reliability and Validity." *Language Testing* 14 (2): 113–39.
———. 2004. "Deluded by Artifices? The Common European Framework and Harmonization." *Language Assessment Quarterly* 1: 253–66. http://dx.doi.org/10.1207/s15434311laq0104_4.
Ghent University. 2016. "Education and Examination Code Academic Year 2016–2017." Last modified May 13, 2016. https://www.ugent.be/en/education/degree/practical/studentadmin/OEREnglish.
Green, Anthony. Forthcoming. "Linking Tests of English for Academic Purposes to the CEFR: The Score User's Perspective." *Language Assessment Quarterly.*

Howell, David C. 1997. *Statistical Methods for Psychology*. Belmont, CA: Duxbury.

Hulstijn, Jan H. 2015. *Language Proficiency in Native and Non-native Speakers: Theory and Research*. Amsterdam: John Benjamins.

International Language Testing Association. 2007. "Guidelines for Practice." Last modified April 28, 2016. http://c.ymcdn.com/sites/www.iltaonline.com/resource/resmgr/docs/ilta_guidelines.pdf.

Interuniversitaire Taaltest Nederlands Voor Anderstaligen. 2016. "Testprincipes." Last modified October 25, 2016. http://www.itna.be/testprincipes.html.

Inter-Univeristy Testing Consortium. 2015. "Interuniversitaire Taaltest Nederlands Voor Anderstaligen. Zelfevaluatierapport." Unpublished policy document.

Kane, Michael T. 2013. "Validating the Interpretations and Uses of Test Scores." *Journal of Educational Measurement* 50:1–73. doi:10.1111/jedm.12000.

KU Leuven. 2016. "Onderwijs- En Examenreglement 2016-2017." Last modified April 28, 2016. https://www.kuleuven.be/onderwijs/oer/2016.

Linacre, John Michael. 2015. FACETS (Version 3.71.4). Beaverton, OR: Winsteps.

McNamara, Tim, and Kerry Ryan. 2011. "Fairness versus Justice in Language Testing: The Place of English Literacy in the Australian Citizenship Test." *Language Assessment Quarterly* 8:161–78. http://dx.doi.org/10.1080/15434303.2011.565438.

Messick, Samuel. 1989. "Validity." In *Educational Measurement*, edited by Robert Linn, 13–103. Washington, DC: American Council on Education/Macmillan.

Norris, John M. 2015. "Statistical Significance Testing in Second Language Research: Basic Problems and Suggestions for Reform." *Language Learning* 65:97–126. doi:10.1111/lang.12114.

———. 2016. *Reframing the SLA-Assessment Interface: 'Constructive' Deliberations at the Nexus of Interpretations, Contexts, and Consequences*. Paper presented at the Language Testing Research Colloquium, Palermo, Italy, June 20–24, 2016.

Phillips, Denis C. 2007. "Adding Complexity: Philosophical Perspectives on the Relationship Between Evidence and Policy." *Yearbook of the National Society for the Study of Education* 106:376–402. doi:10.1111/j.1744-7984.2007.00110.x.

Rawls, John. 2001. *Justice as Fairness: A Restatement*. Cambridge, MA: Belknap Press.

Riazi, Mehdi. 2013. "Concurrent and Predictive Validity of Pearson Test of English Academic (PTE Academic)." *Papers in Language Testing and Assessment* 2:1–27. http://www.altaanz.org/uploads/5/9/0/8/5908292/2_riazi.pdf.

Sen, Amartya. 2010. *The Idea of Justice*. London: Penguin.

Universiteit Antwerpen. 2016. "Procedure Proc/Adond/001.1." Last modified April 12, 2016. https://www.uantwerpen.be/images/uantwerpen/container1160/files/Procedure%20buitenlanders-2016def.pdf.

Zheng, Ying, and John H. A. L. De Jong. 2011. "Research Note: Establishing Construct and Concurrent Validity of Pearson Test of English Academic." Pearson Education Ltd. Last modified September 29, 2016. http://www.academia.edu/11010877/Establishing_Construct_and_Concurrent_Validity_of_Pearson_Test_of_English_Academic.

Chapter 11

Addressing Consequences and Validity during Test Design and Development

Implementing the CAL Validation Framework

JUSTIN KELLY, JENNIFER RENN, and JENNIFER NORTON
Center for Applied Linguistics

ASSESSMENTS ARE BEING USED increasingly by teachers, administrators, and policymakers as tools to inform important decisions that have real-world consequences for students. Given the high stakes role that assessments play, ensuring test validity, or "the degree to which evidence and theory support the interpretations of test scores for proposed uses of tests" (American Educational Research Association, American Psychological Association, and National Council on Measurement in Education [AERA, APA, and NCME] 2014, 11), is crucial. Evaluations of test validity assess the evidence that supports the interpretations and decisions made about test-takers on the basis of their performance on a test, and the appropriateness and adequacy of such interpretations. To establish a validity argument for an assessment, test design and administration must connect to intended and actual score interpretation and consequences. To that end, the Center for Applied Linguistics (CAL) Validation Framework combines two distinct, yet complementary approaches to assessment, Evidence-Centered Design (ECD; Mislevy, Almond, and Lukas 2004; Mislevy, Steinberg, and Almond 2003) and the Assessment Use Argument (AUA; Bachman and Palmer 2010), in order to connect the path from test design to test-taker performance, to the uses and interpretations of test scores, and the subsequent consequences of test use. This framework follows previous argument-based structures developed by Toulmin (2003) and Kane (2002, 2006), and is organized around assertions, or claims, about the assessment. The claims are presented as a series of statements that connect some aspect of the assessment process to the intended purposes of the assessment.

This chapter uses an English language proficiency (ELP) assessment developed at CAL, ACCESS for ELLs (henceforth ACCESS),[1] as an example to demonstrate how the CAL Validation Framework can be used to develop a validity argument. ACCESS is an assessment for students who have been identified as English language learners (ELLs), and is taken annually by nearly two million students in thirty-eight US states and territories. ACCESS scores serve as annual accountability measures of ELLs' ELP gains. Starting in 2015, ACCESS was updated to an online format, called ACCESS for ELLs 2.0 (henceforth ACCESS 2.0).

The CAL Validation Framework: A Roadmap for Assessment

One of the complexities of developing an assessment is addressing a range of stakeholders' concerns with the decisions and consequences of the results. Test developers need a "roadmap" to help them, as well as stakeholders such as state-level administrators, to maintain focus on test scores' impact on examinees as individuals and on society. Additionally, as a roadmap, the CAL Validation Framework is not a how-to guide or a set of rules; rather, it serves as a communication tool to guide thinking, decision-making, and the organization of documentation at each step of the development process, implementation, and use of an assessment. By joining two useful frameworks, Bachman and Palmer's (2010) AUA and Mislevy and colleagues' (2003, 2004) ECD, it connects the conceptual approach of the AUA to ECD's systematic test-design thinking. As this paper will show, the argument-based approach introduced by Kane (2002, 2006) and implemented in the AUA involves documenting claims about the assessment and then providing evidence to support those claims. A claim is a "statement about the inferences to be made on the basis of data and the qualities of those inferences" (Bachman and Palmer 2010, 99). The process of identifying evidence to support claims encompasses the entire assessment endeavor, from using ECD during test design to outlining the consequences of test use.

Origins of the CAL Validation Framework

The CAL Validation Framework was motivated by work on the 2011–15 ASSETS Enhanced Assessment Grant, awarded to the state of Wisconsin to develop ACCESS 2.0. Under this grant, one of CAL's responsibilities was for foundational documents to guide ACCESS 2.0 test development. The state members of the WIDA Consortium,[2] who are the primary intended users of the test, CAL staff, and WIDA staff collaborated on the project. Early work was informed by a National Design Advisory Committee (NDAC)[3] and the ACCESS for ELLs Technical Advisory Committee (TAC). Given the participants' varied perspectives,

some overarching comprehensive framework was needed to help all parties involved in this very complex project (a) understand the complex issues to be addressed, (b) situate their own concerns and the concerns of others, and/or their own work and the work of other researchers and experts, within the larger endeavor, (c) allow all parties to feel their concerns and work was valued and for them to value their own work and the work of others, (d) prioritize the use of limited resources at all levels of the project, and (e) more clearly communicate between internal teams within the complex project and also with external stakeholders. (Kenyon 2016, 3–4)

In 2011, CAL staff began to combine ECD, which is a process for test design planning and development, with the AUA, which analyzes how assessments are used by various stakeholders, from policymakers to individual test-takers. The resulting CAL Validation Framework structure went through several iterations, during which CAL consulted with experts to maximize the effectiveness of the framework.[4] Throughout its evolution, a major goal of the CAL Validation Framework was to communicate with a broad audience, including those with minimal technical background.

CAL used ECD principles in its original design of paper-based ACCESS (developed 2002–5; Kenyon 2007; Boals et al. 2015). CAL recognized that with ECD, Mislevy and his colleagues' approach was quite similar to that of Kane (2002, 2006) and Bachman in using Toulmin's argumentation design (Toulmin 2003) by linking claims and evidences in order to build a foundation for the validity argument. Given the desire to more clearly show the interrelationship between test and item design decisions and the process of building a validity argument, the CAL Validation Framework brought together the two existing approaches of ECD and AUA. Due to the primary focus of its work on test development, CAL wanted to highlight the phases of test development that could be briefly summed up in three somewhat iterative phases: planning, trialing (including the iterative phases of designing, building, and implementing; see Kenyon and MacGregor 2012), and operationalizing. The final framework design is described in the next section.

Overview of the Framework

The CAL Validation Framework, like the work of Kane, Bachman, and Mislevy, is based on Toulmin's (2003) argument structure. According to Toulmin, a good, strong argument consists of six parts: data, claim, warrants, qualifiers, rebuttals, and backing. As illustrated in figure 11.1, when constructing an argument, data, or evidence, are central to formulating a claim. This structure also highlights the necessity of acknowledging limitations in the form of rebuttal data and alternative explanations in order to find the most robust explanation or solution.

In the context of assessment, a claim is a statement regarding the inferences we make about examinees based on their performance on the assessment. So, in developing an assessment, each stage must be supported by data or evidence to justify the claims made by test developers and test users. For example, if we are making a claim that an assessment evaluates an examinee's reading proficiency along the entirety of a given proficiency scale, we need data to corroborate that the assessment did in fact assess reading, that the assessment contained items that assessed each point in the proficiency scale, that the items perform properly from a psychometric perspective, and so on.

Within Toulmin's structure, the connection between the data and the claim must be founded on warrants, which are logical statements that act as bridges between the data and the claim. The warrants themselves have backings, like theoretical rationales or prior research findings, that give them their cogency. For example, in the context of a reading assessment like the one described above, a warrant to support the argument that the assessment did in fact assess reading could be that our test contained reading passages with multiple choice items that test an examinee's understanding of the passage, with backing from prior research on effective reading assessments. Finally, a strong argument must be able to withstand alternative explanations and provide rebuttal data that refute them; when rebuttal data is not available, the alternative explanation may become the "winner." Building on the example above, an alternative argument might be that an examinee may be able to deduce the answers to the reading items if their home language shares a large number of cognates with English. To refute this argument, the test developer might show evidence that the reading passages and multiple choice items were analyzed to ensure that the use of cognates was minimized in the text.

CAL utilizes this model to develop a validity argument for its assessments, starting with decisions made about test design, continuing to claims surrounding test-taker performance, and finally, justifying interpretations of test scores and the subsequent consequences of test use. In this format, claims are presented as a series of statements that connect the assessment development and administration process to the intended purposes of the assessment. The CAL Validation Framework, which is used in CAL assessments, is shown in figure 11.2. As the diagram shows, the CAL Validation Framework brings together the processes and components of ECD as developed by Mislevy and colleagues, covering steps 5–7 at the bottom of the diagram, with Bachman and Palmer's AUA structure covering steps 1–5.

ECD is a framework for test design based on evidentiary reasoning; in other words, the way in which evidence is collected is fundamentally related to the intended

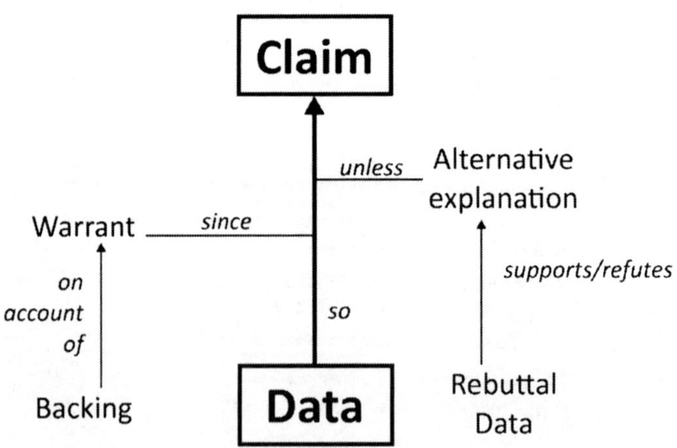

Figure 11.1. Toulmin's argument structure
Source: Mislevy, Steinberg, and Almond (2003, 11).

purpose of the assessment (Mislevy, Steinberg, and Almond 2003, 2; Mislevy, Almond, and Lukas 2004, 2). Likewise, the AUA structure provides a framework for developing assessments that link the decisions made on the basis of test scores (and the consequences of the decisions) to examinee performances on the test and the interpretations of said performances (Bachman and Palmer 2010, 85–92). Both ECD and the AUA structure make explicit use of Toulmin's argument structure, focusing primarily on claims we want to make about an assessment and the data or observations on which we base claims. Thus, Toulmin's argument structure in figure 11.1 is an integral, underlying feature of both the AUA and ECD components of the CAL Validation Framework in figure 11.2.

In addition to the core components of ECD and the AUA in the CAL Validation Framework, the phases of test planning, trialing (including designing and operationalizing), and using are included in the diagram. These are more informal terms that are used to characterize different steps or groups of steps in the framework in a nontechnical sense.

Another significant aspect of the framework is that assessment development and implementation is portrayed as iterative rather than as a simple, sequential process. Rather, to start planning an assessment, test developers must consider the final step, consequences, showing the cyclical nature of the assessment process. In addition, many steps in the development and use of an assessment involve revisiting and revising previous stages. The diagram highlights these iterative processes, reminding

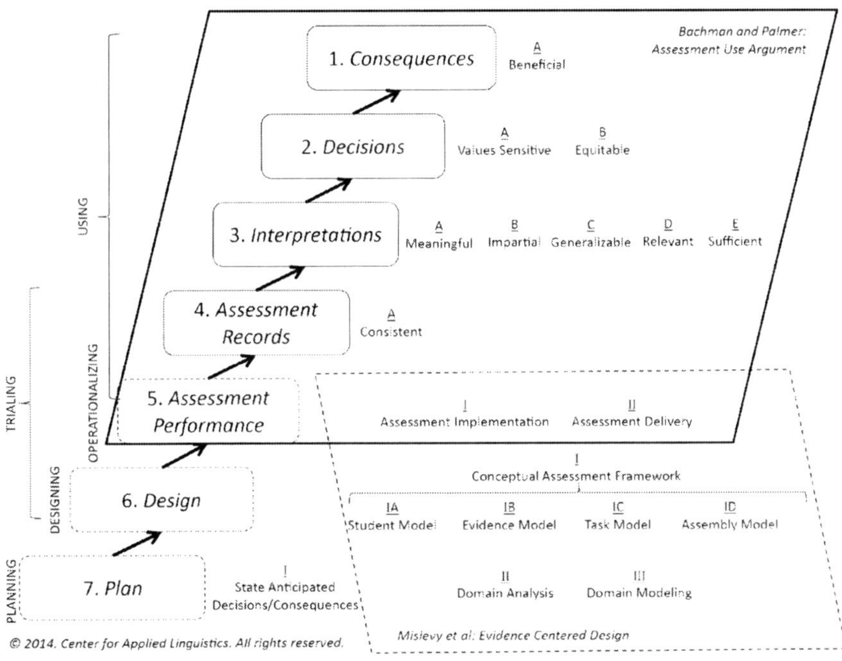

Figure 11.2. The CAL Validation Framework

users to constantly look both forward and backward throughout assessment development and implementation. Each subsequent (higher) step in the framework depends upon the strength of the step below it, including the reasoning that went into each planning decision. In other words, each step in the framework is built upon the decisions made in the step below it, so if a given step is lacking in some way, the faults in that step propagate up to the next higher step.

To give a trivial example to illustrate the importance of thoughtful decisions at all stages of test conceptualization, development, and implementation, consider the planning stage (step 1, domain analysis) of a reading assessment. If the domain analysis happened to include that students must be able to perform mathematical computations, then in the design stage (step 2), item specifications would need to be created for items requiring students to perform mathematical calculations. Of course, this would conflict with the intended decisions and consequences of a typical reading test, and would require revisions to the domain analysis. For this reason, the steps are numbered from seven to one, with one being the culmination but also the start of the assessment cycle. The next sections describe each component of the CAL Validation Framework, first focusing on the ECD portion and then looking at the AUA section.

Evidence-Centered Design

ECD is a framework for test design that is founded on the importance of evidence in the decision-making process; in other words, the way in which evidence is collected, the decisions made about the test-taker, and the intended purpose of the assessment all inform each other in ECD (Mislevy, Steinberg, and Almond 2003, 2; Mislevy, Almond, and Lukas 2004, 2).

ECD typically involves three layers, and each layer comprises multiple components. In the CAL Validation Framework, the assessment performance, design, and plan stages (steps 5–7 in figure 11.2) are derived from ECD. Planning includes both domain analysis and domain modeling. Domain analysis involves asking questions about the decisions and consequences of the assessment to elucidate the construct to be measured within the given context of the proposed use of the test. During domain modeling, overarching connections are made between the assessment to be created, based on the domain analysis, and its use for making decisions about students based on their performance on the assessment. For example, in the planning stage, domain analysis for an ELP test involves defining what is meant by "English language proficiency." The domain model involves further definition of the domain, including information on the proficiency scale, how it is operationalized, and guidance on the type of content to convey in the test.

In the CAL Validation Framework, the design stage (step 6 in figure 11.2) includes the conceptual assessment framework (CAF) from ECD, which consists of four models that build on the domain analysis and domain model: the student model, evidence model, task model, and assembly model. The CAF helps test developers think clearly about the essential components of an assessment from four different perspectives, and these models help us answer questions like "What are we measuring?" and "How do we measure it?" (Mislevy, Almond, and Lukas 2004, 11).

The student model defines what the examinees may possess in terms of knowledge, skills, or other attributes for the given population. For example, in a reading proficiency test where reading proficiency is further broken down into different components of reading ability, the student model would define each of these components, again in terms of the target population. In the evidence model, test developers define the observable student behavior needed to provide the necessary evidence to make claims about the abilities being assessed and identify how that evidence will be collected and converted into scores using an appropriate measurement model. In the task model, test developers describe the nature and characteristics of the assessment tasks that they intend to develop to elicit the observable student behaviors needed to provide the necessary evidence. For the assembly model, test developers consider the relationships between the student, evidence, and task models and determine how to effectively and efficiently collect needed evidence from students. In this model, test developers must balance the need to collect sufficient data in order to make accurate interpretations of student ability with real world constraints, such as the likelihood of fatigue affecting the results of an overlong test (Mislevy, Almond, and Lukas 2004, 7–13).

Assessment implementation and assessment delivery of ECD comprise test development and operational administration of the assessment (step 5 in figure 11.2). For new tests, assessment implementation involves developing item or task prototypes (based on new, untested specifications from the task model). This development includes rounds of review and revision by the test developers, often including feedback from stakeholders, as well as preoperational testing like small-scale pilots and large-scale field testing. For existing operational tests, assessment implementation can include developing new items or tasks based on existing task model specifications, as well as developing new specifications and items. Test items on large-scale tests are often refreshed or replaced annually in order to remove items whose psychometric properties are no longer functioning or that have been exposed to a large number of examinees. New specifications and prototype items or tasks are often designed when there is a desire to keep the test up-to-date and to reflect stakeholders' input. As with new tests, any development of new materials for an operational test also includes preoperational testing as part of the assessment implementation stage. For all assessments, assessment implementation also includes developing or refining required ancillary test materials such as rubrics, scoring materials, and training materials for administrators and scorers.

Assessment delivery is concerned with the actual administration of the test. Within the CAL Validation Framework, the assessment delivery process includes developing the actual materials needed to give the test (e.g., paper or online test forms or item pools for the test delivery platform), as well as creating practice items, sample tests, test administration instructions, score reports, and other ancillary materials needed by stakeholders to use the assessment results for making decisions about examinees. As mentioned earlier, these processes entail revision and refinement and do not occur in a fixed sequence. The assessment implementation and assessment delivery stages are the point at which test administration takes place; this step is the bridge that connects ECD and the AUA in the CAL Validation Framework.

Assessment Use Argument

Within CAL's Validation Framework, the assessment performance stage (step 5) acts as the hinge between ECD and the AUA. As described above, the AUA structure provides a framework for the development of assessments that links the decisions made on the basis of test scores (and the consequences of the decisions) to examinee performances on the test and the interpretations of said performances (Bachman and Palmer 2010, 85–92). In the CAL Validation Framework, step 1 (consequences), step 2 (decisions), step 3 (interpretation), step 4 (assessment records), and step 5 (assessment performance) are derived from the five layers of the AUA structure (although as noted above, assessment performance is the crucial point of overlap between ECD and the AUA structure). Steps 1–4 are each tied to one of the four primary claims of an AUA respectively (Bachman and Palmer 2010, 105–27):

Claim 1: Intended consequences

The consequences of using an assessment and the decisions that are made are *beneficial* to all stakeholders.

Claim 2: Decisions

The decisions that are made on the basis of the assessment-based interpretations take into consideration existing community *values* and relevant legal requirements, and

- are *equitable* for those stakeholders who are affected by the decision.

Claim 3: Interpretations

The interpretations about the ability to be assessed are

- *meaningful* with respect to a particular learning syllabus, an analysis of the abilities needed to perform tasks in the target language use (TLU) domain, a general theory of language ability, or any combination of these;
- *impartial* to all groups of test-takers;
- *generalizable* to the TLU domain in which the decision is to be made;
- *relevant* to the decision to be made; and
- *sufficient* for the decision to be made.

Claim 4: Assessment records

Assessment records are *consistent* across different assessment tasks, different aspects of the assessment procedure, and across different groups of test-takers.

As applied to the CAL Validation Framework diagram, claim 1 drives the first stage (step 1 in figure 11.2), considering the consequences of using the test for decision-making. As both the final and initial step, this stage involves thinking about who is involved, as well as what the assessment intends to do for the examinees. This claim reminds test developers and all stakeholders to think about the intended beneficial consequences for individuals and groups of test users and underscores the need to examine any unintended consequences of decisions made based on test scores.

Claim 2 pertains to step 2 of the CAL Validation Framework, which shows that decisions are made based on interpretations of the test performances and then lead to real world consequences for test-takers. Evidence needs to be collected to support claims that decisions are made in a way that aligns with the *values* of all stakeholders within the larger context of the assessment (including applicable laws and regulations) and that are *equitable* to all test-takers and others affected by the decisions. Again, while consequences and decisions lie at the end of test use, the CAL Validation Framework reminds test developers to develop a clear statement of these at the very beginning of initial test development (step 7 of figure 11.2).

Claim 3 connects with step 3 of the CAL Validation Framework, focusing on interpretations made on the basis of test scores. In this stage, the goal is to identify what evidence supports the claim about understanding something about an examinee on the basis of their test performance. Under this claim, test developers must identify what they need to know about examinees' abilities and how test scores will be interpreted. For example, questions surrounding what it means to score a "2" on a given scale must be considered and researched sufficiently in order to ensure that interpretations are meaningful, impartial, generalizable, relevant, and provide sufficient information for stakeholders to make subsequent decisions.

Finally, claim 4 drives the assessment records stage (step 4 in figure 11.2), in focusing on the information that is derived from the assessment administration. This step focuses on ensuring that test scores are consistent and dependable and relies heavily on claims and data related to the technical and psychometric properties of test scores.

Relationships between ECD and the AUA in the CAL Validation Framework

The CAL Validation Framework does not revolutionize any specific points of either ECD or the AUA; rather, its innovation is in integrating two formerly distinct models into a single framework. As the framework's use at CAL has proliferated, connections between decisions made within the ECD and evidence provided to support claims in the AUA have become ever clearer. For example, if score users are to make meaningful interpretations of performances (step 3), then how score users understand the domain needs to be a critical part of the domain analysis stage in step 7. The following illustration provides concrete examples that highlight how various components of the CAL Validation Framework are employed in assessment development. In particular, we focus on how research and development components of ECD are connected to real world uses of an ELP assessment (as defined within the AUA) and demonstrate how the CAF in ECD provides a foundation for subsequent interpretations.

Operationalizing the CAL Validation Framework: ACCESS 2.0

ACCESS 2.0 is a large-scale, online, high-stakes annual summative assessment of academic English language proficiency for ELLs in kindergarten through grade twelve in the domains of reading, listening, speaking, and writing. Once an ELL's score on ACCESS 2.0 passes a given state-determined threshold, the student is deemed proficient in academic English and is exited from English language support services. Exited students are considered ready to access the grade-level academic content curriculum in the same manner as their non-ELL peers. Therefore, the decisions based on ACCESS 2.0 test scores and the consequences of those decisions can have a significant impact on an ELL's classroom supports and experiences.

Every year, approximately one-third to one-half of test items on ACCESS 2.0 are refreshed. Given the high-stakes decisions and consequences based on the test scores, great care must be taken in the development of new materials for the assessment. This fundamental link between the ACCESS 2.0 test development process and the decisions and consequences based on the test scores is born out in the CAL Validation Framework. In the remainder of this section, we describe how several components of the CAL Validation Framework are operationalized in ACCESS 2.0.

Domain Analysis and Domain Modeling

Within ECD, the domain analysis stage provides a broad definition of the construct to be tested. For ACCESS 2.0, the domain analysis identifies "academic" ELP as a critical foundation for academic success in school, and thus as the primary target of assessment. Essentially, one purpose of the test is to make the inference that a student who scores at or above a specified cut score possesses sufficient proficiency in English to succeed academically without English language services. This claim relies in part on the domain model, a conceptual step between the broad construct definition in the domain analysis and the narrower operationalization of the construct for the specific purposes of the assessment, as defined in the CAF. The domain model is initially defined in a fairly theoretical sense, but it becomes more concrete as the assessment is developed and evidence related to student performance is collected.

For example, the WIDA English Language Development (ELD) Standards, which serve as the theoretical basis of the domain model of the test, describe academic language as "the oral and written text required to succeed in school that entails deep understanding and communication of the language of content within a classroom environment" (WIDA Consortium 2012, 112). In addition, the WIDA ELD Standards further define the construct of academic English in terms of the *language* of the main content areas and the social and instructional context for kindergarten through high school: (1) social and instructional language, (2) language of language arts, (3) language of mathematics, (4) language of science, and (5) language of social studies (WIDA Consortium 2012, 3). Furthermore, the WIDA ELD Standards define six proficiency levels along the continuum of English language development: (1) entering, (2) emerging, (3) developing, (4) expanding, (5) bridging, and (6) reaching (WIDA Consortium 2012). The performance definitions for each level relate to the discourse, sentence, and word or phrase levels of language. That is, the performance criteria describe linguistic expectations or demands in terms of linguistic complexity, language forms and conventions, and vocabulary usage.

The domain analysis and domain model for ACCESS 2.0 consist of a number of documents. The original basis for the domain analysis and domain model was the WIDA ELP Standards and Resource Guide (WIDA Consortium 2007), along with the 2012 Amplification of the WIDA Standards (WIDA Consortium 2012).

At the inception of the ASSETS grant, CAL, WIDA, state-level stakeholders, the NDAC, and the TAC collaborated to develop a number of additional documents that broadened the domain analysis, including the ACCESS 2.0 test framework document (CAL 2014) and a test and item design plan (CAL, n.d.). The domain analysis and domain model undergo continual refinement, through collaboration between CAL, WIDA, and stakeholders, as understanding of academic English language proficiency evolves. For example, additional resources include the conceptualization of the key uses of academic language (Wright and Musser 2014), the WIDA Can-Do Descriptors (WIDA Consortium 2016), and the annual technical reports generated by CAL (e.g., Center for Applied Linguistics 2016). As these resources are analyzed, decisions about what is being tested and how to test it can be made and documented. It is critical to maintain a transparent connection between these foundational resources and the construct definition of the domain model. For example, as our understanding of an underlying construct evolves over time, and this evolution is codified in the domain model, it must also be incorporated into other documents relevant to test development, like test and item specifications, which are in turn used by test developers to ensure that the understanding of the construct is implemented in newly developed test tasks.

Conceptual Assessment Framework

Additional components of ECD as implemented in the CAL Validation Framework provide the details required for test development. The CAF provides a structure for talking about the essential components of the assessment. To illustrate how the CAF is operationalized for ACCESS 2.0, we consider each of its four models, followed by concrete examples of the documentation developed by CAL to codify the CAF for ACCESS 2.0.

The Student Model

For ACCESS 2.0, the population being tested consists of students in grades kindergarten through twelve classified as ELLs in WIDA Consortium member states. The ELL population is linguistically and culturally diverse: some ELLs are recent arrivals to the United States, including refugees, whereas others may be second- or third-generation residents or Native American, and they represent numerous different language backgrounds as well as a wide range of sociocultural, socioeconomic, religious, and regional experiences. Furthermore, ELLs may or may not have received an education in their native language. Our aim is to assess the academic English language proficiency of students in this population in all four language domains (listening, reading, speaking, writing), targeting all five WIDA Standards (social-instructional language, language of language arts, language of math, language of social studies, and language of science), within sociocultural contexts for language use. Much of the documentation related to the student model was developed from the domain analysis and domain model (e.g., the WIDA ELD Standards), as discussed above, primarily in support of claims 1 and 2 of the AUA regarding intended consequences of ACCESS 2.0 and the decisions that will be made based on ACCESS 2.0 scores and interpretations.

The Evidence Model

ACCESS 2.0 is required to measure language proficiency of students up to Level 6 on the WIDA ELD Proficiency Levels through student demonstration of both comprehension and production of written and spoken language. Students demonstrate comprehension through dichotomous selected response items, which are scored automatically, for receptive domains (listening and reading). Students demonstrate production through constructed response tasks for productive domains (speaking and writing); these tasks are scored using a rubric aligned to the WIDA ELD Standards and are scored by trained raters. This model is constrained by a number of primarily logistical factors, including development time, testing time, development and testing cost, scoring time and cost, etc. The evidence model is codified in a number of documents, including a test and item design plan and test maps and blueprints; these documents are also relevant to the assembly model, as discussed below. The evidence model also contains psychometric models used to analyze assessment records. Documentation related to the evidence model is developed cooperatively by CAL, WIDA, state- and local-level stakeholders, and the TAC, and it is updated periodically in order to serve stakeholders and to support claims 2 and 3 of the AUA regarding the interpretations about the abilities assessed by ACCESS 2.0 and the decisions made based on these interpretations.

The Task Model

For ACCESS 2.0, given the domain analysis and domain model, the primary documents related to the task model include test and item specifications and frameworks for the individual language domains (listening, reading, speaking, and writing).

To make the WIDA ELD Standards and performance definitions more concrete, the Standards provide suggested examples of assessable targets, also known as Model Performance Indicators (MPIs), which articulate how academic language may be used or processed at a given proficiency level in a given standard. For example, an MPI for proficiency Level 2 in speaking at grade nine in the language of science is: "Give examples of the effects of modifying a variable using illustrated word banks and sentence frames in small groups" (WIDA Consortium 2012). In ACCESS 2.0, an MPI statement is the core of an item specification from which an item writer can develop an item. Item specifications are developed internally by CAL, but shared with WIDA and stakeholders in the test development process to support claim 3 of the AUA that the interpretations made based on ACCESS 2.0 performance are meaningful, impartial, generalizable, relevant, and sufficient. Item specifications are refreshed annually to ensure that the test continues to adhere to the most current thinking about English language development and instructional practices. For example, item specifications for ACCESS 2.0 are updated regularly to reflect connections to college- and career-readiness content standards, such as the Common Core State Standards and the Next Generation Science Standards, in order to further bridge the theoretical notion of academic English language proficiency with concrete, operationalizable parameters.

The Assembly Model

The assembly model for ACCESS 2.0 consists of a number of decisions regarding the overall test structure, including the number and sequence of items or tasks. Given the domain analysis, the domain model, the evidence model, and the interpretations of student performance on which decisions are based, a test must be long enough to provide the needed evidence regarding student performance, yet not so long that it has adverse effects on the students, like fatigue, stress, and lost instructional time. Given the broad intended scope of ACCESS 2.0, CAL has developed a number of documents that serve to codify the assembly model on an increasingly more granular level. For example, framework and blueprint documents, test specifications, and test maps stipulate for each language domain how many items or tasks targeting each WIDA Standard and proficiency level appear on the test. These documents serve to support claim 4 of the AUA regarding the consistency of assessment records.

Assessment Implementation

Assessment implementation (part of step 5 in figure 11.2) is the crucial link between conceptual test development (steps 6 and 7 in figure 11.2) and the interpretation of test scores (step 3 in figure 11.2). Assessment implementation includes developing test items or tasks, iterative item reviews, trialing, and field testing new items or tasks. It also includes developing and trialing ancillary documents such as test administration manuals, read-aloud directions, and practice items. Given that ACCESS 2.0 is an ongoing operational assessment system, test item refreshment is fundamental to the goal of continually refining the test. While refreshing the test annually prevents item overexposure to students within a given grade cluster, refreshing the test also helps ensure that the CAF underlying the test remains current with the evolving definition of the construct of academic ELP among ELLs in kindergarten through grade twelve classrooms in the United States.

The assessment implementation component of the CAL Validation Framework is a valuable tool to ensure that new item specifications, as well as test items and tasks themselves, align with the domain model and the CAF as defined for ACCESS 2.0. This alignment helps CAL keep the overall goal of validity in mind throughout the test development process. Students receive a score on the test, which receives an interpretation, upon which a decision is based, which has consequences for the student. This causal chain can seem remote to a test developer during the day-to-day work of refining item specifications and test items and tasks. However, using the CAL Validation Framework as a roadmap in test development helps focus on ensuring that claim 3 of the AUA is met and that the interpretation of a test score is valid (i.e., meaningful, impartial, generalizable, relevant, and sufficient to the population being tested). In order to do so, not only does the intended construct need to be defined (in terms of the domain analysis, domain model, and CAF), but the test items or tasks must align to the construct definition. Given the fact that the primary role of test developers is to successfully create items or tasks that align to the construct definition, a focus on the validity of test score interpretation is naturally in the purview of test development activities. Thus, the assessment implementation component truly is the linchpin between connecting the conceptual backbone of a test with the interpretation of empirical test scores.

Throughout the test development process, CAL consults with stakeholders, including WIDA and educators, to review items, tasks, and test administration procedures. As with CAL-internal quality control procedures, the intent of these reviews is to support claim 3 of the AUA that the interpretations about the ability assessed by ACCESS 2.0 are valid. Two of these reviews are discussed below.

During the refreshment process, professional CAL test developers train kindergarten through grade twelve ESL teachers to serve as contracted item writers and item reviewers as part of the continual refinement of the test. Engaging educators as item writers and reviewers contributes to test validity by buttressing the argument that the assessment reflects academic language that is grade-level appropriate, reflects grade-level content topic areas, and is fair and unbiased to all ELLs regardless of subgroup, thus aligning to the domain analysis, domain model, and CAF.

Another important component of the refreshment process embedded within the assessment implementation component of the CAL Validation Framework is trying out new tasks in the productive domains (speaking and writing). For example, CAL works with classroom ESL teachers to administer the tasks to a small number of students and asks the teachers to make qualitative judgments as to whether the task content is grade-level appropriate and whether they think it will elicit language at the target proficiency level. In this manner, CAL further strengthens the alignment of new tasks to the domain analysis, domain modeling, and CAF, and collaboration with educators helps us winnow down to the strongest tasks to move forward to the large-scale field-test pool, thus supporting claim 3 of the AUA.

Summary

The CAL Validation Framework (and its embodiment of ECD and the AUA) links processes for assessment planning and development with how assessments are used by stakeholders. By building a focus on validity into the foundational documents of ACCESS 2.0, CAL integrates validity into the culture of test development at CAL. Given the CAL Validation Framework, the assessment implementation stage bridges the gap between assessment planning, development, and administration, the interpretation of test scores, the decisions based on these test scores, and the consequences of the decisions, much in the same manner that the test development process connects the conceptual underpinnings of a test with the empirical evidence that is the result of an operational test. The purpose of this paper was to illustrate the components of ECD and the AUA that are directly relevant to the process of test development, so we do not explicitly discuss steps 1 through 4 of the CAL Validation Framework. However, throughout this discussion, we have shown how the steps that we have discussed do bear on steps 1–4 by supporting the claims made in those parts of the framework.

Conclusion: Using a Framework to Guide Assessment Development

This illustrative example from the ACCESS 2.0 assessment demonstrates how the CAL Validation Framework is an effective tool for analyzing test design and development questions and for organizing the decisions that must be made for each step test development process. As Kenyon (2016, 16–17) describes, one advantage of the framework is that it encourages specialists to think about the big picture, while also highlighting each stage of the assessment process. This makes the assessment process clear and accessible to a broad audience, since in the past it has been a black box to many users and policymakers. It facilitates understanding by creating a common frame of reference, allowing stakeholders with different perspectives to be on the same page. Given that language testing must consider educational measurement and applied linguistics perspectives as well as those of test developers, test users, policy decision-makers, and even technology specialists, the CAL Validation Framework allows these perspectives to share a vision that is reflected in the seven different steps. Most importantly though,

> the comprehensive diagram reminds all those involved in the language testing endeavor that real decisions about real individuals with real consequences will be made on the basis of the outcome of their work. While the context can determine whether the stakes involved in the testing may be relatively low or relatively high, the use of a comprehensive diagram like the one developed to guide CAL's work reminds all specialists involved that the impact of their work can have tremendous ramifications, and often is itself a reflection of societal values and norms. (Kenyon 2016, 16–17)

The CAL Validation Framework facilitates communication with stakeholders and helps remind test developers, as well as other stakeholders, that the consequences and decisions based on a test's score must remain central to test design considerations. These illustrations from ACCESS 2.0 highlight some of the many ways in which the outcomes for examinees is explicitly considered in the test development process. Above all, everyone involved in assessment must remember that the individuals affected by test scores matter and should be at the forefront of our minds throughout test development in order to produce assessments whose results are consistent, meaningful, impartial, generalizable, relevant, sufficient, values sensitive, equitable, and beneficial.

Notes

1. At the inception of the project, ACCESS served as an acronym, but it is no longer used as such. ACCESS now just serves as the name of the assessment.
2. At the inception of the project, WIDA served as an acronym, but it is no longer used as such. WIDA now just serves as the name of the consortium.
3. NDAC members were Phil Olsen, Audrey Lesondak, Laura Pinsonneault, Alison Bailey, Margaret Heritage, Kimberly Kelly, Robert Linquanti, Edynn Sato, Cheryl Alcaya, Joan Jamieson, Mary Schleppegrell, and Aida Walqui.
4. Experts such as Carol Chapelle and Lyle Bachman and other TAC members contributed their feedback during the development of the CAL Validation Framework.

References

American Educational Research Association, American Psychological Association, and National Council on Measurement in Education. 2014. *Standards for Educational and Psychological Testing.* Washington, DC: American Educational Research Association.

Bachman, Lyle F., and Adrian Palmer. 2010. *Language Assessment in Practice*. Oxford: Oxford University Press.

Boals, Timothy, Dorry Mann Kenyon, Alissa Blair, M. Elizabeth Cranley, Carsten Wilmes, and Laura J Wright. 2015. "Transformation in K–12 English Language Proficiency Assessment Changing Contexts, Changing Constructs." *Review of Research in Education* 39 (1): 122–64.

Center for Applied Linguistics. N.d. *The WIDA Consortium English Language Proficiency Assessment for Grades 1–12: Test and Item Design Plan for the Annual Summative and On-Demand Screener*. Washington, DC: Center for Applied Linguistics.

———. 2014. *The WIDA Consortium English Language Proficiency Assessment Framework: Annual Summative and On-Demand Screener*. Washington, DC: Center for Applied Linguistics.

———. 2016. *Annual Technical Report for ACCESS for ELLs' English Language Proficiency Test, Series 303, 2014–2015 Administration*. WIDA Consortium Annual Technical Report No. 11. Washington, DC: Center for Applied Linguistics.

Kane, Michael. 2002. "Validating High-Stakes Testing Programs." *Educational Measurement: Issues and Practice* 21 (1): 31–41.

———. 2006. "Content-Related Validity Evidence in Test Development." In *Handbook of Test Development*, edited by Steven M. Downing and Thomas M. Haladyna, 131–53. Mahwah, NJ: Lawrence Erlbaum Associates.

Kenyon, Dorry Mann. 2007. "Examining a Large-Scale Language Testing Project through the Lens of Assessment Engineering: What Can Language Testers Learn?" Presentation given at plenary session at the East Coast Organization of Language Testers Conference, Washington, DC, November.

———. 2016. "The Need for a Comprehensive Assessment Validation Framework." Paper presented at the Language Testing Research Colloquium, Palermo, Italy, June.

Kenyon, Dorry Mann, and David MacGregor. 2012. "Pre-operational Testing." In *The Routledge Handbook of Language Testing*, edited by Glenn Fulcher and Fred Davidson, 295–306. New York: Routledge.

Mislevy, Robert J., Russell G. Almond, and Janice F. Lukas. 2004. "A Brief Introduction to Evidence-Centered Design." CSE Report 632. National Center for Research on Evaluation, Standards, and Student Testing, University of California, Los Angeles.

Mislevy, Robert J., Lisa S. Steinberg, and Russell G. Almond. 2003. "On the Structure of Educational Assessments." CSE Technical Report 597. National Center for Research on Evaluation, Standards, and Student Testing, University of California, Los Angeles.

Toulmin, Stephen E. 2003. *The Uses of Argument*. Cambridge: Cambridge University Press.

WIDA Consortium. 2007. *English Language Proficiency Standards and Resource Guide*. Madison: Board of Regents of the University of Wisconsin System.

———. 2012. *2012 Amplification of the English Language Development Standards Kindergarten–Grade 12*. Madison: Board of Regents of the University of Wisconsin System.

———. 2016. *WIDA Can-Do Descriptors*. Madison: Board of Regents of the University of Wisconsin System.

Wright, Laura, and Samantha Musser. 2014. "Operationalizing Key Uses of Academic Language for Test Development." Unpublished White Paper. Washington, DC: Center for Applied Linguistics.

Chapter 12

Using a Validation Framework as a Guide for Planning Analyses and Collecting Information in Preoperational and Operational Testing

CHIH-KAI (CARY) LIN and DAVID MACGREGOR
Center for Applied Linguistics

THIS CHAPTER FOCUSES ON how the validation framework described by Kelly, Renn, and Norton (chapter 11, this volume) shapes qualitative and quantitative research into tests, both in the preoperational phase and after the test becomes operational. In the first half of this chapter we discuss how the validation framework can help in planning and carrying out preoperational testing (Kenyon and MacGregor 2012). Specifically, we discuss how the framework helps in identifying key issues that need to be explored, and in framing the questions that are asked and the evidence collected to address those questions. In the second half of this chapter, we turn our attention to how the validation framework can inform the types of psychometric inquiries to be conducted to collect evidence pertaining to claims about score interpretations and intended test uses.

An argument-based approach to validation (e.g., Bachman and Palmer 2010; Kane 2006) is best understood not as a process that occurs separate from test development, but rather as an integral element that permeates all aspects of test development. This entails having a clear understanding of the decisions and consequences that will be made on the basis of test results and interpretations, and attempting to ensure throughout the development process that all elements of the test lead to beneficial consequences based on accurate information.

One implication of such an approach to validation is that it should inform the planning and carrying out of the piloting and field testing phases of development, which Kenyon and MacGregor (2012) refer to as "pre-operational testing." Kenyon and MacGregor characterize those two phases thusly:

- Piloting is exploratory, and is carried out when major or minor changes to assessment and accompanying pieces may still be made.
- Field testing is confirmatory. It serves as a final check that everything is working as intended and the test is ready to become operational within the context for which it is being developed

In designing a research agenda for either preoperational testing or operational testing, it is important to be purposeful. On the one hand, it is not enough to carry out a series of activities only because they are prescribed by standard procedures, but on the other hand it is important to avoid focusing on trivial issues. A well-defined validation framework can help avoid those dangers. The key is to always keep in mind the critical claims made of the test, and, specifically, the decisions to be made and the consequences of those decisions. With those considerations in mind, test developers can examine the steps of the validation framework to identify the key claims made that buttress the intended use of the test, potential rebuttals that pose the most serious threat to the intended use of the test, and the evidence needed to refute those rebuttals. This approach allows test designers to be strategic in their approach to preoperational testing, and to focus often limited resources on the most critical areas. Additionally, this approach forms the basis to guide efforts in examining the proposed claims about score interpretations and intended test uses in operational testing.

Another crucial consideration is to identify which rebuttals will be explored during the piloting phase, and which during the field testing and operational testing phase. To that end, it is important to keep in mind that, as described above, piloting usually involves small-scale, often qualitative analyses, while field testing tends to be larger scale and more appropriate for sophisticated psychometric analyses. Piloting generally occurs when there is still an opportunity for small or large revisions to items, item specifications, and even test design, while field testing (as defined by Kenyon and MacGregor 2012) occurs at a point where no more changes can be made to items, item design, or test design; at most, evidence collected in field testing can be used in final item selection.

In designing a preoperational testing regime, it is important to be strategic. Preoperational testing cannot be exhaustive, as more threats both great and trivial can always be discerned. To ensure that the preoperational testing program is practical, yet provides sufficient evidence, it is helpful to keep in mind that the purpose of preoperational testing is to provide evidence in the construction of the validity argument, with an eye toward the interpretations to be made based on the results, the decisions to be made based on those interpretations, and, ultimately, the consequences to students and other stakeholders. With that in mind, the key to a successful preoperational testing program is to identify what the key claims are and what the most damaging potential rebuttals could be, and plan the preoperational testing around those.

In this chapter, we discuss some examples from ACCESS for ELLs and Basic English Speaking Test (hereafter BEST Plus), that illustrate these points in preoperational testing and operational testing. The purpose of ACCESS for ELLs is to assess the developing English language proficiency (ELP) of English language learners (ELLs) in grades kindergarten through twelve in the United States, following the 2012 *Amplification of the English Language Development Standards Kindergarten–Grade 12* of the multistate WIDA Consortium (WIDA Consortium 2012). The purpose of BEST Plus is to assess the oral language proficiency of adult ELLs typically found in adult education programs in the United States. BEST Plus measures performance over the full range of proficiency levels represented in the National Reporting System (NRS) Educational Functioning Levels (EFLs). We do not present an exhaustive survey of the preoperational testing and operational testing activities carried out for those tests, but rather an illustrative sample.

Preoperational Testing

In this section, we describe two examples of preoperational testing that address different steps in the validity argument.

Example 1: Student Model

The first example, as described by Renn, DeMarco, and MacGregor (2015), explores one aspect of the student model for ACCESS for ELLs. The fact that, as of school year 2014–15, ACCESS for ELLs is being offered online allows certain affordances, including having test-takers keyboard their responses to writing prompts. However, the possibility of handwriting responses is also included for students who are unable to show their best writing through keyboarding. For students in grades six through twelve, keyboarding is the default, with handwriting offered as an accommodation. For students in grades one through three, keyboarding is not offered. However, for grades four and five, some representatives of state educational agencies from WIDA Consortium states indicated that all their students learned to keyboard from an early age, while others were concerned that keyboarding would be difficult for their ELLs. Thus, the Consortium decided to allow individual states to decide whether keyboarding or handwriting should be the default.

Because a central claim of the test is that it allows students to demonstrate their proficiency in academic English, it is necessary to design the test to minimize the possibility that factors external to their proficiency will impede their performance on the test. In the case of writing, then, the mode of response should not have a negative effect on student performance, nor should it lead raters to assign a lower score to their responses. In order to implement this decision, it was necessary to provide evidence that keyboarding was a viable option for at least some students in grades four and five. Because keyboarding was intended to be one option for those students, along with handwriting, it was not necessary to show that all or even a large number of students could successfully keyboard. Rather, it was necessary to investigate whether at least some students in this age group are able to show their level of

English through keyboarding to the same extent that they can through handwriting. Therefore, a small-scale research project was designed to test the claim that at least some students in grades four and five can keyboard their responses to the writing tasks.

Research Questions

The study was designed to address the following research questions:

1. Do students produce handwritten and keyboarded writing samples that are scored at similar proficiency levels using the WIDA Writing Rubric?
2. What kinds of errors do students make in their writing samples and do they differ depending on the response mode used?

Within the validation framework for the ACCESS for ELLs assessment, data collected in response to these questions would provide the assessment development team evidence to support the claim that the test provides all students the opportunity to demonstrate their academic ELP through the domain of writing.

Participants in the study were fifteen fourth and fifth grade ELLs, with mid to high proficiency, in WIDA states. All participants had already taken the operational ACCESS for ELLs for school year 2014–15 and were identified by their teacher or school as being capable of keyboarding responses on computerized ACCESS for ELLs.

Three CAL staff members administered writing tasks onsite. Two tasks designed to elicit the language of science were administered to each student. One of the tasks was designed to elicit language at Proficiency Level (PL) 4 on the WIDA English Language Development scale, while the other was designed to elicit language at PL 5. Tasks were designed to provide students with enough content to produce an extended response. The students were given twenty minutes to respond to each task.

Half of the participants were randomly assigned to respond to the PL 4 task in the keyboarding mode and the PL 5 task in the handwriting mode. The other half responded to the PL 4 task in the handwriting mode and the PL 5 task in the keyboarding mode. In each group, half of the students responded to the PL 4 task first while half of the students responded to the PL 5 task first.

Analysis

To address research question 1, all responses were double-rated by trained CAL raters using the eleven-point WIDA ELD Writing rubric. Scores on the rubric range from 0 to 6, with the possibility of a "plus" score for score points 1–5 (e.g., 1+, 2+, etc.). Handwritten responses were transcribed digitally, and both handwritten and keyboarded responses were presented in random order to the raters in the same format, with no indication of whether they were handwritten or keyboarded. Raters' scores were compared across administration mode (handwritten versus keyboarded).

To address research question 2, all responses were transcribed and coded using the Systematic Analysis of Language Transcription (SALT) software. Error codes were developed based on the data collected in a small-scale pilot, and were analyzed across the two administration modes to determine whether the type and rate of errors per word differ across the keyboarded and handwritten responses. Individual error codes were evaluated, as well as error type (sentence level, word level, and punctuation).

Results
Research Question 1

Table 12.1 shows the ratings for each student by mode. As can be seen, students were scored similarly across administration modes. Six students scored higher on the keyboarded task, four scored lower on the keyboarded task, and five scored the same on both tasks, and the raters never differed by more than one proficiency level. There was no tendency to perform better in one response mode versus the other.

Research Question 2

Table 12.2 shows the rate per one hundred words of errors by type. The rate for phrase-level errors and miscellaneous errors was similar across modes of response. However, for word-level errors and punctuation errors, the rate of errors was considerably higher in the keyboarded responses. Tables 12.3 and 12.4 break down the word-level errors and punctuation errors respectively by type. These show that students were more likely to commit certain mechanical errors, such as missing capital letters, spelling errors, and missing spaces, in the keyboarding mode than in the handwriting mode. In WIDA's conceptualization of English language proficiency, these types of errors should not affect ratings of student writing, and so in the current study raters were instructed not to rate samples lower due to such errors.

◆ Table 12.1. Ratings for each student by mode

Student	Mode	
	HW	KB
1	2+	3
2	2+	3
3	2	1+
4	2	2
5	1+	2+
6	2+	3
7	2	1+
8	2+	2+
9	3	2
10	2	2+
11	2	2+
12	3	3
13	2+	2+
14	3	3
15	3+	2+

◆ **Table 12.2.** Comparison of error types per 100 words

	Handwriting		Keyboarding	
	Mean	**SD**	**Mean**	**SD**
Phrase Level Errors	2.11	2.23	2.75	3.21
Word Level Errors	14.21	8.79	23.03	16.28
Punctuation Errors	3.24	4.06	9.08	4.92
Misc Errors	1.62	2.46	.82	2.36
All Errors	21.18	14.81	35.67	17.37

◆ **Table 12.3.** Comparison of word-level errors per 100 words

	Handwriting		Keyboarding	
	Mean	**SD**	**Mean**	**SD**
Missing Capital Letter	2.34	2.51	5.84	5.26
Unnecessary Capital Letter	1.22	1.81	.39	1.52
Spelling Error	6.53	7.86	9.62	7.45
Misspelled Homophone	.62	.88	1.18	2.07
Word Choice Error	.54	.89	3.08	6.02
Missing Word	1.25	2.04	1.60	2.60
Unnecessary Word	.99	1.97	.51	1.99
Missing Bound Morpheme	.13	.51	.94	1.35

◆ **Table 12.4.** Comparison of punctuation errors per 100 words

	Handwriting		Keyboarding	
	Mean	**SD**	**Mean**	**SD**
Missing Punctuation	2.15	3.43	2.36	2.90
Incorrect Punctuation	.16	.43	.79	1.04
Unnecessary Punctuation	.92	2.90	.50	1.18
Missing Space	.00	.00	4.32	4.44
Extra Space	.00	.00	1.10	2.49

Discussion

The purpose of the small-scale study described here was to investigate whether it is possible to identify fourth and fifth grade students who would be able to produce responses through keyboarding that would be similar in quality to their handwritten responses. Overall, it was found that such students could be identified. However, these results also have important implications for the claims made regarding assessment records (i.e., scores and ratings resulting from test performance). Specifically, in order to ensure that the ratings are consistent, it is necessary to include in rater training explicit instruction on the types of errors that characterize keyboarded responses, and to ensure that raters do not lower their ratings as a result of those types of errors. In addition, follow-up studies will be carried out when operational data is available to investigate whether the option of keyboarding has had an effect on the overall results of the population.

Example 2: Task model

The second example concerns the task model of the adult oral proficiency test BEST Plus 2.0. In addition to the computer adaptive version, three new versions of the print-based test were created. Since all four forms of the test are intended to be parallel, the existence of both a computer-based form and paper-based forms has implications for claims made about assessment records. Specifically, an important claim regarding the consistency of the records is that student performance on the print-based form (PBF) is comparable to performance on the computer-adaptive test (CAT). If it is found that tasks on the PBF do not allow students to demonstrate their full range of English language proficiency, that would serve as a rebuttal to the claim. Therefore, it was necessary to collect evidence comparing scores on the PBF and the CAT versions of the test.

Background: Design of the paper-based forms

The PBF involves students first taking the same eight-item locator test. Based on their performance on the locator test, students continue to either level 1 (low), level 2 (mid), or level 3 (high). For the lowest scoring students, the test ends after the locator test.

Spoken responses to all questions are scored on a rubric that includes three criteria: listening comprehension (0–2 points), linguistic complexity (0–4 points), and communicative appropriateness (0–3 points). Note that if the linguistic demands of the question are not high (e.g., a yes/no question or a question requiring a one- or two-word response), a student can still get the highest possible scores in comprehension and communicative appropriateness, while only getting a score of 1 in linguistic complexity. That is, students can receive scores of 2-1-4 on tasks that require low levels of linguistic complexity. Results are interpreted in terms of the seven NRS EFLs. An initial comparability study was conducted to investigate whether performances differed on the PBFs and the CAT.

Initial Comparability Study

Eighty-four students from an adult ESL program in a northeastern state took part in the first phase of the pilot study. The eighty-four examinees (thirty-one male and fifty-two female) represented the range of program levels and were sampled from morning, afternoon, and evening classes. The students had been placed into four program levels: ESL 1, ESL 2, ESL3, and ESL 4.

All participants took the CAT and one PBF form. Students in group 1 took PBF A, students in group 2 took PBF B, and students in group 3 took PBF C. A counterbalanced designed was used, such that half of the participants took the CAT first, while half took the PBF first. In the final analysis, the results of six of the students were excluded because they did not take both forms on the same day. In addition, three examinees whose results on the two forms differed by three or more NRS levels were considered outliers,[1] and so excluded. As a result, data from seventy-five students were used in the final analysis.

Results

Table 12.5 shows the descriptive statistics for the three groups. As can be seen, students in groups 2 and 3 scored similarly on both the CAT and the PBF. Students in group 1, on the other hand, scored on average more than twenty points higher on the CAT than on the PBF (on a scale that ranges from 88–999).

To examine whether the differences between scores on the CAT and the PBF were statistically significant, three paired sample t-tests were conducted with an alpha level of .05. The results (group 1, $t = 2.309$, $df = 23$, $p = .030$; group 2, $t = .328$, $df = 25$, $p = .746$; group 3, $t = -2.140$, $df = 24$, $p = .833$) showed the following:

- Examinees' scores on PBF Form A were significantly lower than on the CAT.
- No significant difference was found between scores on PBF Forms B and C and scores on CAT.

Discussion

The pattern of results suggests that some examinees who took Form A were being placed in a lower level than they should have been, creating a ceiling effect on their scores. Because the locator test on each of the forms is the same, it seems unlikely that there was something exclusive to Form A that was causing this ceiling effect. Rather, these results suggest that the average proficiency level of the students in the group who took Form A was higher than the proficiency level of the students who took forms B and C, but that there was something about the locator test that did not allow those students to be placed into the higher-level test where they could demonstrate their level of proficiency.

As a result, the two items on the locator test that were meant to be more challenging were examined, and it was determined that students could respond felicitously to the questions with short answers, and so they did not give enough of a chance for mid- and high-level students to show higher-level speaking skills. Therefore, those items were replaced with more open-ended items that elicit a broader range of speaking ability for mid- and high-performing examinees, and two further comparability studies were conducted to determine if the results of the revised PBF were more consistent with the results of the CAT. While a detailed discussion of these studies is beyond the scope of this chapter, in brief, it was found that with the revised locator question, results on all forms of the PBF correlated highly with results on the CAT. Thus, the results of the piloting phase of the test development process were used to improve the test and to strengthen the claims made.

◆ Table 12.5. Descriptive statistics for the computer-adaptive version and parallel forms of the semiadaptive, print-based versions of BEST Plus

		Computer-Adaptive Scale Scores	Semiadaptive, Print-Based Scale Scores
Group 1	N	24	24
	Mean	498.25	477.67
	Std. Deviation	62.235	66.603
	Minimum	390	327
	Maximum	629	636
Group 2	N	26	26
	Mean	464.65	462.12
	Std. Deviation	66.386	59.124
	Minimum	357	363
	Maximum	590	578
Group 3	N	25	25
	Mean	447.84	449.52
	Std. Deviation	69.767	77.157
	Minimum	292	335
	Maximum	598	629

Operational Testing

In this second half of the chapter, we discuss how the validation framework described by Kelly, Renn, and Norton (chapter 11, this volume) can help to guide and carry out psychometric inquires in the context of operational testing. We direct our attention to the roles of psychometric analyses in test development and test refreshment.

In test development for operational testing, we present two examples from ACCESS for ELLs. In this setting, claims identified in the validation framework inform the types of psychometric analyses to be conducted and guide the analysis designs, while psychometric analyses provide information to evaluate the identified claims. Analysis results can then offer feedback to test refinement or further development with respect to the claims being made. In test refreshment for operational testing, we provide two examples from BEST Plus. In this setting, psychometric analyses serve to evaluate evidence in light of refreshment against the original claims identified in the validation framework. Analysis results then serve to examine whether the original claims still hold and whether refining the claims is necessary.

The Role of Psychometric Inquiries in Test Development for ACCESS for ELLs

ACCESS for ELLs is a large-scale annual assessment of academic ELP for ELLs in kindergarten through twelfth grade in the United States. The listening section of

ACCESS for ELLs is a group-administered paper-based test designed to assess the English listening proficiency of young ELLs. The listening section of ACCESS for ELLs consists of selected-response items, which are dichotomously scored.

Guided by CAL's validation framework, we ask ourselves the following overarching question in relation to the claims we make about the scores from ACCESS for ELLs: *How do we know that scores from ACCESS for ELLs (Listening) are consistent and dependable?* Clearly, this question is a multifaceted one that requires evaluating validity evidence from multiple perspectives. Our discussion here is not intended to be exhaustive; rather, our primary focus is on the role of psychometric analyses in collecting a piece of information to evaluate some of the claims we make by answering the above overarching question. We provide two examples of psychometric inquiries related to this.

Example 1 for ACCESS for ELLs

Our first example draws on the Student Model from the validation framework. As such, we consider whether items measure what they are supposed to measure, which is the academic English listening proficiency defined in the WIDA Standards. Building on the claim that listening items are jointly measuring what they are supposed to measure with satisfactory reliability, we ask the following research question: To what extent are the items reliably measuring academic English listening proficiency?

Cronbach's coefficient alpha is widely used as an estimate of reliability, particularly of the internal consistency of test items. It expresses how well the items on a test appear to measure the same construct. Conceptually, it may be thought of as the correlation obtained between performances on two halves of the test, if every possibility of dividing the test items in two were attempted. Thus, Cronbach's alpha may be low if some items are measuring something other than what the majority of the items are measuring. As with any reliability index, it is affected by the number of test items (or test score points that may be awarded). That is, all things being equal, the greater the number of items, the higher the reliability. Cronbach's alpha is also affected by the distribution of ability within the group of students tested. All things being equal, the greater the heterogeneity of abilities within the group of examinees (i.e., the more widely the scores are distributed), the higher the reliability. In this sense, Cronbach's alpha is sample dependent.

Our example is the kindergarten operational listening test form for academic year 2014–15, which consisted of thirty dichotomously scored items and was administered to a total of 218,288 students. The Cronbach's alpha coefficient was .934. Although Cronbach's alpha is sample dependent, results are based on population data, including all kindergarten ELLs from the WIDA consortium in academic year 2014–15. It demonstrates high internal consistency for the kindergarten listening items.

Example 2 for ACCESS for ELLs

Our second example draws on the evidence model from the validation framework. Again, we consider the psychometric properties of the listening items. Building on the claim that the listening items measure the full range of WIDA proficiency levels, we ask the following research question: To what extent do items with different difficulty levels fit the response patterns expected by the Rasch measurement model?

The measurement model that forms the basis of the psychometric analysis is the Rasch measurement model (Wright and Stone 1979). It has been widely used in many assessment contexts (Bond and Fox 2001). For the kindergarten operational listening test form for academic year 2014–15, Rasch measurement principles served to guide all decisions throughout the development of the assessment and was not just a tool for the statistical analysis of the data. For example, Rasch fit statistics guided the inclusion, revision, or deletion of items during the development of the test. For the kindergarten listening with dichotomously scored items, the Rasch model may be presented as

$$\ln\left(\frac{p_{ni1}}{p_{ni0}}\right) = Examinee_n - Item_i$$

where p_{ni1} refers to the probability of a correct response "1" by examinee n on item i, while p_{ni0} is the probability of an incorrect response "0" by examinee n on item i. Rasch person measure refers to the measure of examinee ability, and Rasch item-difficulty measure refers to the measure of how hard an item is. When the probability of a person getting a correct answer equals the probability of a person getting an incorrect answer (i.e., 50% probability of getting it right and 50% probability of getting it wrong), p_{ni1}/p_{ni0} is equal to 1. The log of 1 is 0. This is the point at which a person's ability equals the difficulty of an item. For example, a person whose ability is 1.56 on the Rasch logit scale encountering an item whose difficulty is 1.56 on the Rasch logit scale would have a 50% probability of answering that question correctly.

Additionally, Rasch analysis provides item fit statistics, which are calculated by comparing the observed empirical data with the data that would be expected to be produced by the Rasch model. We used Rasch item fit statistics to identify items that fit the Rasch measurement model and those that may present potential distortion to the measurement. There are two types of Rasch item fit statistics: infit mean squares aim at unpredicted patterns of responses to items that target examinee ability (e.g., idiosyncratic misperforming), while outfit mean squares aim at unpredicted patterns of responses to items *not* targeting examinee ability (e.g., lucky guesses for low-performing examinees). Fit mean squares have an expected value of 1.0. Items with fit mean squares close to 1.0 indicate items that lead to productive measurement. Linacre (2002) suggested that a fit mean square value larger than 1.5 implies that the item may distort measurement (i.e., underfitting), while fit mean square value smaller than .5 indicates redundancy in measurement (i.e., it does not distort measurement but could be deleted from the set of items without affecting measurement quality).

Infit helps ensure that test-takers within a range of the targeted proficiency levels perform as expected. It is not as sensitive to outliers as outfit. Outfit can be skewed if test-takers with extreme (i.e., high-level or low-level) proficiency do not perform as expected. Generally speaking, large infit mean squares are more of a concern to validity than large outfit mean squares in a selected-response test, because outfit values can be inflated by idiosyncratic examinee behavior for items that are very easy (e.g., concentration lapse or unintended omission by high-performing examinees) or very difficult (e.g., lucky guessing by low-performing examinees). Table 12.6 below shows the infit and outfit mean squares of the kindergarten listening items.

The Rasch item analysis here is based on population data, including all kindergarten ELLs from the WIDA consortium in academic year 2014–15. Results presented in table 12.6 show that no kindergarten listening item is shown to have large infit issues (i.e., an infit mean square value above 2.0). Only five out of the thirty items (17%) have large outfit mean squares, but this is expected in any selected-response test because such a test format allows for random guessing. Together with the result of high internal consistency for the kindergarten listening items, these findings suggest that the items jointly and reliably measure a unidimensional construct of academic English listening proficiency, as represented by the constellation of the items on this test.

The Role of Psychometric Inquiries in Test Refreshment for BEST Plus

BEST Plus is an individually administered, face-to-face, computer-adaptive oral interview designed to assess the English listening and speaking proficiency of adult English language learners in the United States. Informed by CAL's validation framework, we ask ourselves the following overarching question in relation to the original claims we make about the scores from BEST Plus in light of refreshment: *How do we know that scores from BEST Plus are consistent and dependable?*

Again, our discussion here is not intended to be exhaustive. We focus our discussion on the role of psychometric analyses in collecting a piece of information to reexaminee some of the claims we make by answering the above overarching question in light of refreshment. We provide two examples of psychometric inquiries related to this.

Example 1 for BEST Plus

Our first example draws on the evidence model from the validation framework. As such, we consider whether scores on BEST Plus maintain the same meaning across years. Referring to our original claim that item difficulty levels remain stable or

◆ **Table 12.6.** Infit and outfit mean squares of kindergarten listening items

Type of Misfit	Infit		Outfit	
	Count	%	Count	%
>2.0, "distorting or degrading measurement"	0	0	5	17
>1.5–2.0, "unproductive but not degrading"	0	0	1	3
0.5–1.5, "productive for measurement"	30	100	23	77
<0.5, "less productive but not degrading"	0	0	1	3
Total	30	100	30	100

invariant across test administrations, we ask the following research question: To what extent has item difficulty drifted over time for continuing items?

An important assumption underlying CATs such as BEST Plus is that item parameter estimates remain stable across different test administrations. Item parameter change across test administrations is known as item parameter drift (Goldstein 1983) and the degree to which it exists should be investigated for items that are used in multiple test administrations. If there has been a great deal of change in an item's parameters, the contribution of performances on that item to examinees' measurement may lead to distortion. If drift happens across many items, interpretations made on the basis of examinees' performances on those items may no longer be valid.

In order to investigate item parameter drift for BEST Plus, item parameter estimates from recent datasets (2011–13) were examined in relation to the items' original parameter estimates in 2003. The datasets used to investigate item drift were responses from operational administrations (n = 4,314) of BEST Plus carried out by adult ESL programs in different parts of the United States during program years 2011–13. Responses from 258 items (the total item bank) were included in the data: 168 items that will remain in the item bank going forward and 90 items that will be replaced by new items. The focus of the item drift analyses was on the 168 continuing items and the points of reference for potential drift were their original item estimates from when BEST Plus was initially constructed in 2003.

To screen for item drift among the 168 continuing items, the Robust Z-statistic (Huynh and Meyer 2010; Kim, Barton, and Choi 2010) was estimated to screen for items showing item drift across test administrations. Researchers (e.g., Huynh and Meyer 2010; Kim, Barton, and Choi 2010) have advocated using a statistic such as the Robust Z-statistic, which uses median item difficulty rather than mean item difficulty, in conjunction with (or in place of) a mean-based statistic such as the displacement index because mean-based statistics can be susceptible to extreme values. Readers interested in the psychometric details of the Robust Z-statistic are directed to Kim, Barton, and Choi (2010). Results indicated that only 6 (3.6%) of the 168 continuing items were flagged for drift using the Robust Z-statistic.

One very positive result of the analysis is to discover that very few items, even after several years of exposure, were flagged for drift. Additionally, among the six items flagged by Robust Z statistics, there seems to be a relationship between item types and the direction of item drift, such that several easy items appear to have become even easier while several difficult items appear to have become more difficult. There were no discernible patterns among this group of flagged items by item type; that is, items flagged for drift come from both challenging and easy items. These results indicate that for the most part, difficulty estimates for the continuing items in the item bank have been very stable over the many years of the operational testing program. Maintenance of the item parameters in the item pool for a CAT is an important aspect of maintaining the validity of BEST Plus score results. More importantly, the current analysis serves to inform our ongoing effort in maintaining the BEST Plus item bank. The six items flagged in this analysis will be one of our priorities in the next phase of enhancing item-bank integrity by either replacing these items with new items or updating their item difficulty parameters.

We also undertook a follow-up study investigating the relationship between item exposure and item parameter drift. The focus of the item drift analysis was on the 168 continuing items that will remain in the updated item bank moving forward. Thus, the follow-up study aimed to investigate whether there was a relationship between item exposure rates and item drift among the 168 continuing items. It is important to investigate this because items that are more exposed may be compromised by their familiarity and thus become easier with the passage of time. We categorized item exposure into four groups with ascending item exposure: items with very low exposure rates, items with low exposure rates, items with medium exposure rates, and items with high exposure rates. Next, items flagged for item drift by the Robust Z-statistic were coded as "1" and those not flagged for drift were coded as "0," creating a binary variable for each item in relation to item drift.

Because the exposure-count categories are ordinal, an ordinal test of independence was conducted between item exposure rates and item drift. When there is a true association between the ordinal variable and the binary variable, an ordinal test using M^2 statistic ($df = 1$) is more sensitive in detecting the association (Agresti 1996). Results show that the M^2 statistic is not significant ($M^2 = 1.683$, $df = 1$, $p = 0.195$). Thus, there is no evidence that more exposure is related to BEST Plus items being flagged for item drift across different test administrations.

Example 2 for BEST Plus

Our second example also draws on the evidence model from the validation framework. Because the computer-adaptive algorithm of BEST Plus can select different questions on each administration of the test, we consider the comparability of scores on different administrations of BEST Plus in light of the refreshment of the ninety new items. Referring to our original claim that BEST Plus scores are comparable across test administrations, we ask the following research question: Are BEST Plus scores comparable across test administrations in light of refreshment?

In 2014, we conducted a study in which thirty-three adult ESL students representing a range of English proficiency levels took the test twice with two different administrators, using the updated BEST Plus item bank (258 items) including 90 new items. The examinees were paired so that one took the test with Administrator A while the other took it with Administrator B, and then the pair immediately switched administrators for the retest.

We compared the descriptive statistics of the examinees' scale scores on the two BEST Plus test administrations and examined the correlations between scale scores achieved on the two administrations to analyze their relationship. Table 12.7 presents the descriptive statistics for the thirty-three students across the two computer-adaptive administrations. It demonstrates the similarity of the average performance across the students in the study.

In addition, a correlation was calculated between the two CAT administrations. In the comparability study, the test-retest reliability of scale scores for the computer-adaptive version was .829. Considering that BEST Plus is a performance-based assessment, that different sets of questions were administered each time, and that two different administrators were doing the scoring, this figure is quite high and provides

◆ Table 12.7. Descriptive statistics for BEST Plus administrations

	N	Scale Score Mean	Std. Deviation	Min.	Max.
Computer-Adaptive Test 1	33	492.61	60.84	380	659
Computer-Adaptive Test 2	33	484.58	58.66	343	619

Note: Test 1 refers to the first test administered and Test 2 is the second test administered.

evidence that examinees will obtain similar results on alternate administrations of the test in light of the 90 refreshed items. Additionally, to examine whether there was a statistically significant difference between scale scores on the CAT administrations, we conducted a paired-sample t-test (paired-difference mean = 8.030; t = 1.319; df = 32; p = .197). Results show that the difference between performances on the two CAT administrations was not statistically significant, which ensures the comparability of scores on different test administrations of BEST Plus in light of refreshment.

Discussion

Our examples of psychometric inquiries in the test development of ACCESS for ELLs and in the test refreshment of BEST Plus demonstrate how a validation framework, such as the one described by Kelly, Renn, and Norton (this volume), can guide us in a principled way in identifying the claims we make about test scores, designing the types of psychometric analyses to be conducted, and collecting information needed to examine our claims. Specifically, the validation framework helps us set priorities in our research resources, narrow down our research questions in addressing the claims we make about score interpretations, and provide feedback to guide test refinement and further test development.

Conclusion

The examples in this chapter have discussed a wide range of investigations and analyses of two very different tests, during both the test development phase and the operational testing phase. They range from small-scale, largely qualitative studies to large-scale investigations of the psychometric properties of a test. However, all are ultimately intended to further the validation argument of the test, as laid out in our validation framework. We have endeavored to show how each activity described here is motivated by that framework and the claims made within it. Our intention in doing so is not to present the current framework as the only or best approach to test validity, but rather to show an example of how modern conceptualizations of test validation (e.g., Bachman and Palmer 2010; Chapelle, Enright, and Jamieson 2008, 2010; Kane 2006) can and should inform all phases of the test development process. As Bachman and Palmer (2010) remind us, it is vital to keep in mind the intended decisions to be made based on test results and the consequences of those decisions, and to strive throughout the development and administration of a test to ensure that those decisions and consequences are beneficial.

Note

1. Students who participated in the study were compensated with a gift card for $20, and were aware that they were participating in a study. These cases were considered outliers as they performed worse on the CAT than on the operational PBF, a result that may reflect a lack of motivation on their part.

References

Agresti, Alan. 1996. *An Introduction to Categorical Data Analysis*. New York: Wiley.

Bachman, Lyle, and Adrian Palmer. 2010. *Language Assessment in Practice*. Oxford: Oxford University Press.

Bond, Trevor, and Christine M. Fox. 2001. *Applying the Rasch Model: Fundamental Measurement in the Human Sciences*. Mahwah, NJ: Lawrence Erlbaum Associates.

Chapelle, Carol A., Mary K. Enright, and Joan M. Jamieson, eds. 2008. *Building a validity argument for the Test of English as a Foreign Language*. New York: Routledge.

———. 2010. "Does an Argument-Based Approach to Validity Make a Difference?" *Educational Measurement: Issues and Practice* 29 (1): 3–13.

Goldstein, Harvey. 1983. "Measuring Changes in Educational Attainment over Time: Problems and Possibilities." *Journal of Educational Measurement* 20 (4): 369–77.

Huynh, Huynh, and Patrick Meyer. 2010. "Use of Robust Z in Detecting Unstable Items in Item Response Theory Models." *Practical Assessment, Research & Evaluation* 15 (2): 1–8. http://pareonline.net/getvn.asp?v=15&n=2.

Kane, Michael. 2006. "Validation." In *Educational Measurement*, 4th ed., edited by R. L. Brennan, 17–64. Westport, CT: Praeger Publishers.

Kenyon, Dorry M., and David MacGregor. 2012. "Pre-operational Testing." In *The Routledge Handbook of Language Testing*, edited by Glenn Fulcher and Fred Davidson, 295–306. New York: Routledge.

Kim, Dong-In, Karen Barton, and Seung W. Choi. 2010. "Sample Size Impact on Screening Methods in the Rasch Model." Paper presented at American Educational Research Association, Denver, Colorado, May.

Linacre, John M. 2002. "What Do Infit and Outfit, Mean-Square and Standardized Mean?" *Rasch Measurement Transactions* 16:878.

Renn, Jennifer, Nicole DeMarco, and David MacGregor. 2015. "Composing at the Keyboard: An Investigation into the Effects of Mode of Response to Writing Tasks." Paper presented at the annual meeting of the East Coast Organization of Language Testers, Washington, DC, October.

WIDA Consortium. 2012. *2012 Amplification of the English Language Development Standards Kindergarten–Grade 12*. Madison, WI: Board of Regents of the University of Wisconsin System.

Wright, Benjamin D., and Mark H. Stone. 1979. *Best Test Design: Rasch Measurement*. Chicago: MESA Press.

Chapter 13

◆ Addressing Diversity in CALL Evaluation through Arguments and Theory-of-Action

JIM RANALLI
Iowa State University

THE DIVERSE AND EVER-CHANGING list of technologies encompassed by computer-assisted language learning (CALL) presents evaluators with a challenging moving target. At a time when CALL can include everything from school-based telecollaborative projects to Massive Online Open Courses (MOOCs), to smartphone- and tablet-based apps, previous approaches to evaluation reveal their inadequacies. The checklists that once predominated (see Susser 2001) assumed the focus of evaluation to be tutorial software known as "courseware," which now constitutes a much-diminished part of the CALL landscape. Methodological frameworks like the one proposed by Hubbard (2006) assume the role of an instructor and a course in which the technology is situated, which is countered by increasingly autonomous and self-directed applications of CALL (Reinders and White 2016). And sets of criteria based in principles of interactionist second language acquisition (SLA; Chapelle 2001) seem less than ideal for evaluating technologies designed for individual use whose function is primarily facilitative of second language (L2) usage, such as online dictionaries or translation tools.

But the continually shifting and expanding nature of technological forms in L2 learning is only the most obvious type of diversity with which CALL evaluators must contend. We can see diversity in other aspects as well: the contexts in which CALL evaluations take place, the purposes for which they are conducted, the audiences for whom they are intended, the theoretical and methodological perspectives that inform their work, and the standards by which CALL interventions are deemed successful or not.

Consideration of the context of learning is essential in CALL evaluation because the value of technology for L2 learning can only be judged with reference to the needs and characteristics of particular participants in particular situations at particular times. Meanwhile, the contexts of contemporary CALL usage evidence diversity in the extreme. They include classrooms across formal and informal educational settings, distance and online learning spaces, institutional self-access centers, and countless opportunities for individual, self-directed learning through technology. There is also diversity in the scales at which CALL contexts can be conceptualized. Gruba and Hinkleman (2012) discuss different concerns of evaluation at the micro (e.g., classroom), meso (e.g., institutional), and macro (e.g., policy) levels.

We also see diversity in the purposes for which CALL evaluations are conducted. While decision-making is an important function of evaluation—one for which checklists and methodological frameworks were designed—it is not the only purpose. Evaluation in our field has also contributed to the development of a base of knowledge about technology for language learning. While we address questions about whether a CALL intervention works, we are also interested in why and how it works and under what conditions its benefits may transfer to other users and contexts. Some CALL experts, such as Levy and Stockwell (2006), differentiate between *evaluation* and *research* to refer to these decision-making and knowledge-building functions, respectively, but, as argued by Chapelle (2001), information about why something works can also serve the purpose of decision-making. Importantly, evaluation can likewise inform the iterative development of CALL interventions and artifacts, which are rarely deemed beyond further improvement.

In addition, the audiences for CALL evaluations are diverse. Chapelle (2007) puts them on a continuum from *insiders* (e.g., software developers and other CALL researchers) on one end to *outsiders* (e.g., other applied linguists and program- or policy-level decision-makers) on the other, with *informed critics* (e.g., learners and instructors) in the middle. Other audience types exist as well; for example, in my own situation, a graduate program that trains future CALL professionals, members of thesis or dissertation committees are tasked with appraising student development and evaluation projects. The information needs of these different audiences, the types of evidence that will be most meaningful to them, and the aspects of the evaluation that best align with their concerns and values, will likewise vary.

There is also diversity in terms of the theoretical and research perspectives that CALL evaluators can draw on in conducting their investigations. An analysis of use of the term *theory* across twenty-five years of issues in the *CALICO Journal*, one of the field's major publications, identified 113 unique descriptors, although many of these represented theories within the fields of linguistics and education (Hubbard 2008). Given the necessary relationship between how phenomena are conceptualized and how they will be measured, it is thus not surprising to find diversity in the research approaches and methods employed by CALL researchers, not simply in terms of the qualitative-quantitative spectrum but also the starting points for investigations (e.g., exploring the use of a generic technology for its applicability to L2 learning versus identifying a problem in L2 instructional practice and developing a technology-based solution; Stockwell 2012). Emerging technologies also bring with them the potential for new ways to document and analyze variables of interest.

Finally, there is diversity in the standards by which the success of CALL interventions is evaluated. Looking at the multitude of published CALL studies addressing the question "Does it work?" may give the impression that effectiveness is the only relevant criterion. While a new tool or task can produce gains in learning, it may yet go unadopted by instructors and learners, in which case it has in an important sense failed. Thus, sustainability of CALL interventions is arguably as important as effectiveness. The fact that CALL is rife with one-off projects (Kennedy and Levy 2009) must of course be attributed in part to the ever-changing nature of technology, but it is a well-known if not well-understood fact that CALL interventions shown to be effective may nevertheless remain stubbornly resistant to widespread adoption in L2 classrooms, such as the use of corpora (Ebrahimi and Faghih 2016).

Given all these forms of diversity, how should evaluation be defined in CALL, and how should it be approached? With respect to the first part of the question, Norris's definition of language program evaluation seems to encompass many if not all of the facets mentioned above: "[Language program evaluation is] a pragmatic mode of inquiry that illuminates the complex nature of language-related interventions of various kinds, the factors that foster or constrain them, and the consequences that ensue. [Evaluation] enables a variety of evidence-based decisions and actions, from designing programs and implementing practices to judging effectiveness and improving outcomes. [It] may provide a heuristic for generating new knowledge; raising awareness; and transforming the ... circumstances of individuals and communities" (2016, 169). If we insert the term *technology-mediated* between *language-related* and *interventions*, substitute *CALL intervention* for *programs*, and exchange *stakeholder groups* for *communities*, we have what may be considered a working definition of evaluation in the field.

To complement this inclusive definition, could a single approach to evaluation likewise be found that is capable of embracing the diverse range of contexts, purposes, audiences, theoretical bases, and research approaches, in addition to the manifold forms of technology themselves? This question aligns with the concerns of the organizers of the 2016 Georgetown University Round Table on Languages and Linguistics (GURT) with making evaluation useful, as well as with the specific focus of the CALL evaluation colloquium at that meeting. In responding to these concerns, I wish to propose here that, to the extent a single approach is possible and desirable, it might be found in the idea of arguments.

What Do Arguments Have to Offer?

Conceptualizing evaluation as argument is not new. In the field of program evaluation, House asserts that evaluations are acts of persuasion aimed at "winning a particular audience to a point of view or course of action by an appeal to the audience's reason and understanding" (1977, 6). In introducing their approach to the evaluation of e-learning and distance education, Ruhe and Zumbo describe a "rigorous, evidence-based argument in support of evaluative claims" (2008, 11). In the field of CALL specifically, Chapelle, inspired by the work of Bachman (2005) on validity arguments, proposes that evaluation be conceptualized as "a situation-specific argument" (Chapelle 2001, 52) in which one marshals empirical evidence to show the extent to which a particular CALL task meets six key criteria derived from SLA theory and research. Since the publication of this groundbreaking CALL evaluation framework, Chapelle has conducted pioneering work with validity arguments in the field of language testing (see Chapelle, Enright, and Jamieson 2008, 2010; Chapelle, Cotos, and Lee 2015) and has recently returned to the notion of CALL evaluation argument to elaborate its potential (Chapelle 2014, 2017). In the following sections, I review Chapelle's current proposal, as well as some argument-based validation research that intersects with CALL evaluation, to illustrate how arguments can be used to this end.

Implicit Arguments in Existing CALL Studies

In a plenary address at the EuroCALL conference at the University of Groningen, Chapelle (2014) proposed using arguments as a conceptual starting point for planning, conducting, and appraising CALL evaluations. In contrast to checklists, methodological frameworks, or SLA-derived sets of criteria, evaluation arguments begin with the *claims* one wants to make about a particular CALL intervention; that is, statements about the value of specific aspects of technology for language learning that are framed with reference to the needs and concerns of the particular audience(s) at whom the evaluation is directed. The evaluator's role is to make these claims explicit and "to plan an investigation that will determine the extent to which the claims can be supported. The results of the investigation are then used in support of an argument about the credibility of the claims" (Chapelle, 2017, 380).

For Chapelle, the lens of evaluation-as-argument can provide significant advantages to the way evaluations are planned, conducted, interpreted and appraised. In particular, it can help novice evaluators, such as graduate students evaluating CALL interventions as part of thesis or dissertation projects, avoid the trap of assuming that evaluation can only be accomplished by comparing between technology and nontechnology conditions. Rather than characterizing this as a new approach, Chapelle asserts that arguments are already evident in much published CALL research. Adopting a perspective of evaluation as argument allows them to be recognized and understood as such.

Chapelle's review of the professional literature in peer-reviewed CALL journals has identified five main types of evaluation argument. These are arguments based on: (1) comparisons, (2) corpus linguistics, (3) authenticity, (4) SLA theory, and (5) general pedagogical principles (Chapelle 2014, 2017). Briefly, comparison arguments are based on studies in which technology and nontechnology conditions are contrasted. Quantitative analysis of scores on outcome measures is typically used to determine if differences in L2 learning gains can be identified across conditions. The second type of argument, based on authenticity, focuses on common, authentic uses of technology for communication outside the classroom, using these as models and rationales for incorporating technology into formal language learning; for example, classroom tasks involving the use of smartphones or tablet computers. The third type of argument also deals with authenticity, but in this case it is with respect to the linguistic forms to which learners are exposed. In this type of argument, corpus linguistics techniques and data, in combined forms referred to as data-driven learning, are claimed to provide more authentic language samples, which in turn are seen to benefit learning. Theory-based arguments constitute the fourth type in Chapelle's taxonomy. Such arguments make claims based on SLA theory about the value of having students engage in certain technology-mediated activities or conditions such as group discussion via text chat. The theory allows connections to be made between qualities of the students' engagement and interpretations about its value for language learning. The fifth and final type are arguments based on pedagogical principles that do not directly relate to enhanced language proficiency. Teachers' or CALL developers' interpretations of good pedagogical practice provide the rationales for having students engage in activities such as telecollaboration tasks, which are claimed to develop intercultural competence.

In addition to the advantages of evaluation-as-argument identified by Chapelle, there are others related to the diversity concerns outlined earlier. CALL interventions based on emerging technologies that push beyond the parameters of existing frameworks or evaluative criteria will always be expressible in terms of claims. And whereas Chapelle (2017) rightly sees the broad range of theories and research approaches encompassed in evaluation-as-argument as a challenge, it is also an affordance because it can capture so much of the diversity that CALL practitioners already find themselves working with.

However, there are also important limitations in this approach. To the extent that novice evaluators must draw from the professional journals for models, they may confront biased sampling, since evaluations in the professional literature whose primary purpose is local decision-making or ongoing evaluation may be relatively less common compared to those whose primary purpose is knowledge-building. Similarly, there will be bias in favor of effectiveness to the neglect of sustainability, and novice evaluators may likewise find insufficient guidance for shaping evaluations to the needs of audiences other than researchers communicating among themselves in peer-reviewed venues.

Another problem is the difficulty of appraising arguments embedded in a genre of communication that requires appraisal on its own terms, and which, by virtue of its complexity, may mask inadequacies in the argument's content or structure. It is a cognitively demanding task to produce and to interpret a research article, and writers' and readers' concerns will tend to default to the requirements of the genre. When all is said and done, a research article may boil down to the provision of support for a single claim, and while such an article may be judged favorably, the argument embedded within it may yet lack clarity and completeness, with important claims and assumptions left unelaborated or insufficiently developed.

Finally, even if a coherent and complete argument can be discerned in the text of a research article, the finished product provides no clue as to how the argument was developed. To borrow Bachman's description of the challenges of previous approaches to test validation, embedded CALL evaluation arguments may in essence represent groupings of "more or less independent qualities and questions, with no clear mechanism for integrating these into a set of procedures" (2005, 1). What may be helpful, then, is a way to delineate the components of a CALL evaluation argument in notation form, separately from the requirements of conducting and reporting research, and to facilitate more thorough identification of claims, underlying assumptions, and the types of evidence that might be gathered to investigate them. We turn to such a procedure in the next section.

Explicit Arguments in CALL-Related Validation Studies

Validation is to assessment what evaluation is to instruction. Both are concerned with appraising the extent to which the qualities of a test or task can support the claims that are made about it. Like evaluation, validation is a complex process that must encompass broad and diverse sets of considerations. Contemporary language testers recognize the need to address traditional validation concerns, such as connecting test performance to reported scores, while also dealing with the consequences of test use, such as how scores are employed in decision-making. Arguments can support such a unitary approach to validation by showing how issues of test interpretation and use can be considered at the same time and by allowing diverse forms of validity evidence to be identified, prioritized, and appraised in relation to a larger whole. Because validation may involve a multitude of claims aimed at a variety of stakeholders, especially in the case of high-stakes assessments, explicitness is important. Explicitness can be accomplished by means of an explicit argument structure.

Language testers have drawn in particular upon the argument-based validation work of Kane (2012), who proposed a linear structure in which logical connections are represented by inferences named according to their place in the chain of reasoning. The *evaluation inference*, for example, links the actual observation of performance to its quantification in a test score, while the *utilization inference* links the score to some form of decision-making. Each inference is associated with claims regarding the particular assessment in question, and bridging the inferences requires the provision of support for the claims and their underlying assumptions. In Kane's (2013) approach, validation involves two stages: (1) an interpretation-use argument, in which the inferences, claims, assumptions, and relevant forms of support are specified; and (2) a validity argument, in which the evidence is gathered and then appraised in relation to the overall argument structure. According to Chapelle, the validity argument should take the form of "a narrative that points to a plausible conclusion" (2008, 319).

One of Kane's innovations was to undergird the validity-argument components with a model of inference developed by Toulmin (2003), which provides useful concepts and structures for teasing out logical relationships and anticipating counterarguments. In Toulmin's model, an observation, or "datum," is connected to a claim by an inference. What allows one to infer the claim from the datum is a warrant, a statement which is subject to challenge and which itself rests on one or more assumptions. Supporting the warrant involves the provision of backing for its underlying assumptions. Backing can take the form of empirical, theoretical, or commonsensical evidence. The model allows for conditions of rebuttal, which can also be backed by evidence and which may render the warrant inapplicable, thus undermining the inference. Importantly for the test-validation process, Kane (2012) says the model can provide guidance in the allocation of research effort. Claims can be prioritized for investigation according to how central they are to the interpretation-use argument or on the basis of assumptions considered especially problematic.

The potential of explicit arguments such as these to inform the development of CALL evaluation arguments is evident in recent validation studies involving technology-based formative assessments; that is, assessments that support learning and teaching. Chapelle, Cotos, and Lee (2015) present a validity argument for the use of an automated writing evaluation (AWE) tool to support classroom-based English-as-a-second-language (ESL) writing instruction by providing grammatical feedback and encouraging multiple drafts. The argument for one of these tools, the Criterion Online Writing Evaluation service, includes five inferences and their associated warrants, which are themselves based on twenty-two assumptions. The authors present empirical evidence related to the evaluation inference, which is based on the warrant that the AWE feedback "provides students with accurate information to target relevant areas for revision/improvement/learning," which in turn is based in part on the assumption that "*Criterion* feedback is accurate" (2015, 3). In reviewing their finding that more than half of Criterion's feedback had gone ignored by students, possibly as a result of inaccuracies in the feedback, the authors identified a potential rebuttal for future investigation, stating that students lack confidence in the AWE system. This study is useful first as an example of an explicit argument in which claims and assumptions regarding the value of technology for L2 learning are specified in detail and supporting evidence is gathered and appraised. It is also notable that, while other recent classroom-based AWE research has focused on issues of effectiveness, such as improvements in grammatical accuracy across drafts (e.g., Li, Link, and Hegelheimer 2015), the argument in Chapelle, Cotos, and Lee (2015) directed the authors' attention to sustainability concerns.

A follow-on investigation to this study conducted by myself and two colleagues (Ranalli, Link, and Chukharev-Hudilainen 2016) shows how explicit arguments can serve the purpose of decision-making and help in communicating among stakeholders. I undertook this study in my dual capacity as both a researcher and a coordinator for the ESL writing program in which the Chapelle, Cotos, and Lee (2015) study was conducted. In my latter capacity, I sought help in deciding whether Criterion should continue to be used in the course I oversaw. Our research team investigated assumptions underlying the evaluation and utilization inferences in the Chapelle, Cotos, and Lee (2015) argument and found that students in a lower-level course were better able to make use of the Criterion feedback in correcting errors than their higher-level counterparts, which led to our recommendation that Criterion should be used in the lower- but not the higher-level course. In addition to facilitating this finding, the explicit argument also helped the research and course coordination teams clarify expectations among themselves regarding the extent to which the major writing assignments were intended to support L2 development versus the development of writing expertise, a key consideration that until then had gone unrecognized.

Another recent study straddling argument-based validation and CALL evaluation is Gleason (2013), which focuses on blended learning in college-level Spanish classes. Practitioners of blended learning seek a middle ground between completely online and completely face-to-face language instruction, guided by the question "Which tasks are best delivered in which format?" Gleason develops an interpretation-use argument and then reviews evidence related to the evaluation inference to determine whether students' engagement in tasks across face-to-face and online conditions demonstrate comparable learning opportunities, with the learning tasks conceptualized as "micro-formative assessments" (2013, 3). The evidence consists of discourse analysis of language produced by students during the tasks, which provides backing for some of the comparability claims but not others; among the latter is the assumption that the online condition affords equivalent chances for learners to spontaneously focus on meaning. Gleason discusses how her findings could support the work of blended-learning designers, thus illustrating how arguments can be used as the basis of formative evaluations informing ongoing CALL development.

Explicit interpretation-use arguments, then, as this very brief review suggests, facilitate greater detail and completeness in the specification of claims and assumptions, helping evaluators identify priority areas for investigation and allowing appraisal of diverse forms of evidence in relation to the larger argument. They expand the scope of concerns beyond mere effectiveness of the intervention and can feed valuable information back into the development process. While making an argument explicit is no guarantee that all stakeholders will be appeased (Bachman 2005), it does increase transparency and the likelihood of more viewpoints being considered. Given the increasing interest in integrating instruction and assessment, as evidenced in many talks at the GURT 2016 meeting, and the ways that technology is allowing new and more powerful means of simultaneously scaffolding and assessing learning, it seems likely that validity arguments involving CALL used for formative assessment will become more common in the future.

One might suppose, then, that validity arguments and CALL evaluation arguments will largely overlap, except insofar as the object of their focus will be, in the case of the former, an assessment, and in the latter, a CALL intervention. There are, however, limitations to the value of applying the Kanean framework to CALL evaluation. Firstly, the validation argument structure will require that a CALL intervention be construable as an assessment, which will not always be possible nor desirable. And while the linear chain of reasoning connecting observations to scores to uses is well suited to language testing, it may not be a good fit for CALL interventions that entail a greater diversity of claims in more complex causal networks. What is needed, then, is a similar method of making evaluation arguments explicit while affording greater flexibility in delineating relationships among components. In the next section, I discuss the potential of Theory of Action (ToA) models to fulfill this purpose.

Theory of Action As a Way Forward

ToA is a concept from the field of program evaluation whose origins lie in efforts to make social programs more goal-oriented and thus likely to succeed. ToA and related approaches such as Logic Modeling and Theory of Change were developed in part to test the readiness of programs to be evaluated by conceptualizing them as identifiable sets of activities and inputs linked to specific outcomes, with these linkages being both logical and testable (Patton 2008). According to Patton, logic models connect outcomes but do not necessarily specify the causal factors that underlie them. When causal mechanisms are added to a program's logic model, it becomes a Theory of Change. If the scale of evaluation is narrower than a complete program or policy intervention, such as a particular strategy to address a specific problem within a specific time frame (e.g., the "action"), the term Theory of Action is used (Patton 2008, 339).

Procedurally, ToA starts with the specification of the intended long-term outcomes, from which program designers and developers then work backward toward shorter term outcomes, outputs, inputs, and so on that constitute preconditions. A simplification of the theory in notation or diagram form helps stakeholders to develop a theory of action for themselves. As for who is responsible for elaborating a program's ToA, some theorists emphasize the role of program staff and intended beneficiaries while others see the need for social scientists' knowledge and expertise. Another approach is to involve both, with practitioners able to contribute knowledge of how a ToA model gets translated into reality while researchers can complement the model's intended outcomes with other, unintended outcomes that previous research or theory suggest may be likely to occur.

Part of the value of this approach is that, in delineating a ToA model, assumptions underlying the causal linkages among inputs, outputs, and intended outcomes are more readily identifiable. Evaluation theorists have termed these "validity assumptions" (Patton 2008; Suchman 1967). In social programs, a common validity assumption is that acquiring relevant knowledge will lead to beneficial changes in behavior, despite much research and evaluation casting doubt on the universal applicability of this assumption (Weiss 2000, cited in Patton 2008). This is relevant to the situation in CALL, where one-off projects are rife and instructors often fail to buy into technological innovations despite research evidence.

Thus, we can see potential productive overlap between ToA and an argument-based approach to evaluation for use in CALL as outlined above. There are clear parallels between the focus on intended outcomes in the former and claims in the latter, and both stress the need to tease out underlying assumptions. ToA is also agnostic in terms of data types and research methodologies. It lends itself to linear chains of reasoning resembling those found in the validity argument, and yet it can be used to model more complex adaptive systems in which a medium-term outcome has more than one cause or serves as a precondition for more than one long-term outcome.

Kane (chapter 14, this volume) discusses the importance of using ToA in conjunction with argument-based validation when assessments are formative, since the outputs from such assessments serve as inputs to instruction, and these inputs have intended outcomes of their own. The only project in applied linguistics to have combined the argument-based validation and ToA approaches so far is the CBAL project coordinated by Educational Testing Service. CBAL, which stands for Cognitively Based Assessment of, for, and as Learning, is a research initiative to develop a comprehensive kindergarten through twelfth grade assessment system integrated into classroom instruction that provides students and teachers with worthwhile educational experiences. The project, which focuses on English language arts and makes substantial use of computer-based materials, has been described in a report detailing how evidence for the ToA is gathered and appraised in conjunction with a validity argument. According to Bennett (2010, 71), the CBAL ToA includes

1. the intended effects of the assessment system;
2. the components of the assessment system and a logical and coherent rationale for each component, including backing for that rationale in research and theory;
3. the interpretive claims that will be made from assessment results;
4. the action mechanisms designed to cause the intended effects; and
5. potential unintended negative effects and what will be done to mitigate them.

The first, second, and fourth elements are recognizable as conventional parts of ToA or logic modeling, although the term *effects* has been substituted for *outcomes* and the term *components* for *inputs* and *outputs*. The third and fifth elements, meanwhile, are more clearly associated with validity arguments (i.e., interpretive claims about consequences and uses of assessments and unintended effects that could constitute rebuttals to the claims). According to Bennett (pers. comm. with the author, May 19, 2016), interpretation-use arguments in general, and the Toulmin model of inference in particular, can naturally complement ToA because the former's focus on warrants, assumptions, and rebuttals can help elaborate the explicit and implicit claims in a ToA model or the evidence needed to elaborate those claims.

While the CBAL example is instructive for language testers working with formative assessments, a more CALL-focused illustration will be helpful for present purposes. In the following section, I set forth an example of a CALL evaluation conceptualized using ToA and the Toulmin inference structure.

An Example

As part of my doctoral work, I developed and evaluated a web-based, technology-mediated course in strategy instruction (SI). The evaluation, which is described in Ranalli (2013), did not include an explicit argument, but I have reconceptualized it in such a form here to illustrate some of its shortcomings and to show how these might have been improved upon if ToA and Toulmin's model of inference had been used as the basis of the evaluation.

Background

The SI course, which was called Virtual Vocabulary Trainer or VVT, was created to teach college-level ESL writing students an integrated form of dictionary skills and language awareness of features of pattern grammar (Hunston and Francis 2000). Pattern grammar encompasses a variety of different ways that lexical words can combine with other lexical words as well as function words; in particular, verb transitivity, complementation, and grammatical collocation. Although providing students of English with information about syntactic patterning is a primary purpose of learner dictionaries, such dictionaries are often misused or underused for a variety of reasons, including lack of understanding about syntactic features of English vocabulary (Ranalli and Nurmukhadev 2014).

The online course comprised multimedia tutorials consisting of videos and accompanying text-based exercises. The tutorials aimed at developing students' declarative knowledge about learner dictionaries and about pattern grammar—its wide variety of forms, its frequency in English, and the way it helps determine which sense of a word is intended—as well as procedural knowledge in terms of students' abilities at syntactic parsing to identify potential patterns and to perform related searches in learner dictionaries quickly and efficiently so as to minimize cognitive load. An instructional design framework for training complex cognitive skills (Van Merriënboer 1997) was used to differentiate these aims, with declarative aims addressed under the name *nonrecurrent* skills, procedural knowledge addressed under the name *recurrent* skills, and the integration of these subcomponents termed *whole-skill practice.*

The original evaluation was based largely on a between-groups experimental design contrasting a VVT condition with a comparison condition that involved learners in repeated dictionary consultations for usage information but no instruction. Participants were assigned randomly to one of the two conditions, which were administered online through a learning management system (LMS). An online task used as a pre- and posttest measure of strategy performance required participants to correct pattern-grammar errors in sentences and to choose among a selection of online dictionaries to assist them in doing so. The results showed large effect sizes for between-groups differences at posttest and within-group differences for the VVT group from pre- to posttest. In addition, user perception data, which was collected via online questionnaires, showed generally positive views of the VVT materials and a majority of participants indicating they would use what they had learned beyond the course.

In the semesters following the original evaluation, the VVT course was used sporadically. It was made available to any interested instructor of the writing course, some of whom chose to use it while others did not. The requirement that students access the course via a separate LMS from that used for the writing course made integration of the materials difficult. Another problem was that instructors who were unfamiliar with pattern grammar expressed uncertainty about the aims of the course, assuming it focused on teaching specific lexical patterns, and were reluctant to better familiarize themselves by completing the course on their own, no doubt because of the investment of time involved. Many opted instead to use a paper-based dictionary consultation assignment that had originally constituted the vocabulary component of the course. The VVT materials, now in need of design and functionality upgrades, are not currently hosted or available online.

Reconceptualizing the Evaluation As a ToA Argument

The original evaluation, then, focused narrowly on effectiveness, with little concern for the needs and views of a key stakeholder group, instructors, and thereby failed to address some of the contextual issues that would influence integration and sustainability. As such, the project may be representative of many CALL interventions that show promise but fail to take root. To illustrate how a ToA argument can work to inform the process of CALL evaluation (as well as iterative development), we can first reimagine the original project as an initial ToA model (figure 13.1).

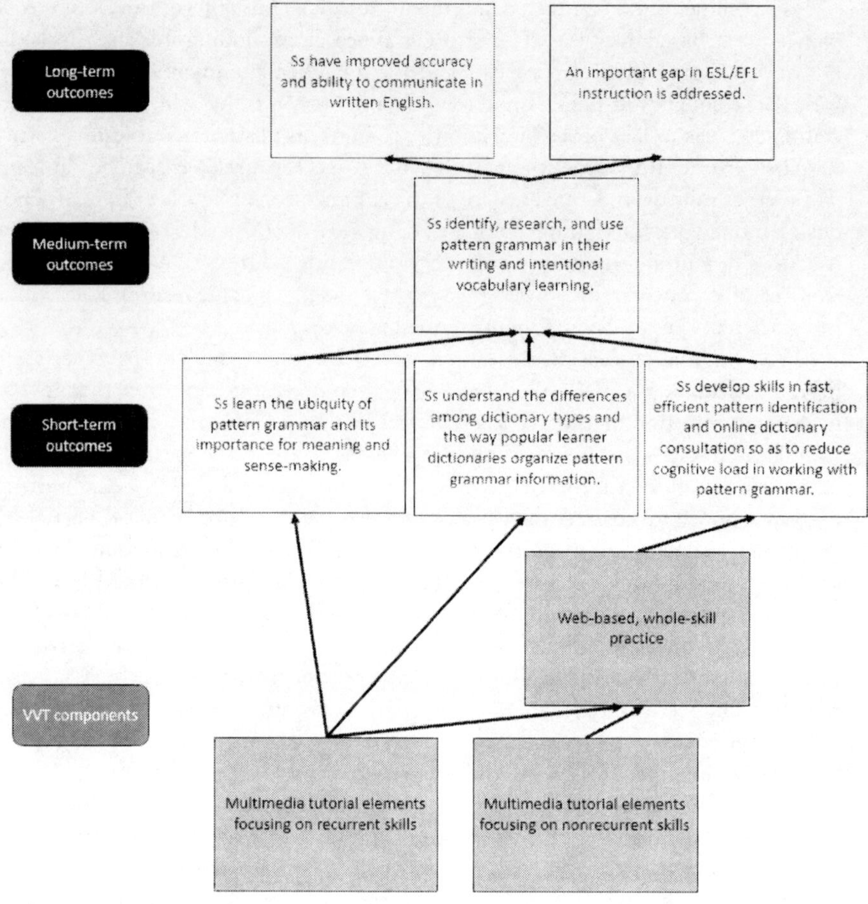

◆ Figure 13.1. Initial ToA model for the VVT online strategy instruction project

Development of the model starts near the top with specification of the long-term outcomes (cf. use of the term *effects* in Bennet 2010). Outcomes represent "changes in awareness, knowledge, skill, or behavior" (Knowlton and Phillips 2009, 8); in the present case, students will have improved accuracy and communication of lexical meaning in their writing and vocabulary use, and an important gap in ESL and EFL (English as a foreign language) instruction will have been addressed.

Working backward from these ultimate intended outcomes, a medium-term outcome is specified: that students identify, research, and use pattern grammar in their writing and intentional vocabulary learning—in other words, that they transfer application of the strategy to new contexts of use where it is also relevant. This single outcome is then shown to be dependent on three short-term outcomes that constitute preconditions focusing on the relevant declarative and procedural knowledge described above. Below these, the SI components represent the inputs (i.e., the differentiated forms of instruction) and outputs (i.e., descriptive indicators of what activities the inputs generate; Knowlton and Phillips 2009) that are claimed to result in the short-term outcomes. Together, the elements resemble a logic model, albeit a high-level specification of one for demonstration purposes that could be broken down into a more detailed representation to address specific evaluation needs.

The next steps in developing the ToA model would be (1) to specify any assumptions underlying the causal linkages between project components and outcomes in the model, and (2) to specify forms of empirical or theoretical support that would render these causal inferences warranted. The ToA model would then be appraised for plausibility, coherence, and completeness. The outcomes (i.e., claims), assumptions, and backing could at this point be reviewed by the evaluator to determine which parts of the model are most in need of empirical support. It is interesting to consider where data from the original evaluation study would fit into this model. Scores from the pre- and posttest could be used as support for the inferences linking the VVT components to the short-term outcomes, while the user-perception data could be used as backing for the linkages from one or more of the short-term outcomes to the medium-term outcomes—although in the latter case, this would constitute very limited support, a fact which the model would make more evident.

The process would not stop here, however. The next step in developing the ToA model would be to share it with key stakeholders including, in this case, thesis committee members as well as instructors in the writing course where the study was based. One immediate advantage of using the model for this purpose instead of a research proposal, pilot study report, or other lengthier verbal description, might be to better facilitate understanding that the focus of the intervention is a complex cognitive skill involving use of a certain type of lexical feature rather than direct improvements of L2 proficiency, which was a very common misunderstanding about the project.

More importantly, however, the lack of attention to sustainability issues may have been immediately evident. Instructors, in talking through the model with the researcher, might have raised questions about the causal connection between the short- and medium-term outcomes, noting that it rests on the assumption that possession of new knowledge and skills will necessarily entail students' using these in new contexts of use. Such observations could constitute a potential rebuttal (figure 13.2) stating that the lack of links to pattern grammar in the summative and formative assessment on the writing course would mean that students would be likely to abandon a concern for it beyond the VVT training.

Types of appropriate backing could then be specified for the assumption and rebuttal, yielding evaluation questions for possible investigation. Alternatively, in recognition of the fact that much previous research favors the rebuttal over the assumption, the model could be elaborated to address the lack of attention to integration and sustainability in the project.

Such elaborations are depicted in the revised model (figure 13.3). A new set of short-, medium-, and long-term outcomes is specified that would (hypothetically) address the needs of instructors. In addition, components of the VVT project have been specified at the bottom, consisting of two workshops and integration of the VVT course into the LMS used by the course instructors to facilitate ongoing

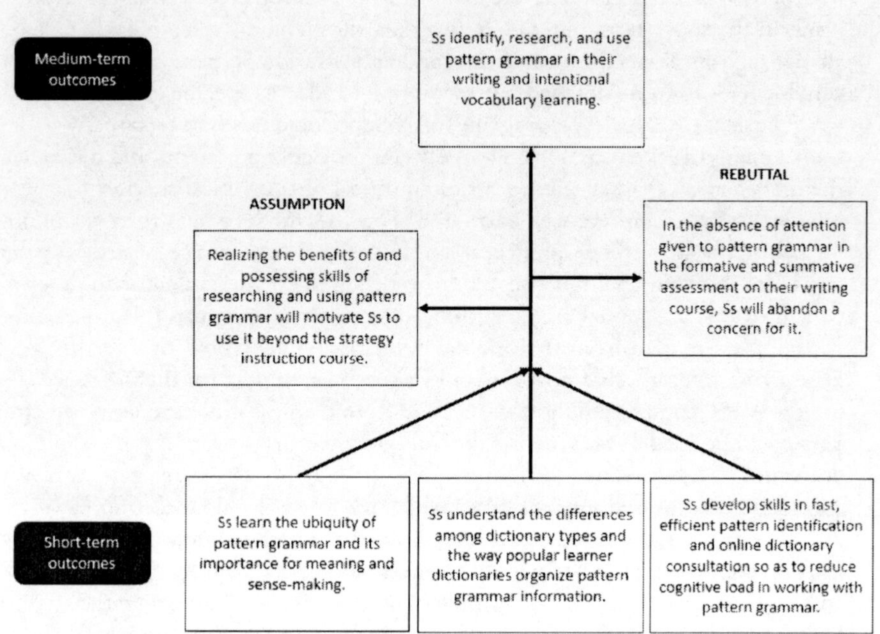

◆ **Figure 13.2.** Inference in the VVT ToA model linking three short-term outcomes to a medium-term outcome, with an assumption on which that inference depends and a potential rebuttal to the inference

administration and grading. Short-term outcomes focus on important forms of pattern grammar–related knowledge that instructors need to possess; medium-term outcomes address the actions intended to result from that knowledge; and long-term outcomes constitute worthwhile professional development goals in their own right, which are distinct from the original goals of the project.

The next step in the process would be to specify assumptions underlying the causal links in this new section of the model and identify forms of evidence that could be used to support these additional claims. Following this, the evaluation would proceed by gathering and assembling these forms of evidence according to priorities established in consultation with stakeholders. The final step would be to compose the evaluation argument itself; that is, a single narrative in which the evidence is reviewed for all specified claims to determine the extent to which they are supported and in which the coherence and completeness of the ToA argument structure is also assessed. Exemplification of these next steps is beyond the scope of the present chapter, but it is hoped this brief illustration provides a glimpse into the ways a ToA argument can structure and enhance the process of CALL evaluation.

Summary and Conclusion

This chapter has discussed the potential benefits of arguments to support the task of CALL evaluation in all its diversity of focuses, purposes, contexts, and audiences.

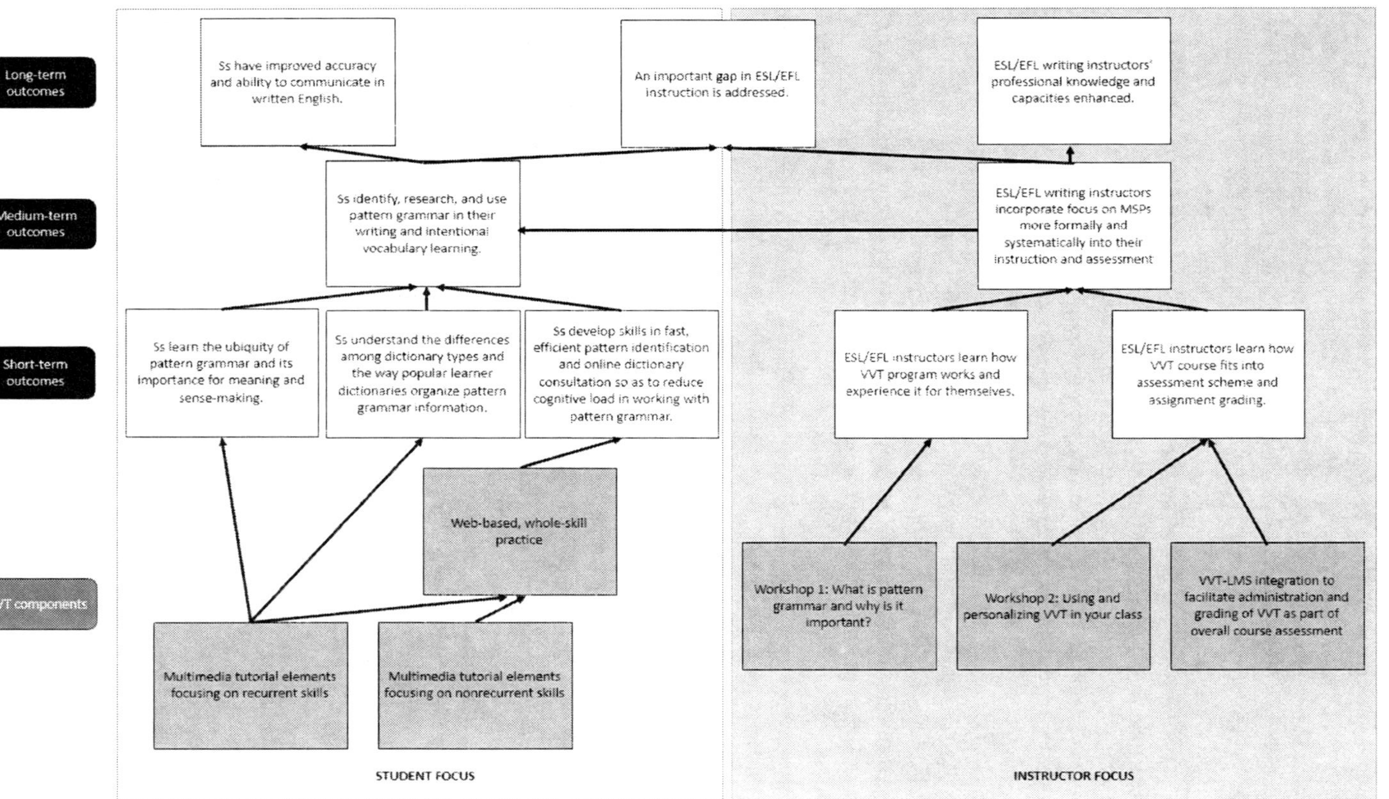

Figure 13.3. The revised ToA model for the VVT project, with new intervention components and outcomes targeted at writing-course instructors

Compared to checklists, methodological frameworks, and sets of evaluative criteria, arguments support a broader and more comprehensive approach to evaluation by focusing on the claims one wants to make about a particular CALL intervention and helping clarify assumptions underlying those claims that might otherwise go unrecognized or underappreciated.

Beyond a general recommendation for use of arguments, this chapter has proposed a particular approach based on the notion of Theory of Action. ToA is a participatory approach that can complement social-science expertise with the vital perspectives of stakeholders and thus highlight issues of sustainability as well as effectiveness. It supports decision-making by requiring the contextual characteristics of an intervention to be incorporated into modeling but can also serve purposes of knowledge building and iterative development. It affords attention to the needs and values of particular audiences and allows diverse theoretical and research perspectives to be utilized in principled ways. Used in conjunction with the Toulmin model of inference, ToA arguments may potentially engender a new approach to CALL evaluation similarly to the way interpretation-use arguments enabled a new approach to language-test validation. They provide a flexible yet powerful methodology for understanding how and why CALL can support the needs of learners and instructors as well as mechanisms for accountability and the guidance of research. Importantly, they align with current views of technology mediation in language education, in which the main question posed is no longer "Is it effective?" but rather "Under what conditions, and for whom?" (Chun 2016).

This potential needs to be developed. Among other things, there is a need to adapt ToA to better accommodate aspects of arguments. Differences between the way one frames claims versus intended outcomes may be subtle but important. ToA typically consolidates assumptions in one area of a model, whereas the Toulmin approach entails modeling assumptions for individual claims. This, along with the potential for large and complex arrangements of claims depending on the CALL intervention in question, will present challenges to graphical depiction. To identify and address such challenges, actual evaluations must be conducted, including developmental evaluations undertaken in the early stages of CALL projects so that reciprocities between development and evaluation can be explored.

References

Bachman, Lyle F. 2005. "Building and Supporting a Case for Test Use." *Language Assessment Quarterly* 2 (1): 1–34.

Bennett, Randall E. 2010. "Cognitively Based Assessment of, for, and as Learning (CBAL): A Preliminary Theory of Action for Summative and Formative Assessment." *Measurement* 8:70–91.

Chapelle, Carol A. 2001. *Computer Applications in Second Language Acquisition: Foundations for Teaching, Testing, and Research*. Cambridge: Cambridge University Press.

——. 2007. "Challenges in Evaluation of Innovation: Observations from Technology Research." *Innovation in Language Learning and Teaching* 1 (1): 30–45.

——. 2008. "The TOEFL Validity Argument." In Chapelle, Enright, and Jamieson, *Building a Validity Argument*, 319–52.

———. 2014. "Arguments for Technology and Language Learning." Plenary address at the annual EuroCALL Conference, Groningen, Netherlands, August.

———. 2017. "Evaluation of Technology and Language Learning." In *The Handbook of Technology in Second Language Teaching and Learning*, edited by Carol A. Chapelle and Shannon Sauro. Malden, MA: Wiley-Blackwell, 378–392.

Chapelle, Carol A., Elena Cotos, and Jooyoung Lee. 2015. "Validity Arguments for Diagnostic Assessment Using Automated Writing Evaluation." *Language Testing* 32 (3): 385–405.

Chapelle, Carol A., Mary K. Enright, and Joan M. Jamieson, eds. 2008. *Building a Validity Argument for the Test of English as a Foreign Language*. New York: Routledge.

———. 2010. "Does an Argument-Based Approach to Validity Make a Difference?" *Educational Measurement: Issues and Practice* 29 (1): 3–13.

Chun, Dorothy M. 2016. "The Role of Technology in SLA Research." *Language Learning and Technology* 20 (2): 98–115.

Ebrahimi, Alice, and Esmail Faghih. 2016. "Integrating Corpus Linguistics into Online Language Teacher Education Programs." *ReCALL* 29 (1): 120–35.

Gleason, Jesse B. 2013. "An Interpretive Argument for Blended Course Design." *Foreign Language Annals* 46 (4): 588–609.

Gruba, Paul, and Don Hinkelman. 2012. *Blending Technologies in Second Language Classrooms*. New York: Palgrave Macmillan.

House, Ernest R. 1977. *The Logic of Evaluative Argument*. CSE Monograph Series in Evaluation 7. Los Angeles: Center for the Study of Evaluation.

Hubbard, Philip. 2006. "Evaluating Call Software." In *Calling on CALL: From Theory and Research to New Directions in Foreign Language Teaching*, edited by Lara Ducate and Nike Arnold, 313–38. San Marcos, TX: CALICO.

———. 2008. "Twenty-Five Years of Theory in the CALICO Journal." *CALICO Journal* 25 (3): 387–99.

Hunston, Susan, and Gill Francis. 2000. *Pattern Grammar: A Corpus-Driven Approach to the Lexical Grammar of English*. Amsterdam: John Benjamins.

Kane, Michael. T. 2012. "Validating Score Interpretations and Uses: Messick Lecture, Language Testing Research Colloquium, Cambridge, April 2010." *Language Testing* 29 (1): 3–17.

———. 2013. "Validating the Interpretations and Uses of Test Scores." *Journal of Educational Measurement* 50 (1): 1–73.

Kennedy, Claire, and Mike Levy. 2009. "Sustainability and Computer-Assisted Language Learning: Factors for Success in a Context of Change." *Computer Assisted Language Learning* 22 (5): 445–63.

Knowlton, Lisa W., and Cynthia C. Phillips. 2009. *The Logic Model Guidebook: Better Strategies for Great Results*. Los Angeles: Sage Publications.

Levy, Mike, and Glenn Stockwell. 2006. *CALL Dimensions: Options and Issues in Computer-Assisted Language Learning*. Mahwah, NJ: Lawrence Erlbaum.

Li, Jinrong, Stephanie Link, and Volker Hegelheimer. 2015. "Rethinking the Role of Automated Writing Evaluation (AWE) Feedback in ESL Writing Instruction." *Journal of Second Language Writing* 27:1–18.

Norris, John M. 2016. "Language Program Evaluation." *Modern Language Journal* 100 (S1): 169–89.

Patton, Michael Q. 2008. *Utilization-Focused Evaluation*. 4th ed. Thousand Oaks, CA: Sage Publications.

Ranalli, Jim. 2013. "Online Strategy Instruction for Integrating Dictionary Skills and Language Awareness." *Language Learning & Technology* 17 (2): 75–99.

Ranalli, Jim, Stephanie Link, and Evgeny Chukharev-Hudilainen. 2016. "Automated Writing Evaluation for Formative Assessment of Second Language Writing: Investigating the Accuracy and Usefulness of Feedback as Part of Argument-Based Validation." *Educational Psychology* 37 (1): 8–25.

Ranalli, Jim, and Ulugbek Nurmukhadev. 2014. "Learner Dictionaries." In *The Encyclopedia of Applied Linguistics*, edited by Carol A. Chapelle, 1–6. Malden, MA: Wiley-Blackwell.

Reinders, Hayo and Cynthia White. 2016. "20 Years of Autonomy and Technology: How Far Have We Come and Where to Next?" *Language Learning and Technology* 20 (2): 143–54.

Ruhe, Valerie, and Bruno D. Zumbo. 2008. *Evaluation in Distance Education and E-Learning: The Unfolding Model*. New York: Guilford Press.

Stockwell, Glenn. 2012. "Diversity in Research and Practice." In *Computer-Assisted Language Learning: Diversity in Research and Practice*, edited by Glenn Stockwell, 147–63. Cambridge: Cambridge University Press.

Suchman, Edward A. 1967. *Evaluative Research: Principles and Practice in Public Service and Social Action Programs*. New York: Russell Sage Foundation.

Susser, Bernard. 2001. "A Defense of Checklists for Courseware Evaluation." *ReCALL* 13 (2): 261–76.

Toulmin, Stephen. 2003. *The Uses of Argument*. Updated ed. Cambridge: Cambridge University Press.

Van Merriënboer, Jeroen J.G. 1997. *Training Complex Cognitive Skills: A Four-Component Instructional Design Model for Technical Training*. Englewood Cliffs, NJ: Educational Technology Publications.

Weiss, Carol Hirschon. 2000. "Which Links in Which Theories Shall We Evaluate?" *New Directions for Evaluation* 2000 (87): 35–45.

Chapter 14

◆ Validating Assessments for Meaning and Usefulness

MICHAEL T. KANE
Educational Testing Service

EDUCATIONAL ASSESSMENTS ARE DESIGNED to yield scores that are meaningful and useful in some way, and they are validated by showing that the proposed interpretation and use are adequately supported. To validate an interpretation and use, it is necessary to specify the claims being made in enough detail that their plausibility can be evaluated, and then to evaluate these claims using appropriate forms of evidence.

Traditional, scale-based assessments (e.g., college admissions tests) have been designed to reflect some general level of performance on a continuous, linear scale, or on a few such scales. These scale-based interpretations can be quite helpful in making summative decisions (e.g., pass or fail, selection), but they are not very useful in guiding instruction or learning, except perhaps on a global level (e.g., placement). They can provide an indication of a student's relative standing on a scale of achievement, but as such, they do not provide much, if any, specific information about what students can or cannot do.

For score interpretations to be useful in guiding instruction (i.e., a formative use), they need to reflect a more detailed analysis of what students can and cannot do in terms of models of performance or distinct levels of performance. Such formative assessments are generally more difficult to develop and validate than assessments designed to yield a simple scale score, but they can also be more useful in making instructional decisions.

One way to address the need for a relatively detailed characterization of student performance is to model the performances in terms of student competencies and task characteristics that influence performance in the domain (e.g., Gorin and Embretson 2006; Mislevy 2006). In cases in which such performance models can be developed for a performance domain, they can provide detailed specifications of relevant student competencies and therefore can be very useful in guiding instruction, but such models are difficult to develop and tend to be limited in their scope.

Rather than try to model performance in detail, *learning progressions* (Bennett 2010; Graf and van Rijn 2016) are specified in terms of a series of levels of performance or competence. The levels can be defined in terms of the kinds of tasks that students can perform, rather than trying to specify exactly how the students perform the tasks. As a result, learning progressions are likely to provide less detailed instructional guidance than might be possible if we had an explicit theory of performance, but they are also likely to be much easier to develop for most instructional contexts. Developmental interpretations (e.g., in terms of learning progressions) tend to provide less detailed models of student performance, but they tend to be more flexible, and therefore can be applied more broadly than model-based interpretations.

The structure of learning progressions (a hierarchical sequence of qualitatively different performances) tends to be tied to the structure of a corresponding instructional program and can be tuned to provide useful guidance for instruction within that program. Traditional psychometric analyses have tended to focus on descriptive, scale-based interpretations, but developmental interpretations tend to be more useful in teaching and learning, because they indicate what students can and cannot do, and thereby what they might be prepared to learn next.

In any case, it is important that the claims inherent in the proposed interpretation and use of the scores be evaluated by appropriate evidence and that any claims about the usefulness of scores in teaching and learning be evaluated by examining whether the scores are, in fact, useful in promoting learning. The interpretive frameworks (e.g., learning progressions) for formative assessments are different from those for traditional scale-based assessments, and the evidence needed for their validation will be quite different; the goal of this essay is to highlight some of these differences.

Validating Score Interpretations and Uses

To validate an interpretation or use of assessment scores is to evaluate the claims based on the scores. Argument-based approaches to validation (Bachman 2005; Chapelle, Enright, and Jamieson 2010; Cronbach 1988; House 1980; Kane 2006; Messick 1989; Mislevy, Steinberg, and Almond 2003; Norris 2008) involve an explicit statement of the claims based on the scores and an evaluation of the plausibility of these claims. The proposed interpretation and use of the scores can be stated as an *interpretation-use argument* (IUA) consisting of a network, or sequence, of inferences leading from a student's performance on assessment tasks to the student's score on the assessment, and then to proposed interpretations of this score in terms of its meaning and implications, and to any decisions based on these claims. A second argument, the *validity argument*, examines the plausibility of the claims made in the IUA (Kane 2013).

By developing a clear, explicit statement of the proposed interpretation and use of the scores, the IUA provides a framework for the validity argument. The validity argument is to provide an overall evaluation of the claims in the IUA, and would address three general issues: the clarity and completeness of the argument, the coherence of the argument, and the plausibility of the inferences and assumptions included in the argument. It is particularly important to avoid making implicit assumptions that, being implicit, are neither examined nor subjected to any kind of challenge.

The IUA should accurately represent the intended interpretations and uses of the scores and include all of the proposed interpretations and uses of the scores. In many cases, there may be only one main interpretation and use of the scores, but it is not unusual to have additional ancillary interpretations and uses of scores (e.g., using admission assessment scores for placement decisions). In any case, it is not appropriate to put forward a relatively simple interpretation of scores (e.g., in terms of content coverage and a reliability estimate) for validation, and then to use its validation to justify a more ambitious interpretation (e.g., in terms of future performance in different contexts) or ambitious uses (e.g., involving instructional or placement decisions).

The individual inferences and assumptions need to be plausible, and alternative assumptions should be considered. The claims being made need to be subjected to serious criticism. As Cronbach (1980, 103) suggests, "The job of validation is not to support an interpretation, but to find out what might be wrong with it. A proposition deserves some degree of trust only when it has survived serious attempts to falsify it." In evaluating the claims inherent in the proposed interpretation and use of assessment results, it is important to adopt a somewhat critical stance that challenges its most questionable inferences and assumptions. If the IUA survives serious scrutiny and is found to be coherent, complete, and plausible, it can be accepted (for the time being). An IUA that has survived serious attempts at falsification can be accepted with confidence.

The IUA can be thought of as a mini-theory about the relationship between assessment performances, assessment scores, and the inferences that can be drawn about students based on their assessment scores. If the IUA does not claim much, it can be adequately supported without much effort. More ambitious interpretations would require more evidence to support the additional claims being made. If the scores are to be used to guide instruction, evidence indicating that the guidance is appropriate and effective is called for. For the proposed interpretations and uses to be considered valid, the claims in the IUA need to be supported by the evidence. Therefore, it is important to neither overstate nor understate the claims being made.

The IUA defines the goals of the validation effort and provides criteria for evaluating how well a proposed interpretation and use has been validated. It also limits the evidence needed for validation, because there is no need to evaluate claims that go beyond the IUA. If we interpret the score on a set of performances (e.g., on the tasks in an assessment) simply in terms of the quality of those performances, the claims being made are limited to those performances, and the evidence needed to support these claims is limited to evidence that the criteria used to evaluate the performances (e.g., the scoring key or rubrics) are appropriate and are applied consistently and accurately. If we extend the interpretation to a claim about how well the student performs this kind of task in general, we have an additional claim that a score for this specific set of performances is generalizable across tasks (of this kind), occasions (over some period), and contexts (over some range), and these claims need to be evaluated.

Validity is a matter of degree; the IUA may be strongly supported (all inferences and assumptions are supported by adequate evidence), moderately well supported (most inferences are adequately supported and none are contradicted by the evidence) or not supported (some inferences are not supported by any evidence or are contradicted), and the degree of support may change as new evidence is developed or the interpretations or uses expand or contract. Interpretations and uses that make sense and are adequately supported by evidence are valid, while interpretations or uses that are contradicted by the evidence are said to be invalid (Messick 1989).

Scale-Based Score Interpretations

Classical test theory (CTT) assumes that each student's observed score consists of two components: a true score for that student plus an error, which is assumed to be independent of the true score and to have an expected value of zero. Given these simple assumptions, it is possible to estimate true-score variances, error variances, and reliability coefficients, and in practice, the main use of CTT is to estimate reliability coefficients and associated standard errors of measurement.

CTT has a scale-based interpretation because it assumes that the assessment is to assign each student to a point on a unidimensional scale, in more or less the same way that a meter stick might be used to measure the length of a bookshelf. The model and its assumptions are statistical, and the model is used mainly to provide quantitative estimates of the dependability of the results (e.g., reliability coefficients, standard errors) over replications. Students are to be assigned to points on a scale, and the model provides an indication of how precise these point estimates are.

Note that CTT, in itself, does not indicate how the scores can be interpreted or used. In the CTT context, our sense of the meaning of the scores is derived from the nature of the assessment tasks and scoring rules (i.e., content-based analyses). Potential uses may be evaluated in terms of empirical studies relating scores to outcomes in various contexts (i.e., criterion-related studies). The main thing that the CTT model yields is an estimate of the precision with which we are measuring whatever it is that we are measuring; this is an important but limited service.

Domain-sampling interpretations also generate a scale, but the scores are defined in terms of expected values over a *target domain* of possible performances specifying the range of performances included in the interpretation. The expected value of a student's score over the target domain, or *target score*, is akin to the true score of CTT, but it has a substantive interpretation in terms of the target domain. If the assessment performances are a random sample from the target domain, and the sample is large enough to control sampling error, the observed score can be generalized to the target score.

However, real target domains (e.g., literacy, numeracy) tend to be broadly and roughly defined and the performances are complex and contextualized. To promote fairness and reliability, the assessment performances are standardized to make them simpler, more context free, and easier to score. Because the observed sample of performance is neither a random nor a representative sample from the target domain, a simple statistical generalization from the observed score to the target score is not plausible. The assessment performances are generally not sampled randomly from the target domain, but from a narrower *assessment domain*, which is limited to assessment performances.

The I UA for a domain-based interpretation would reflect what we actually do with the scores and would involve three main inferences (Kane, Crooks, and Cohen 1999). First, we evaluate the observed performances, yielding an observed score. Second, we generalize this observed score over the assessment domain. Third, we extrapolate to the target score.

The first inference, from observed performance to observed scores, relies mainly on expert judgment, rater consistency, and scaling models. The second inference, from observed scores to the expected value over replications of the assessment is a statistical generalization. It requires evidence that the observed sample of performance is large enough and representative enough to control sampling error, and it is evaluated in terms of reliability or generalizability studies, and, perhaps, evaluations of rater consistency.

The third inference is an extrapolation from the context of assessment to the target domain. An evaluation of the extrapolation inference generally relies on analyses of the extent to which the assessment tasks require more or less the same competencies as the full range of tasks in the target domain and do not require any irrelevant skills that are not generally required by the tasks in the target domain (Messick 1989). The extrapolation inference can also be evaluated in terms of correlations between the assessment scores and other indicators of the target scores.

Typically, the I UA would include other inferences in addition to this basic set of three, depending on the proposed interpretation and use of the scores. To validate the proposed interpretation and use of the scores is to evaluate the I UA as a whole.

Formative Assessment

As we develop new assessments for new and existing uses, we need to develop I UAs and validity arguments that reflect the structures and goals of these assessment programs. In particular, interpretations that focus on qualitative differences, rather than continuous linear scales, require new kinds of validity evidence.

Formative assessments are intended to provide information that is useful in instruction and learning in some way, and are usually employed within an instructional program. The general idea is to determine what the student (or a class or other group of students) knows or can do and to use this information to make instructional choices. For example, if a student has already mastered a skill or topic, it would not generally make sense to provide additional explicit instruction on that skill or topic (although additional practice might be useful); in contrast, if the lack of a skill is impeding a student's progress in some domain, intensive instruction on the skill could be appropriate.

A *Theory of Action* (ToA) for the assessment would specify how student scores might be used with other information about the students (e.g., interests, social skills) to make instructional decisions (e.g., picking the next activity for students, given their current level of achievement) and the impact that these decisions might have on the students' achievement (Bennett 2010); the ToA is to indicate how the goals of a score-base intervention are to be achieved. We don't expect the instructional decisions to always lead to the intended outcome, but the score-based decisions should generally lead to the intended outcomes indicated by the ToA.

In developing an assessment, it is clearly important to attend to the technical measurement issues, like precision and accuracy, but in formative contexts, the usefulness of the results in promoting learning takes center stage; the technical issues play an essential supporting role, rather than the other way around, as was the case in CTT. We want score interpretations that are both instructionally useful and psychometrically sound.

The development of formative assessments in terms of a ToA requires that this ToA be specified in some detail, and the validation of such theory-based interpretations requires that the theory be supported by adequate evidence. The primary source of evidence supporting a ToA would be evidence that the instructional decisions based on the assessment scores and on the theory of action achieve their intended effects. For IUAs that include ToAs, validation would resemble program evaluation (Norris 2008).

Learning Progressions

Learning progressions have been proposed as useful frameworks for developing formative assessments and for interpreting scores resulting from such assessments (Bennett 2010; Graf and van Rijn 2016). The general idea is to specify a sequence of levels that learners are expected to master as they make progress in some area of instruction. The levels are ordered from less sophisticated to more sophisticated and can be defined in terms of what students at each level can do.

Each learning progression would have an entry level and a highest level (the target level), and intermediate levels that can be considered stages or steps leading from the entry level to the target level (Graf and van Rijn 2016). The performance levels are defined by kinds of tasks and evaluative criteria associated with each level and in terms of the competencies required to perform these tasks (e.g., conceptual understanding, specific skills). Each level would be defined in terms of a cluster of related skills, understandings, and competencies that are required to perform certain kinds of tasks.

The number and "spacing" of the levels in a learning progression can be adjusted to reflect the breadth of the instructional area being modeled and the uses to be made of the results. As students work through the learning progression from one level to the next, the tasks and evaluative criteria for the performances become increasingly sophisticated, and students at a given level are assumed to have mastered all lower levels and to perform more or less adequately on the tasks at their level. As a result, learning progressions are likely to be most useful in domains conceived of in terms of increasing proficiency and sophistication in some activity (e.g., learning to write or to develop explanations in science) rather than the mastery of domains of content or skills.

Learning progressions are designed to provide a succinct but rich and instructionally meaningful description of each student's level of achievement in terms the kinds of tasks that the students can perform adequately. We give up the very fine-grained information (which may not be very useful in any case) suggested by a continuous scale and adopt a coarser-grained developmental sequence, which can be more informative.

Learning progressions differ from traditional scale-based interpretations of assessment scores in several ways. First, rather than focus on a more or less continuous score scale (akin to length as measured by meter sticks or tapes), as in CTT, learning progressions focus on a sequence of levels (akin to the steps in a staircase or a stepladder) defined in terms of mastery of the core concepts, principles, and skills in a domain. Students' performances are thought of in terms of their levels in the progression and not in terms of points on the scale.

Second, the assessment would be designed to reflect the structure of the progression. It would be natural for the assessment to involve tasks associated with the different levels in the learning progression. If a student does well on the tasks drawn from the first n levels, but can't generally perform those at the $(n + 1)$–th level, it would be reasonable to assign the student to the n-th level. In contrast, the development of assessments for scale-based interpretations is not so closely tied to a developmental model.

Third, learning progressions tend to be more closely tied to instructional programs than would generally be the case for scale-based assessments. Developing a learning progression that corresponds to distinct levels of student performance tends to be easiest if both the instructional program and the learning progression reflect natural stages in mastering the domain. To the extent that instruction is consistent with the learning progression in the sense that the competencies and tasks defining the entry level are taught first, followed by the competencies and tasks defining the next higher level, one would expect a student to progress from one level of the learning progression to the next in a relatively orderly way. Thus, a correspondence between the instructional sequencing and the learning progression is highly desirable if the learning progression is to provide a coherent interpretation of the assessment results.

Fourth, assuming that the learning progression provides a realistic model of student development, a student's placement in the learning progression is likely be more helpful in guiding instruction than a scale-based interpretation would be. For example, a student who has mastered some levels in the progression and is working on the competencies required at the next level in the progression could be encouraged to work on the activities at that level, and on the specific competencies associated with that level.

The levels of the learning progression provide at least a general model of growth. Because the levels represent well-defined, increasing levels of competence, they can provide a performance-based description of the student's progress in mastering the domain, and, as a result, they can provide useful suggestions for instruction and learning. Note that the growth model may be specific, to a large extent, to a particular instructional context, but that is not a problem as long as it is to be used in that context.

An assessment designed to assign students to levels in a learning progression would need to involve tasks that require the kinds of performances associated with the different levels in the learning progression. It is expected that most students at a level of achievement will be at roughly the same levels on all or most of these competencies. Assuming that this is the case and that students are distributed across a number of achievement levels, the measures of the specific competencies should be positively correlated with each other; students with high scores on some of these competencies would be expected to have relatively high scores on the other competencies.

Good teachers employ models similar to learning progressions, but do not typically specify the levels formally (Kane 2006). They know that students are operating at different levels, and they tend to update judgments about levels attained as they interact with the students. They also have some idea of the specific competencies each student has mastered. Learning is seen as a process of student growth, involving the gradual assimilation of core concepts, theories, skills, and so on, and the ability to apply these cognitive assets to perform certain kinds of tasks, rather than as a movement along a unidimensional scale.

Evaluating IUAs Based on Learning Progressions

In developing a learning progression and an associated formative assessment system, we would generally begin with the development of a preliminary learning progression and ToA that seem appropriate for a specific instructional context. The initial descriptions of the levels could be based on experience, on theory, or on some combination of theory and data, and the generality of the levels and the spacing between levels would depend on the domain. The theory of action would indicate how students might be helped to progress from one level to the next (e.g., by explicit instruction on the competencies or tasks at the next level or by practicing these tasks).

With this framework in place, we could develop assessment tasks corresponding to the different achievement levels. This might involve extended-response tasks that allow for qualitatively different levels of performance (e.g., different levels of sophistication in developing an argument or in designing an experiment) or objective items involving different levels of analysis needed to answer the questions; it is expected that the tasks requiring more sophisticated performances will be more difficult than those requiring less sophisticated performances. The tasks could also be differentiated in terms of the scaffolding provided to guide students toward an adequate performance and the scoring criteria applied to student performances.

The tasks at each level would be designed to be similar in the sense that they would require more or less the same competencies at more or less the same level of sophistication. If these tasks were assigned to an appropriate sample of students, we would expect the assessment tasks at each level to have similar empirical difficulty levels, and we would also expect the tasks at lower levels to be completed successfully by a higher percentages of students than those at higher levels. To the extent that these conditions did not hold empirically, the assessment tasks or the learning progression might need to be revised (Gotwals and Songer 2013).

In the ideal case, we would expect each student to be at a specific level (in the sense that their performances are consistent with the description of that level), such that the student can perform some of the tasks at that level, can perform most tasks at lower levels, especially far lower levels, and would not be able to perform most tasks at higher levels, especially far higher levels. Under these conditions, the level assignment is easy to make and is highly informative about what students can and cannot do: they can do most tasks below their level, they can't do most tasks above their level, and they can complete some tasks at their level.

More generally, task performance is likely to be less regular than this ideal model, in part because of factors (e.g., familiarity of specific content) that are not included in the model. Under these conditions, scale scores could be derived from observed performances (e.g., using item response theory [IRT] models) and students with scores in successive ranges on the scale associated with the levels could be used to assign students to levels in the learning progression (van Rijn, Graf, and Deane 2014).

Assuming that we have a ToA indicating how score-based instructional activities are likely to be helpful in the student's progressing to the next higher level, we also have a clear indication of what to do next. Instructional effectiveness could be evaluated using several kinds of data. First, the ToA (Bennett 2010) can be evaluated in terms of its plausibility in light of theory and previous research. Evidence (e.g., interview or observational data) indicating that teachers find the data helpful and are using them in the ways anticipated in the ToA would indicate that it is being implemented appropriately. Statistical studies (longitudinal or comparative) indicating how teacher behavior and student achievement change with implementation of the program could be used to evaluate the effectiveness of the assessment-based interventions. An optimal approach to evaluating the efficacy of the program, at least initially, would probably involve qualitative, descriptive studies of how the program is functioning, its impact on what's happening in classrooms, and small-scale outcome studies. At this stage, if defects are identified, they can be fixed.

Validating Score Interpretations and Uses Based on Learning Progression

Learning progressions are likely to be most useful in providing a framework for score interpretation and use in cases in which the goal of instruction is to develop increasing student sophistication in some activity (e.g., critical thinking). The goal is to move students through a series of levels or stages, starting at some entry level and ending at the fully realized target performance level. The levels are to be defined in terms of the kinds of tasks that students at each level can perform and in terms of the quality of the student performances (e.g., their accuracy, thoroughness, style).

By identifying the inferences and assumptions inherent in this kind of interpretation, we can identify the kinds of evidence needed to evaluate the proposed interpretation and use. Learning progression–based interpretations typically involve at least five inferences.

As is the case for essentially all assessments, the first inference involves an evaluation of student performances on the assessment tasks and the assignment of scores, but for a learning progression, the scoring rule would be primarily designed to assign each student to an appropriate level in the learning progression (van Rijn, Graf, and Deane 2014). The scoring rule might assign the student to a point or points on one or more scales as an intermediate step in scoring, but ultimately each student is to be assigned to a level in the progression. In any case, the scoring needs to be tied to the requirements associated with the different levels.

A major component in evaluating the scoring inference would be expert analyses of the extent to which the tasks and scoring criteria associated with the different levels are consistent with the definitions of the levels, and to which the rules used to combine data from different tasks are appropriate, given the structure of the learning progression. In developing the assessment, a major concern would be the expectation that the tasks assigned to a level would have similar difficulty levels. For learning progressions, the empirical difficulties of the tasks at a given level should be similar and should be different from those associated with higher and lower levels; if they are not, the situation might be improved by tightening the level definitions or by having fewer levels that are further apart.

The second inference involves a claim that the student's level, in itself, provides a good indication of what student can do and not do on the performances of interest. The model is basically hierarchical and relies on a number of related assumptions. Students at level n would be expected to effectively perform many level-n tasks and most tasks at level $n - 1$, and to be even more likely to perform well on tasks at level $n - 2$ and below. Similarly, students at level n would be expected not generally to do well on tasks at level $n + 1$, and to be even less likely to be perform tasks at levels $n + 2$ and above. It is assumed that the performances at each level all require roughly the same mix and level of competencies, and therefore, a student's level in the progression indicates what the student can and cannot do.

This inference can be evaluated by determining whether students at a given level are able to perform most tasks at lower levels, especially tasks two or more levels below, and cannot perform most tasks at higher levels, especially tasks two or more levels above. These assumptions can be evaluated empirically (see van Rijn, Graf, and Deane 2014). In addition, it is expected that the hierarchical structure of the data should be more or less the same across groups (e.g., racial or ethnic, gender).

The data may not satisfy these requirements for a number of reasons. It may be that the levels are not well defined, or the tasks or scoring criteria are not consistently related to the level descriptions. It may also be the case that the levels are too close together, or that the tasks contain sources of irrelevant variance that are not related to the learning progression. Such problems might be alleviated by changes in the learning progression or by improvements in the assessment.

It may also be the case that the performance domain is not strongly hierarchical. Assessments built on curricula that focus mainly on knowledge and skills, such that "higher-level" tasks do not build on lower-level tasks and do not require the competencies developed at "lower levels," are not likely meet the requirements for a learning progression. It should be easier to develop effective learning progressions for instructional programs that focus on developing a high level of mastery on a limited set of core competencies and that do so by having students perform increasingly sophisticated tasks that rely on these competencies (Gotwals and Songer 2013).

Third, the scores are expected to be *generalizable* in that students are generally assigned to the same or adjacent levels on repeated assessments. Note that the assumptions entailed by the generalization inference for learning progression are stronger than they are for traditional scale-based interpretations. For scale-based interpretations, it is generally sufficient that the scores be highly correlated across replications of the assessment, because the scores can be statistically adjusted to eliminate mean differences (e.g., that scores on Form A of an assessment were generally higher than those on Form B for the same test-takers). A learning progression–based interpretation makes claims about what students can and cannot do, so replications that make different level assignments across replications are problematic, even if the level assignments are positively correlated (i.e., the ordering of level assignments over students is generally consistent across replications).

If assignments are not replicable, it may be possible to improve the dependability of the results in several ways. If there are indications that the level definitions are too broad or too vague, it may be necessary to tighten their definitions by specifying the kinds of performance expected at the different levels in more detail. In some cases, it may be possible to improve dependability by having fewer levels that are further apart; making fine distinctions between closely packed levels can be difficult. Another option is to increase the length of the assessment; averaging over a larger sample of performance tends to suppress various sources of random error.

Fourth, the interpretation in terms of position in the learning progression would be extended to claims about performance in the classroom and other nonassessment contexts. It is possible that assessment results provide distorted estimates of student performance because of systematic effects associated with the design and implementation of the assessment. For example, the assessment result could overestimate students' levels in the learning progression if the assessment tasks provide excessive scaffolding that helps students perform better than they would in most other contexts. Or the assessment might underestimate student competency level if students do not fully understand what is expected of them; Gotwals and Songer (2013) found that students could perform better in developing scientific explanations in interviews than was indicated by their assessment-based level in a learning progression.

Fifth, the levels are assumed to be educationally meaningful in that it is possible to help students to move from one level to the next. These efforts might focus on specific new competencies needed at the next level (or at the current level if it has not been fully mastered), or on continuing practice on tasks at the current level or the next higher level. Evidence on how well this assumption is satisfied could involve investigations of how well the interventions designed to help students move from one level to the next are functioning, of whether these interventions are successful across groups, and of the extent to which they generate undesirable side effects (e.g., narrowing of the curriculum, adverse impact). By checking whether the program using the formative assessment works as intended, we evaluate the formative assessment and the program as a whole (Norris 2008).

Validation and Program Evaluation

The argument-based approach to validation has roots in several earlier developments in educational measurement, including construct validity and program evaluation.

In Cronbach and Meehl's (1955) exposition of construct validation, the construct being assessed was to be defined implicitly in terms of its role in a theory, and the construct interpretations and the theory were both evaluated by deriving predictions from the theory and checking these predictions against empirical results. If the predictions did not agree with observations, then something was amiss, and either the theory or the construct measures (or some assumption in the study design) was to be rejected. If the predictions were confirmed by the data, both the theory and the interpretation of scores in terms of the theoretical constructs were supported.

In the argument-based approach, the IUA plays the role that a scientific theory plays in the original version of construct validity. It lays out the proposed interpretations and uses of the scores and provides a framework for validation and criteria for the adequacy of the validation. If the IUA were coherent and complete and all of its empirical implications had survived serious challenges, the interpretation and use of the scores would be acceptable, or valid. If any part of the IUA were not plausible, the interpretation or use would not be considered valid. Validation can proceed systematically by specifying an IUA and by checking its inferences and assumptions.

House (1980) and Cronbach (1982, 1988) propose that the logic of evaluation argument could be employed in evaluating assessment programs, and this general notion provided a framework for the argument-based approach to validation. As is the case for educational and social programs in general, assessment programs are designed to achieve certain goals and are expected to avoid serious side effects. A thorough evaluation of any program would incorporate the evidence for and against the claims being made for the program and would consider plausible alternate interpretations. The analysis "should make clear, and to the extent possible, persuasive, the construction of reality and the value weightings implicit in a test and its application" (Cronbach 1988, 5).

In cases in which assessment programs are designed to achieve some specific goal or goals, the linkage between program evaluation and validation can be especially clear. For example, in accountability systems, assessment scores at some level of aggregation may be used to estimate the effectiveness of educational units (e.g., schools, teachers, classes), with the explicit goal of improving their performances. In these cases, the precise content domain covered by the assessment and the specific interpretation assigned to assessment scores can be of less interest to policymakers than the impact of the accountability system on the performance of the units being evaluated. In such cases, the assessment program is being used mainly as an educational intervention, rather than as an assessment tool per se. The use depends on a score interpretation, but that interpretation may be quite general (e. g., achievement in mathematics). In these cases, an evaluation of the assessment program is essentially program evaluation.

Similarly, in evaluating assessments that are intended to inform instruction and promote learning, the validation of score interpretations and uses and the evaluation of program outcomes tend to run together. If the instructional program is not as effective as it is expected to be, the fault may lie in any of several parts of the system. It may be that the assessment program is not functioning as intended (e.g., because the scores have large standard errors of measurement or are subject to sources of irrelevant variance) or because the instructional program is not functioning well (e.g., not providing clear instruction or not motivating students). It may also be the case that both the assessment and the instruction are functioning well, given their designs, but they are not well matched.

Concluding Remarks

It is the proposed interpretation and uses of scores that are validated, not the assessment or the scores themselves, and the validity of a proposed interpretation or use depends on how well the evidence supports the claims being made. The inferences and assumptions entailed by the claims being made can be specified as an interpretation-use argument (IUA). The validity argument can then evaluate the IUA's coherence and completeness and the plausibility of its inferences and assumptions.

We have long experience and a vast literature on the development and evaluation of scale-based interpretations, and, as a result, we have well-developed methodology for such assessments. However, newer assessment models, like learning progressions, raise new questions, and these new questions require a fresh look at our validation models. For example, the scores generated for learning progressions are ultimately level assignments. And these assignments can be considered generalizable to the extent that students are assigned to the same category over replications of the assessment. In this context, the correlation between scores (i.e., assignments to levels) over replications is not an adequate measure of precision.

In addition, learning progressions assume that a student's progress in mastering a domain involves a series of qualitatively different stages, or levels, that are typically achieved in the order specified in the progression. Learning progressions abandon the scale-based interpretation in favor of a hierarchical model in which progress is defined in terms of a levels rather than scale values, and the assumptions inherent in such interpretations need to be verified empirically.

Formative assessments are designed to support instructional programs, and to be useful, they will have to provide effective guidance to teachers and students. In such cases, validation has a lot in common with program evaluation.

References

Bachman, Lyle. 2005. "Building and Supporting a Case for Assessment Use." *Language Assessment Quarterly* 2 (1): 1–34.

Bennett, Randy E. 2010. "Cognitively Based Assessment of, for, and as Learning (CBAL): A Preliminary Theory of Action for Summative and Formative Assessment." *Measurement: Interdisciplinary Research & Perspective* 8 (2–3): 70–91.

Chapelle, Carol. A., Mary. K Enright, and Joan Jamieson. 2010. "Does an Argument-Based Approach to Validity Make a Difference?" *Educational Measurement: Issues and Practice* 29 (1): 3–13.

Cronbach, Lee. J. 1980. "Validity on Parole: How Can We Go Straight?" *New Directions for Testing and Measurement: Measuring Achievement over a Decade* 5:99–108.

———. 1982. *Designing Evaluations of Educational and Social Programs.* San Francisco: Jossey-Bass.

———. 1988. "Five Perspectives on Validity Argument." In *Assessment Validity,* edited by Howard Wainer and Henry I. Braun, 3–17. Hillsdale, NJ: Erlbaum.

Cronbach, Lee. J., and Paul. E. Meehl. 1955. "Construct Validity in Psychological Assessments." *Psychological Bulletin* 52 (4): 281–302.

Gorin, Joanna. S., and Susan. E. Embretson. 2006. "Item Difficulty Modeling of Paragraph Comprehension Items." *Applied Psychological Measurement* 30 (5): 394–411.

Gotwals, Amelia W., and Nancy B. Songer. 2013. "Validity Evidence for Learning Progression-Based Assessment Items that Fuse Core Disciplinary Ideas and Science Practices." *Journal of Research in Science Teaching* 50 (5): 597–626.

Graf, Edith, and Peter van Rijn. 2016. "Learning Progressions as a Guide for Design: Recommendations Based on Observations from a Mathematics Assessment." In *Handbook of Assessment Development*, 2nd ed., edited by Susan. Lane, Mark Raymond, and Thomas Haladyna, 165–89. New York: Routledge.

House, Ernest. R. 1980. *Evaluating with Validity.* Beverly Hills: Sage Publications.

Kane, Michael. 2006. "Validation." In *Educational Measurement*, 4th ed., edited by Robert Brennan, 17–64. Westport, CT: American Council on Education and Praeger.

———. 2013. "Validating the Interpretations and Uses of Test Scores." *Journal of Educational Measurement* 50 (1): 1–73.

Kane, Michael, Terence Crooks, and Allan Cohen. 1999. "Validating Measures of Performance." *Educational Measurement: Issues and Practice* 18 (2): 5–17.

Messick, Samuel. 1989. "Validity." In *Educational Measurement*, 3rd ed., edited by Robert L. Linn, 13–103. New York: American Council on Education and Macmillan.

Mislevy, Robert. 2006. "Cognitive Psychology and Educational Assessment." In *Educational Measurement*, 4th ed., edited by R. L. Brennan, 257–305. Westport, CT: American Council on Education and Praeger.

Mislevy, Robert, Linda Steinberg, and Russell Almond. 2003. "On the Structure of Educational Assessments." *Measurement: Interdisciplinary Research and Perspectives* 1 (1): 3–62.

Norris, John. 2008. *Validity Evaluation in Language Assessment.* New York: Peter Lang.

Van Rijn, Peter, Edith Graf, and Paul Deane. 2014. "Empirical Recovery of Argumentation Learning Progressions in Scenario-Based Assessments of English Language Arts." *Psicología Educativa* 20 (2): 109–15.

Yuko Goto Butler is an associate professor of educational linguistics in the Graduate School of Education at the University of Pennsylvania. She is also the director of the Teaching English to Speakers of Other Languages (TESOL) Program at Penn. Her research interests include language assessment and second and foreign-language learning among children.

Svetlana V. Cook is a second language acquisition specialist at the National Foreign Language Center at the University of Maryland. Her research interests include cognitive aspects of second language acquisition and foreign language assessment. Her publications appeared in *Bilingualism: Language and Cognition*, *Frontiers in Psychology*, and *The Mental Lexicon*, among others.

John McE. Davis is Evaluation Specialist at the Foreign Service Institute, US Department of State (contractor with Yorktown Systems Group). His research interests include language program evaluation, language assessment, and questionnaire research methods.

Larry Davis is a managing research scientist in the Center for English Language Learning and Assessment at Educational Testing Service. His primary research focus is speaking assessment, including speaking constructs, task design, scoring rubrics, rater expertise and behavior, and applications of automated scoring technology.

Chris Davison is head of the School of Education, University of New South Wales Australia, and a specialist in school-based English language assessment and teacher education. She is founding co-editor of the Springer series on English language education and editor in chief of the *Australian Review of Applied Linguistics*.

Bart Deygers is a postdoctoral researcher at the University of Leuven, Belgium. He has conducted research into university admission language testing. The chapter in this volume is part of that larger research, in which he empirically examined the main assumptions that support the admission policy. Apart from the assessment of language for academic purposes, his main research interests include validity, fairness, and justice.

Catherine J. Doughty is the Romance Languages Division director at the Foreign Service Institute of US Department of State, and an affiliate professor of second language acquisition at the University of Maryland.

Martin East is a language teacher educator and current associate dean (research) in the Faculty of Education and Social Work at the University of Auckland, New Zealand. His research interests lie in effective and innovative approaches to language teaching, learning, and assessment, and he publishes widely in these areas.

Michael Evans conducts research focused on second language education. He codirected a national study of the impact of government policy on language learning in schools (2006–9) and directed *Language Development and School Achievement: Opportunities and Challenges in the Education of EAL Students* (2016). He is series coeditor of Cambridge Education Research (Cambridge University Press).

Michael J. Ferreira is an associate professor of Portuguese linguistics, director of the Portuguese Language Program and director of graduate studies in the Department of Spanish and Portuguese at Georgetown University. He coordinates the Georgetown Teletandem Initiative and the DC Area Celpe-Bras Exam. Areas of expertise include Portuguese as a foreign language, interaction, corpus linguistics, paleography and textual edition, and lexicography.

Viviane Bagio Furtoso is an assistant professor in the Department of Modern Foreign Languages at State University of Londrina, Brazil, with a specialization in teaching English and Portuguese to speakers of other languages. Her research interests include language assessment, teacher education, and internationalization of higher education.

Kira Gor is an associate professor of second language acquisition and Russian at the School of Languages, Literatures, and Cultures at the University of Maryland. Her publications appeared in *Applied Psycholinguistics*, *Bilingualism: Language and Cognition*, *Frontiers in Psychology*, *Journal of Memory and Language*, *Language and Cognitive Processes*, *Language Learning*, *Slavic and East European Journal*, *Studies in Second Language Acquisition*, and *The Mental Lexicon*.

Lin Gu is a research scientist in the Center for English Language Learning and Assessment at Educational Testing Service. Her main research interests include speaking assessment, automated scoring of speaking performance, and young English language learners.

Liz Hamp-Lyons, a former president of ILTA, was the chair professor of English at the Hong Kong Polytechnic University from 1996 to 2003, and honorary professor of education at the University of Hong Kong from 2006 to 2012. Since 2008, she has been a member of the Centre for Research in English Language Learning and Assessment (CRELLA) at the University of Bedfordshire, where she supervises doctoral students and researches language teacher assessment literacy.

Tuija Hirvelä is a project researcher in the National Certificates of Language Proficiency (NCLP) in the Centre for Applied Language Studies at the University of Jyväskylä, Finland. She is a statistical expert in various language testing methods, specializing in item response theory in the NCLP from 2002.

Ari Huhta is a professor of language assessment in the Centre for Applied Language Studies at the University of Jyväskylä, Finland. His research interests include assessments that support learning (e.g., diagnostic and formative assessment), self-assessment and feedback, computer-based assessment, and combining second language acquisition research and language testing perspectives in research.

Scott R. Jackson holds a degree in linguistics from the University of Arizona. His work spans several subfields, including formal linguistics, psycholinguistics, neurolinguistics, and second language acquisition. He has worked at the University of Maryland Center for Advanced Study of Language since 2009, with a primary focus on language aptitude.

Michael T. Kane is the Messick Chair in validity at the Educational Testing Service. His research interests are validity theory, generalizability theory, and standard setting. Dr. Kane holds a PhD in education, an MS in statistics from Stanford University, and a BS in physics from Manhattan College.

Justin Kelly is a test development manager at the Center for Applied Linguistics. His research interests include assessing the receptive language domains, assessment at the boundaries of proficiency levels, and formal grammars.

Richard Kiely is a reader in TESOL applied linguistics in the Department of Modern Languages at the University of Southampton. He is the coauthor of *Programme Evaluation in Language Education* (with Pauline Rea-Dickins) and *Exploratory Practice for Continuing Professional Development: An Innovative Approach for Language Teachers* (with Assia Rolls). He is currently researching the development of student self-assessment in the language curriculum.

Keiko Koda is a professor of second language acquisition and Japanese in the Department of Modern Languages at Carnegie Mellon University. Her research interests include second language reading and biliteracy development. Currently, she is involved in several studies addressing crosslinguistic variations in reading acquisition and text comprehension in typologically diverse languages.

Alia Lancaster holds an MA in applied linguistics from Boston University and is a doctoral student in the Second Language Acquisition Program at the University of Maryland. Her research interests include phonological and lexical representations in second language learners and bilinguals and individual differences among learners.

Constant Leung is a professor of educational linguistics in the School of Education, Communication and Society, King's College London. He is a fellow of the Academy of Social Sciences. His research interests include additional and second language curriculum and assessment, language policy, and teacher professional development. He is joint editor of *Language Assessment Quarterly*.

Chih-Kai (Cary) Lin is a psychometrician at the Center for Applied Linguistics (CAL). At CAL, Dr. Lin's primary responsibility is to conduct psychometric and statistical analyses to support large-scale language assessment programs. Major assessment programs in which he is involved include ACCESS for ELLs 2.0, BEST Plus 2.0, and CAL English Proficiency Test.

Yongcan Liu is a lecturer in the Faculty of Education, University of Cambridge and founder convener of Cambridge Research in Community Language Education Network. His research interests lie in multilingualism in education and Vygotsky's sociocultural theory of mind. He has recently been involved in a series of linked projects on the schooling experience and assessment of English as an Additional Language (EAL) children.

David MacGregor is currently an assessment researcher for the WIDA Consortium. Previously he worked for over ten years at the Center for Applied Linguistics on psychometric and validation issues for ACCESS for ELLs. He received his PhD in applied linguistics from Georgetown University.

Margaret E. Malone is Director of the Assessment and Evaluation Language Resource Center (AELRC) and Research Professor at Georgetown University and Director of the Center for Assessment, Research and Development at ACTFL. Her current research focuses on language assessment literacy, oral proficiency assessment, and the relative difficulty of learning different languages.

Todd H. McKay is a PhD candidate in applied linguistics and research assistant with the AELRC at Georgetown University. His research interests include language assessment, language program evaluation, and applied measurement, with emphases on the less commonly taught languages and language programs in South Asia.

Reeta Neittaanmäki is a project researcher and statistician in the National Certificates of Language Proficiency in the Centre for Applied Language Studies at the University of Jyväskylä, Finland. Her expertise covers quantitative research methods in the field of language testing with special focus on item response theory.

John M. Norris is Senior Research Director of the Center for English Language Learning and Assessment at the Educational Testing Service, USA. His primary research interests include educational uses of language assessment, program evaluation, task-based language teaching, and research synthesis.

Jennifer Norton is the director of test development at the Center for Applied Linguistics, Washington, DC, where her work has focused on language proficiency assessment development, standards, online testing, and teacher input into assessment.

Gary J. Ockey is an associate professor in the Applied Linguistics and Technology Program at Iowa State University. He received a PhD from the University of California, Los Angeles in applied linguistics. He conducts research on L2 assessments with the aim of making them as fair as possible.

Sari Ohranen is a project researcher in the National Certificates of Language Proficiency (NCLP) in the Centre for Applied Language Studies at the University of Jyväskylä, Finland. She has worked as a researcher in the NCLP since 2011 and in projects focusing on Finnish language placement tests for adult migrants in 2014–16.

Nickolas B. Pandža is a doctoral student in the Second Language Acquisition Program at the University of Maryland and a faculty research specialist at the Center for Advanced Study of Language. His research interests include lexical access, speech perception, executive control, and psychometrics.

Eric Pelzl is a doctoral student in the Second Language Acquisition Program at the University of Maryland, College Park.

James E. Purpura is an associate professor of linguistics and education at Teachers College, Columbia University, where he teaches L2 assessment and research methods. His research interests include grammar and pragmatics assessment, learning-oriented assessment, scenario-based assessment, and the sociocognitive underpinnings of L2 assessment. He is author of *Strategy Use and L2 Test Performance* (Cambridge University Press) and *Assessing Grammar* (Cambridge University Press), and is currently coauthoring "Learning-Oriented L2 Assessment" (Routledge) A former president of ILTA, he is coeditor of *Language Assessment Quarterly*, series coeditor of New Perspectives in Language Assessment (Routledge) and series coeditor of Language Assessment at ETS: Innovation and Validation (Routledge).

Jim Ranalli is an assistant professor of TESL/applied linguistics at Iowa State University. His research focuses on the intersection of second language writing, technology, and self-regulated learning. He is currently investigating innovative applications of digital technologies for providing formative feedback on students' writing products and processes.

Jennifer Renn is the director of adult language and literacy education research at the Center for Applied Linguistics. She is the director of the English for Heritage Language Speakers Program, and her research interests include language variation, language education, and working with diverse learners.

Young-A Son is a PhD candidate in the Department of Linguistics at Georgetown University. Her research interests include the assessment of foreign and heritage language learners. More specifically, her work examines validation of language tests and other indicators of language proficiency for research as well as instructional purposes.

Elina Stordell is a language assessor and item writer at Testipiste, a language assessment center for adult migrants located in Helsinki, Finland. She is interested in listening comprehension, writing, and study skills, and she has been responsible for statistical analyses and standard setting.

Shauna J. Sweet holds a degree in evaluation, measurement, and statistics from the University of Maryland, College Park. She collaborates with subject matter experts across a variety of fields, with a particular interest in assessment development.

Taina Tammelin-Laine is a research coordinator in the Centre for Applied Language Studies (CALS) at the University of Jyväskylä, Finland. Her research interests include L2 Finnish acquisition of low-educated adult immigrants and assessment of language skills below A1 at CEFR. She is also an active member of LESLLA.

Veronika Timpe-Laughlin is an associate research scientist in the Center for English Language Learning and Assessment at Educational Testing Service. Her research interests include L2 pragmatics, task-based language teaching, technology in L2 instruction and assessment, and program evaluation. Before joining ETS, Veronika taught in the English Department at TU Dortmund University, Germany.

Koen Van Gorp is the head of foreign language assessment at the Center for Language Teaching Advancement (CeLTA) at Michigan State University. His research interests include task-based language teaching and assessment and multilingual education.

Junko Yamashita is a professor at the Graduate School of Humanities, Nagoya University, Japan. Her research interests are in factors affecting second language reading performance, crosslinguistic influences on language processing, and second language literacy acquisition. Her publications have appeared in several journals such as *Applied Psycholinguistics*, *Language Learning*, *Reading in a Foreign Language*, and *TESOL Quarterly*.

Index

Note: tables are indicated with *t* and figures are indicated with *f*